A Voyage round the World, in the years 1803, 4, 5, and 6, performed by order of his Majesty Alexander the First, in the ship Neva, etc. With an appendix of vocabularies, tables of the ship's route, etc.

Yury Fedorovich Lisyansky

A Voyage round the World, in the years 1803, 4, 5, & 6, performed by order of his ... Majesty Alexander the First, ... in the ship Neva, etc. [With an appendix of vocabularies, tables of the ship's route, etc.]
Lisyansky, Yury Fedorovich
British Library, Historical Print Editions
British Library
1814
4°.
212.e.7.

The BiblioLife Network

This project was made possible in part by the BiblioLife Network (BLN), a project aimed at addressing some of the huge challenges facing book preservationists around the world. The BLN includes libraries, library networks, archives, subject matter experts, online communities and library service providers. We believe every book ever published should be available as a high-quality print reproduction; printed on- demand anywhere in the world. This insures the ongoing accessibility of the content and helps generate sustainable revenue for the libraries and organizations that work to preserve these important materials.

The following book is in the "public domain" and represents an authentic reproduction of the text as printed by the original publisher. While we have attempted to accurately maintain the integrity of the original work, there are sometimes problems with the original book or micro-film from which the books were digitized. This can result in minor errors in reproduction. Possible imperfections include missing and blurred pages, poor pictures, markings and other reproduction issues beyond our control. Because this work is culturally important, we have made it available as part of our commitment to protecting, preserving, and promoting the world's literature.

GUIDE TO FOLD-OUTS, MAPS and OVERSIZED IMAGES

In an online database, page images do not need to conform to the size restrictions found in a printed book. When converting these images back into a printed bound book, the page sizes are standardized in ways that maintain the detail of the original. For large images, such as fold-out maps, the original page image is split into two or more pages.

Guidelines used to determine the split of oversize pages:

- Some images are split vertically; large images require vertical and horizontal splits.
- For horizontal splits, the content is split left to right.
- For vertical splits, the content is split from top to bottom.
- For both vertical and horizontal splits, the image is processed from top left to bottom right.

BL

UREY LISIANSKY

K.G. & V.

A

VOYAGE ROUND THE WORLD,

IN

THE YEARS 1803, 4, 5, & 6;

PERFORMED,

BY ORDER OF HIS IMPERIAL MAJESTY

ALEXANDER THE FIRST, EMPEROR OF RUSSIA,

IN

THE SHIP NEVA,

BY

UREY LISIANSKY,

CAPTAIN IN THE RUSSIAN NAVY,

AND

KNIGHT OF THE ORDERS OF ST. GEORGE AND ST. VLADIMER.

LONDON:
PRINTED FOR JOHN BOOTH, DUKE STREET, PORTLAND PLACE; AND
LONGMAN, HURST, REES, ORME, & BROWN, PATERNOSTER ROW;
BY S. HAMILTON, WEYBRIDGE, SURREY.

1814.

Jos: Banks

B L

TO

HIS IMPERIAL MAJESTY

ALEXANDER THE FIRST.

Sire,

The veneration and gratitude which prompted me to dedicate to your Most Gracious Majesty the History of my Voyage, in the Russian language, again impel me to offer to your Sacred Person the present Edition of it in English.

Deign, Sire, to accept a Work that will convey to the British Nation the knowledge of the paternal care for the welfare of your subjects, which so eminently distinguishes Your Majesty, under whose auspices the Russian Flag was first carried round the Globe.

I am,

Sire,

Your Imperial Majesty's

Most devoted and most faithful Subject,

UREY LISIANSKY.

London, March 25, 1814.

CONTENTS.

Preface xiii

CHAPTER I.

PASSAGE FROM CRONSTADT TO FALMOUTH.

Departure of the two Vessels. Russian Custom on taking leave of the Port-admiral. Arrival in Copenhagen Roads. Stay at Copenhagen. Method of purifying confined Air. Vessel of a curious Construction. Departure from Copenhagen. Separation of the two Ships in a Storm in the North Sea. Arrival at Falmouth . Page 1

CHAPTER II.

PASSAGE FROM FALMOUTH TO TENERIFFE.

Departure from Falmouth. Remarkable Meteor. Method of preventing Bilgewater. Precautions against Disease. Sublime Appearance of the Peak of Teneriffe from the Sea. Fortunate Escape from a Hurricane. Account of the Towns of Laguna and Santa Cruz, in the Island of Teneriffe. Bad Anchorage of the Bay of Santa Cruz. A Mummy, supposed to have been embalmed by the ancient Inhabitants of Teneriffe, given to our Ambassador 11

CHAPTER III.

PASSAGE FROM TENERIFFE TO THE ISLAND OF ST. CATHARINE.

Departure from Teneriffe. Precautions for Health on entering the warm Latitudes. Amusements of the Crew. Make the Island of St. Antony, one of the Cape de

Verd Islands. Variation of the Chronometers. Impolicy of passing through the Cape de Verd Islands in going to the Cape of Good Hope. Rejoicings on Crossing the Line. Importance of attending to the Sea Currents. Seek in vain for the Island of Ascension. Cape Frio. Island of Alvaredo. Singular Peril of the two Ships. Arrival and Stay at St. Catharine. Account of that Island, its Productions, and Inhabitants . . . . Page 20

CHAPTER IV.

PASSAGE FROM THE ISLAND OF ST. CATHARINE TO EASTER ISLAND.

Departure from St. Catharine. Danger of the Neva from striking upon the Body of a dead Whale. Change of Climate, and bad Weather. Perceive Staten Land. Currents. Supposed Difficulty of passing Cape Horn erroneous. Advice to Navigators doubling that Cape. The Neva and Nadejda separate in a Fog. The Neva proceeds alone for Easter Island. Arrival there. Survey of the Coasts. Account of the Inhabitants. Latitude and Population of the Island different from what Captain Cook makes them 41

CHAPTER V.

PASSAGE FROM EASTER ISLAND TO THE WASHINGTON ISLANDS.

Departure of the Neva from Easter Island. State of the Winds. Make the Marquesas. Take a Survey of this Group. Visited by Canoes from the Island of Noocahiva, one of the Washington Islands. The two Ships meet. Anchor in the Bay of Tayohaia. Receive a Visit from the King of the Bay. Attempts of the Women to gain Admittance on Board. Traffic for Provisions. Further Visits of the King, with some of his Relations. Trick played us by His Majesty. Misunderstanding with the Inhabitants. Visit the King, with Captain Krusenstern. Palace. Burying-ground. A Grappling stolen from one of our Boats. The King dines on Board the Neva. The Neva visited by the Queen. Excursion to Jegawe Bay. Excellent Anchorage there. Prepare for Departure from Noocahiva. Further Account of the Religion, Government, and Customs of the Inhabitants . 61

CONTENTS.

CHAPTER VI.

PASSAGE FROM THE WASHINGTON ISLANDS TO THE SANDWICH ISLANDS.

Nautical Difficulties on leaving Noocahiva. Search in vain for an unknown Land, seen by Marchand. Surprise of the Crew at the Sight of a Shark which we caught. Make the Island of Owyhee. The Nadejda leaves us to proceed to Camchatca. Anchor in the Bay of Carocacoa. Traffic with the Inhabitants. Reason for refusing to admit Women on Board. Excursion on Shore with the Chief of the Bay. Habitations. Temples. Visited by Mr. Young, who governs the Island in the Absence of the King. Village of Tavaroa. Leave Owyhee. Island of Otooway. Visited by its King. Island of Onihoo . . . . Page 95

CHAPTER VII.

ACCOUNT OF THE SANDWICH ISLANDS.

Government of the Sandwich Islands. Particulars of the Institution of Taboo. Division of Time. Priests. Human Sacrifices. Funereal Customs. Nobility. Customs as to Eating. Advance of the Inhabitants towards Civilisation. Reign of the present King Hamamea. Mr. Young. Cattle. Feathered Tribe. Division of Owyhee into Provinces, Districts, and Farms 115

CHAPTER VIII.

PASSAGE FROM THE SANDWICH ISLANDS TO CADIACK AND SITCA SOUND.

Unfavourable State of the Weather on quitting the Sandwich Islands. Make Cheericoff Island. Pass the Islands of Sithoonack and Toohidack. Visited by Bidarkas from Cadiack. Danger of the Ship from the Unskilfulness of the Pilot. Anchor in the Harbour of St. Paul. Accept a Proposal of assisting the Commander-in-chief of the Russian Settlements against the Sitcans. Delayed by contrary Winds. Proceed for Sitca. Arrive in Cross Bay. Cautious Conduct of a Sitcan Boat. Visited by Boats from the Company's Ships, the Alexander and Catharine. Find the Commander-in-chief absent. Cautious Conduct of other Native Sitcans. Endeavour in vain to take a Boat in which was the Son of our principal Enemy. Skill of the

Sitcans in the Use of Fire-Arms. The Commander-in-chief arrives. Curiosities found by him. Aleutian Tents, Hunters, and Dances. Take Possession of a Settlement of the Enemy. Overtures on the Part of the Sitcans. Attack the Sitcans, and are repulsed by them. Fresh Overtures. Flight of the Enemy from their Fort. Horrible Massacre of Infants previous to their Flight. Fort described. Loss sustained by the Russian Party in the Contest with the Sitcans. Sea-Lions killed by our Sportsmen. One of our Fishermen shot. Fabulous Origin of the Sitcan Nation. Eloquence of their Toyons . . . . Page 138

CHAPTER IX.

RETURN TO THE ISLAND OF CADIACK, TO PASS THE WINTER.

Particulars of our Run from Sitca to Cadiack. Moor the Ship for the Winter. Winter Amusements. State of the Weather. Set out to explore the eastern Part of Cadiack. Settlement of Ihack. Conversation with the Chief. New volcanic Island. Visited by an old Shaman, or Wizard. Bay of Ihack, Bay of Kiluden, and Settlement of Oohasheck. Land at a Settlement, that has only Women and Children. Curiosities at Drunkard's Bay. Harbour of Three-Saints. Fugitive Settlement. Account of Mr. Shelechoff. Huts appropriated for Women. Curiosities at Cape Bay. Tea and Supper in a Barabara. Stupidity of the Aleutians. Singular Custom on the Death of Relatives. Tame Eagle. Mountain tumbled into the Sea by an Earthquake. Straits of Sulthidack. Female Surgeon. Return to the Harbour of St. Paul. Explore the western Part of Cadiack. Account of Cook's River. Intelligence respecting the Russian Settlement of Nooscha 169

CHAPTER X.

DESCRIPTION OF THE ISLAND OF CADIACK.

Climate of the Island. Plants. Wild Beasts. Birds. Number of Inhabitants. Customs. Dress. Food. Marriages. Burials. Manner of catching Fish, wild Animals, and Birds. Instruments used for the Purpose. Shamans. Games. Building of Bidarkas. Building of Barabaras. Filthiness of the Inhabitants. Nature of the Government 190

CHAPTER XI.

SECOND PASSAGE FROM CADIACK TO SITCA.

Feelings of the Russian Inhabitants on our leaving Cadiack. Arrive at New Archangel. Improved State of this Settlement. Account of the Destruction of the old Settlement. Explore the Coast round Mount Edgecumbe. Sitcan Embassy, and Ceremonies attending it. Excursion to the Top of Mount Edgecumbe. Arrival, at New Archangel, of another would-be Ambassador. Hot Baths. Plan of the ensuing Course of our Voyage . . . . Page 216

CHAPTER XII.

DESCRIPTION OF THE SITCA ISLANDS.

Reason of this Group of Islands being so denominated. Advantageous Situation of the new Russian Settlement. Productions of these Islands. Climate. People. Dress. Character. Food. Houses. Canoes. Custom of burning the dead. Arts. Tribes or Casts. Religion. Power of the Toyons. Custom respecting Females of cutting the Lip when they arrive at Womanhood 235

CHAPTER XIII.

PASSAGE FROM SITCA SOUND TO CANTON.

State of the Weather on leaving Sitca. Number of Sick from Fatigue. Precautions for future Health. Ill Effect from the Use of Bread. Curious Shells. Clouds mistaken for Land. New Disappointments as to the Discovery of Land. Danger of the Ship from grounding on a coral Bank. Discover a new Island. Particulars relating to it. Discover a new Bank. Limit the Crew in their Allowance of Bread. Advice respecting the westerly Winds in the Southern Ocean. Make the Islands of Saypan and Tinian. Encounter a Hurricane. Putrid State of the Ship's Cargo. Loss sustained by it. Enter the Chinese Seas. Arrive at Macao, and meet Captain Krusenstern. Pirates. Macao described. Proceed to Whampoa to dispose of the Neva's Cargo. Chinese Customs relative to Commerce. Repair of the Neva. The

Nadejda and Neva detained by Order of the Chinese Government. Services rendered by Mr. Drummond in this Business. The Ships released . . . . . Page 245

CHAPTER XIV.

DESCRIPTION OF CANTON.

Houses. Population. Commerce. Despotic and mercenary Character of those in Authority. Productions. Wretchedness of the lower Class of Inhabitants. Sumptuous Fare of the Rich. Customs as to eating. Dress. Character. Religion. Temples. Military Force. Boats. Laws. Country-house of a Mandarin. Price of Provision. Weights and Measures 278

CHAPTER XV.

PASSAGE FROM CANTON TO CRONSTADT.

Departure of the Nadejda and Neva from Canton. Islands and Straits in the Chinese Seas. Advice to Navigators respecting them. Islands of Two Brothers. Make the Islands of Java and Sumatra. Erroneous Situation of several Places rectified. One of the Crew of the Neva dies. Strait of Sunda. The two Ships separate. Navigation round the Cape of Good Hope. Currents. Make the Western Islands. Pass immense Quantities of Sea-weeds. Arrival and Stay at Portsmouth. Arrive at Cronstadt. The Ship visited by the Emperor Alexander and the Empress-mother. Honours and Rewards conferred on the Officers and Crew 298

CONTENTS.

APPENDIX.

No. I. *A Vocabulary of the Language of Noocahiva* . . . . . Page 323
   II. *A Vocabulary of the Language of the Sandwich Islands* . . . 326
  III. *A Vocabulary of the Language of the Islands of Cadiack and Oonalashca, the Bay of Kenay, and Sitca Sound* 329
  IV. TABLES *of the Route of the Neva, during the Years 1803, 4, 5, & 6:—From the Time of its leaving Europe to its Return* . . 339

Table I. *Passage from Falmouth to Teneriffe* 341
  II. *Passage from Teneriffe to the Island of St. Catharine* 343
 III. *Passage from the Island of St. Catharine to Easter Island* . . . 349
 IV. *Passage from Easter Island to the Washington Islands* 357
  V. *Passage from the Washington Islands to the Sandwich Islands* . 359
 VI. *Passage from the Sandwich Islands to the Island of Cadiack* . . 362
 VII. *Passage from the Island of Cadiack to Sitca or Norfolk Sound* . 365
VIII. *Passage from Sitca or Norfolk Sound, to the Island of Cadiack* . 366
 IX. *Passage from the Island of Cadiack to Sitca or Norfolk Sound* . 367
  X. *Passage from Sitca or Norfolk Sound to Canton* 368
 XI. *Passage from Canton to Portsmouth* 377

PREFACE.

The Russian American Company,* having experienced great difficulty in supplying their colonies on the north-west coast of America with all kinds of provisions and necessaries, on account of the length and tediousness of the journey by land to Ochotsk, resolved to try if the conveyance by sea would not prove more favourable to their views. A plan was accordingly framed of an expedition from Cronstadt round Cape Horn for the purpose of ascertaining the practicability of this project, and was laid before the then minister of commerce, count Roomantsoff, and admiral Mordwinoff, minister of the marine. This plan being approved of by them, was presented to his Imperial Majesty for his sanction, who extended the

---

* This Company was established in the reign of the empress Catharine the Second, for the purpose of giving solidity and effect to the fur trade; and the better to promote those purposes, all the islands lying between Camchatca and the Russian part of the north-west coast of America, were granted to them in perpetuity. His present majesty, Alexander the First, has extended the privileges of the Company, and graciously declared himself their immediate patron.

objects of the voyage, by commanding, that it should be converted into a voyage of discovery and circumnavigation; and that, at the same time, a Russian ambassador should be carried out to Japan. Two ships, the Nadejda and Neva, were accordingly ordered to be equipped. The command of the Nadejda, and the expedition in general, was conferred on captain Krusenstern, who was also directed to conduct the Russian ambassador and his suite to the court of Jeddo. The Author of the following narrative had the honour to be appointed to the command of the second ship, the Neva, with instructions to proceed to Cadiack, and the north-west coast of America.

Thus, for the first time, was the voyage round the globe undertaken and carried into effect by the government of Russia. On the return of the expedition to Cronstadt, a separate account of the voyage of each vessel, with an atlas of charts and engravings, was ordered to be printed at the expense of the emperor. A translation of the first two volumes of the narrative of captain Krusenstern has already appeared in English.

The British public may justly inquire into the claims of the present work, on the same subject, to general attention. They are as follow:—From the different destination of the two vessels on their arrival in the Pacific Ocean, and from their frequent and unavoidable separation, it fell to the lot of the Author, to visit, without his companion, the Easter and Sandwich Islands, to pass more than one whole year on the island of Cadiack and at Sitca or Norfolk Sound, and to discover an island and a shoal, hitherto unknown, but of no small importance to the navigation of the South Sea. During the time the two ships were in company, the mere journal of each must necessarily be similar, and some occurrences may have been noticed in common by both; but, even in that case, the Author of the present work trusts, that his observations will seldom be found to be a mere repetition of those already before the public, as the same objects are often viewed under different aspects by different men, conformably to their various education, dispositions, and character. Even where the descriptions coincide, the coincidence may not be wholly useless, as affording an evidence to the accuracy of both observers.

With a view to render the narrative of this volume more interesting to the general as well as to the professional reader, such a style of relation has been attempted, as, it is hoped, may induce the former not to throw it aside as a mere naval log-book; while the seaman will probably conceive it entitled to his attention, from the many nautical observations interspersed, as well as the charts and drawings giving new light to the hydrography of the seas. For the fidelity of these charts, the Author holds himself strictly responsible, having drawn them from an actual survey.

It has been observed by an English writer of great reputation,* that a reader peruses a book with more pleasure when he knows something of the author. In compliance with a feeling so natural to the human mind, and from no motive of vanity, the Author of the following narrative will conclude this preface, by stating a few particulars of himself.

He was born in the town of Negin, in Little Russia, on the 2d of April, 1773, of noble parents.

Being destined for the navy, he was sent, when ten years of age, to the Marine Academy at Cronstadt, where he remained studying the theory of his future profession till he was fifteen.

In the year 1788, having finished his education, he was made a midshipman in the Russian navy. In that situation he continued during the Swedish war, and was in almost all the general engagements in the Baltic, and especially in that memorable

---

* Addison.

defence of Revel in the year 1790, when the Russian squadron, under the command of admiral Basil Chichagoff, being moored across the bay, sustained the attack of the whole Swedish fleet, three times stronger than itself, and obliged it at last to retire with the loss of two ships, of which one, the Prince Charles, was taken, and the other burnt in the offing of the bay.

In 1793 he was made a lieutenant, and had the honour of being chosen, by her late imperial majesty, Catharine the Second, to be sent to England, to serve as a volunteer in the British navy.

On his arrival in England, he devoted a few months to the study of the language of the country, and early in the spring of 1794 sailed for North America, in the L'Oiseau frigate, commanded by captain (now admiral) Robert Murray, together with the squadron under the command of the honourable George Murray, rear-admiral of the white.

Near the coast of the United States he was at the taking of a large fleet of American ships, which were bound to France with provisions, under the convoy of the French frigate La Concorde, and other armed vessels. It was then he saw, for the first time, the activity of the British ships in chasing an enemy.

By her superior sailing, the L'Oiseau captured, besides many merchant-vessels, an armed brig, called Chigamoga, on board of which was Monsieur Belgard, a black general, well known in the French West-India islands.

After this capture, the L'Oiseau repaired to Halifax to refit, and then sailed on a winter cruise. During this cruise she was blown off the coast of the Chesapeak, sprung a leak, and was carried to the West-Indies.

There the writer of these memoirs was attacked by the yellow-fever, which raged through all the islands; and he has no doubt that he should have fallen a victim, but for the kindness of captain Murray, who not only gave up for his accommodation a part of his own cabin, but employed every means in his power to counteract the violence of the distemper.

In the year 1795 he left the frigate L'Oiseau, and proceeded on a course of travels in America. He passed through the United States, from Boston to the Savanna; and, after spending the winter in Philadelphia, returned in the following year to Halifax; where, finding that his old commander and friend had sailed for England, he entered on board the frigate La Topase, commanded by captain Church. In this frigate he was in a very smart engagement with L'Elizabeth, a French frigate of equal force, which ended in the capture of the enemy.

In the year 1797, he returned to England in the Cleopatra, commanded by captain (now admiral) Penrose. This frigate brought home admiral George Murray; who, having unfortunately been struck by apoplexy, was obliged to resign his command of the Halifax squadron, to the great affliction of all who served under him.

As the chief object of the writer of this sketch was to see, if possible, every part of the world, he availed himself of an opportunity, which offered, of going to the Cape of Good Hope, in the Raisonnable line-of-battle ship, under the command of captain (now admiral) Charles Boyles. On his arrival at the Cape, he was appointed by admiral Pringle to the Sceptre, of sixty-eight guns, commanded by captain Edwards. Being however indisposed, he was obliged to reside chiefly on shore; and he afterwards travelled several hundred miles into the interior of the country, for the benefit of his health.

In the year 1798, he sailed in the Sceptre, with the troops commanded by general Baird, which were dispatched from the Cape, on account of the well-known war with Tippoo Saib, for Madras, and afterwards for Bombay.

PREFACE.

There he received from his Imperial Majesty, Paul the First, a promotion to the rank of master and commander, with orders, at the same time, to return to Russia. In consequence of this, instead of going to China, as he had intended, he took his passage in a country ship, and in 1799 arrived in England, where he spent a whole winter.

In 1800 he returned to Russia; and, on his arrival, was appointed to the command of a frigate; and the next year had the honour of being knighted with the military order of St. George of the fourth class.

In 1802 the expedition round the world was planned. He bought and equipped both ships in England, and had the command of the Neva conferred on him. The voyage, as will be seen, occupied three years of his life; namely, from August 1803, to the same month in the year 1806.

In 1807 he commanded a squadron in the Baltic, consisting of six sloops of war and four cutters; and was the same year appointed commander-in-chief of all the private yachts and vessels of his Imperial Majesty.

In 1808, he had also the command of a line-of-battle ship, of seventy-four guns; but, finding his constitution in a debilitated state, from the different climates he had visited, and the many years he had spent at sea, he found himself under the necessity, in 1809, of retiring from the service, with the half-pay of a post-captain.

LIST

OF

THE OFFICERS AND SEAMEN

BELONGING TO

THE SHIP NEVA, OF 350 TONS AND 14 GUNS.

Commander.
Urey Lisiansky.

Lieutenants.
Pavel Arboosoff.
Petre Powalishin.

Midshipmen.
Fedor Kowedyaeff.
Vaseeley Berg.

Master.
Danilo Kaleeneen.

Master's Mate.
Fedool Malhzoff.

Physician.
Moretz Laband.

Surgeon's Mate.
Alexey Mootofkin.

Purser.
Nicoly Korobeetzeen.

Chaplain.
Father Hedion.

Boatswain.
Petre Roosacoff.

Quarter-Masters.
Oseep Averianoff.
Semen Zeleneen.
Petre Kaleeneen.

Seamen.
Vaseeley Maklashoff.
Ivan Popoff.
Fadey Nikeeteen.
Petre Borisoff.
Oolian Mihyloff.

Seamen.
Ivan Havreeloff.
Stefan Konopleff.
Andrey Hoodyacoff.
Ilia Ivanoff.
Vaseeley Stepanoff.
Egor Salandin.
Alexandre Potyarkin.
Vaseeley Ivanoff.
Petre Serheyeff.
Fedot Feelatieff.
Beek-morza Usoopoff.
Emelian Kreevoshein.
Andrey Wolodeemeroff.
Ivan Andreyeff.
Ameer Mansooroff.
Dmetrey Zabiroff.
Larion Afanassieff.
Radion Epeefanoff.
Potap Kvashneen.
Ivan Vaseelieff.
Ivan Alexeyeff.
Ivan Horboonoff.
Mitrofan Zeleneen.

Gunners.
Fedor Egoroff.
Mosey Kolpakoff.

Carpenter.
Ivan Korukeen.

Carpenter's Mate.
Terentey Nekludoff.

Sail-Maker.
Stefan Vacooreen.

Cooper.
Pavel Pomeeleff.

DIRECTIONS TO THE BINDER.

The Portrait, *to face* the Title.
The Chart of the World, *to face* ....Page 1
The Chart of the Harbour of St. Catharine, *to face* 40
The Chart of the Washington Islands, *to face* 61
The Chart of the Harbour of St. Paul, *to face* 144
Plate I., *to face* 150
Plate II., *to face* 163
The Chart of the Island of Cadiack with its Environs, *to face* 169
View of the Harbour of St. Paul, *to face* 191
Plate III., *to face* 205
View of New Archangel, *to face* 218
The Chart of the Coast from Behring's Bay to the Sea-Otter Bay, *to face* 221
The Chart of the Harbour of New Archangel, *to face* 235
The Chart of the Island of Lisiansky, *to face* 256

ERRATA.

Page 12, line 6, *for* 13° 55′, *read* 13° 28′.
—, — 7, *for* 13° 28′, *read* 13° 55′.
22, — 7, *for* 26° 23′, *read* 25° 23′.
—, — 13, *for* the acceleration of No. 50, *read* that of No. 50.
28, — 20, *for* evening, *read* morning.
31, — 9, *for* harbour, *read* Fort.
46, — 21, *for* Blay, *read* Bligh.
51, — 21, *for* thirty, *read* thirty-seven.

Page 61, at the beginning of the chapter, *for* 26th, *read* 21st.
63, — 8, *for* west, *read* north-west.
115, — 11, To the list of islands, add Onihoo.
169, — 9, *for* Dranker's Bay, *read* Drunkard's Bay.
311, — 8, *for* the Cape, *read* St. Helena.
328, last line, *for* g, *read* h.

B&L

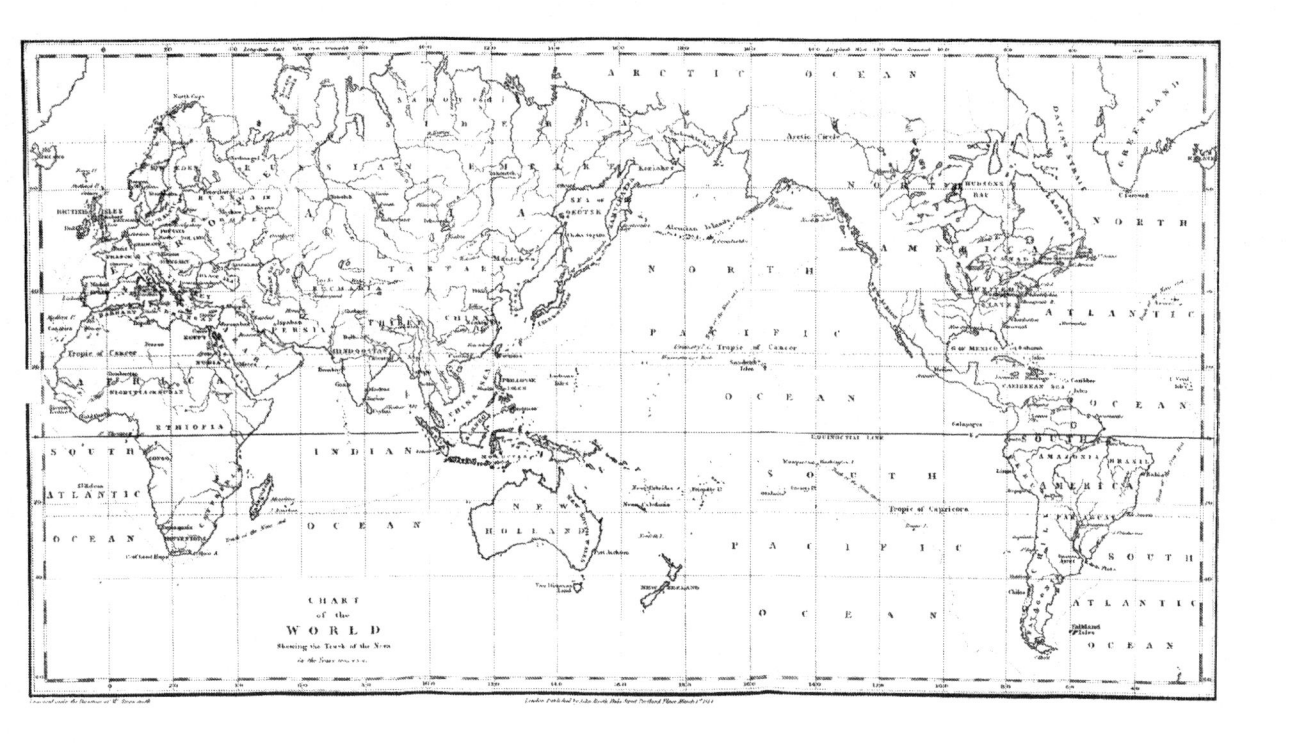

CHART
of the
WORLD

A VOYAGE ROUND THE WORLD.

CHAPTER I.

PASSAGE FROM CRONSTADT TO FALMOUTH.

Departure of the two Vessels. Russian Custom on taking leave of the Port-admiral. Arrival in Copenhagen Roads. Stay at Copenhagen. Method of purifying confined Air. Vessel of a curious Construction. Departure from Copenhagen. Separation of the two Ships in a Storm in the North Sea. Arrival at Falmouth.

THE two vessels were ready for sea, and moved from the harbour of Cronstadt into the roads on the 19th of July, 1803. They were however detained by contrary winds till the 7th of August, when, at ten o'clock in the morning, the ambassador, Mr. Rezanoff, his majesty's chamberlain, arriving on board the Nadejda, they departed with a fair southerly wind.

We should have found the delay we had experienced tedious and disagreeable, but for the continual visits of our friends and relations, who were curious to see the preparations for so remote a voyage, and anxious for their countrymen, who were about to undertake it for the first time.

1803.
August.

On our passing the guard-ship, admiral Hanicoff, port-admiral and commander in chief of Cronstadt, came on board to take leave of us; and, agreeably to the ancient Russian custom, he presented me with a loaf of bread and some salt; the first of which I carefully kept during the whole voyage, and gave him back, in perfect preservation, on my return to Russia.

Being now in deep water, I ordered the ship's company to be mustered on the quarter-deck; and, in the best manner I was able, I represented to them the magnitude of the enterprise, the courage, patience, and perseverance we should be called upon to exert, in order to succeed in it, and the pleasure and benefit that would result to them from cordiality with one another, due obedience to their superiors, and the observance of perfect cleanliness in every thing relating both to the ship and to themselves.

The wind varied much in its strength till half past ten in the evening, when it changed to the south-west, and continued there for four days, during which both ships were obliged to ply to windward, and could get no further than the Isle of Hogland. On the 11th, after a calm of some hours, it shifted to the south-east, and carried us briskly forward.

11th.

During the prevalence of the contrary winds, I employed myself in arranging the distribution of provisions to my ship's company; and I regulated the allowance thus:—To each man per day, one pound of meat, one pound of biscuit, and a glass of brandy; and to each man per week, a pound of butter, a mess of pea-soup, a casha or grit pudding, and what might be deemed a sufficient quantity of mustard and vinegar. As we found, upon trial, that our beef, though lately prepared, was rather too salt, I gave orders for it to be regularly soaked two days previously to its distribution.

On the 13th, though the wind fell considerably, we cleared the Gulf of Finland, having passed Cape Dagerort the day before.

We now found that our fresh water began to smell rather strong; it was therefore exposed to the air in a tub made for the purpose, and worked with Ostrige's purifying machine.

On the 14th we had easterly winds and fine weather; and at five o'clock the next morning the Isle of Gottland appeared to the north-west. About this time one of our best seamen, in drawing up a bucket of water, fell overboard, and, notwithstanding our utmost endeavours to recover him, was unfortunately drowned. What will appear extraordinary in this accident is, that, though an expert swimmer, he sunk the instant he fell, and never rose afterwards.

At half past five in the morning of the 16th, the thick weather clearing up, we descried the island of Bornholm at no great distance, and found ourselves in the midst of a multitude of ships of different nations, some beating to windward, and others, like ourselves, making the best of the fair breeze. I was much pleased to see that my ship was the best sailer amongst them.

At nine in the evening the wind died away; and as the weather again grew thick, we could only approach the place called Ste-

1803.
August.
vens, and we came to an anchor not far from our companion, the Nadejda.

17th. At day-break of the 17th we got under way, and, with a light north-easter, reached the island of Draco, where we were becalmed, and we again cast anchor. The current was so strong, that I might have reached Copenhagen with ease, had I not deemed it proper to wait for captain Krusenstern. Fortunately, we lost nothing by the delay; an easterly wind soon springing up, which brought both ships into the Copenhagen roads at four in the afternoon.

19th. In the morning of the 19th our ships warped up close to the harbour, to take in with more ease the different things that had previously been provided for us. About midnight, a tremendous squall, accompanied with heavy rain and with thunder and lightning, came on, and raged till nearly day-light. As my marine barometer, however, had some time before indicated its approach, I was prepared for its reception, and sustained the shock without damage.

While the articles alluded to above were conveying on board, I ordered all the water casks to be taken on shore, and well burnt;* and our beef, which, from having been put into unsound casks, had acquired a bad smell, to be re-salted.

---

* For burning the inside of these water casks, shavings were used, and the burning was continued till the inside of the cask was converted to a coal, of about the eighth part of an inch thick. By this proceeding, and by putting a small quantity of charcoal powder into each cask, we had not a drop of bad water during the voyage. I kept a cask for

Every thing else on board being now overhauled, to be more safely stowed, I found, to my very great regret, the whole of our sour crout in the highest state of corruption. This proceeded from the negligence of the company's servants, who had put it into large and improper casks. We thus found ourselves deprived of a quantity of this valuable antiscorbutic vegetable, that would have been more than sufficient for half the voyage.

At this place I had an opportunity of making acquaintance with Mr. Bugge, a gentleman whose name, as an astronomer, ranks very high. I ordered my chronometers to be taken on shore, and delivered to him, to be regulated: and I cannot forbear acknowledging, how much I am indebted to him for his polite attentions. He showed me the observatory of his Danish majesty, which I found very complete, and in the most perfect order; as well as his own collection of astronomical instruments, which were many in number, and all excellent. He rendered me a still more important service in giving me a receipt for purifying the air of any confined place by fumigation; which consisted of *magnesia nigra* and common salt, in equal quantities, with a proportional mixture of oil of vitriol: and I found by experience, that it answered the purpose in the most satisfactory manner.

Though I had many things to occupy me, in the necessary preparations for continuing our voyage, I still found leisure for

---

trial; and on my return to Cronstadt, her majesty, the empress mother, having honoured me with a visit on board, tasted the water; and pronounced it, except in colour, to be as good as she had ever drank.

1803.
August.
gratifying my curiosity in the city of Copenhagen: but as this place has been described by many abler pens than mine, I will not obtrude upon the reader any detail of it, especially as my stay in it was so short. At the same time, I cannot pass over in silence a very curious ship, of 500 tons burthen, which I saw in the harbour. When fully loaded, she drew eight feet of water, and had not a single square timber in her construction, being entirely built of deal planks, with a stern in form of a reversed triangle, and a rudder on each side of its base. She had been built by Mr. du Crest about six years before, and at the time I saw her had already made several voyages, and withstood some very tempestuous weather. The commander of her assured me, that she sailed well, and was an excellent sea-boat.

Sept. 7th.
At eight o'clock in the evening of the 7th of September, we came out of the harbour into the roads, to take advantage of the first favourable wind.

8th.
Although it blew on the 8th from the north-west, and the weather was very unsettled, we got under way in the afternoon of that day, and arrived at Elsineur about eleven at night.

15th.
From the prevalence of the wind in the same quarter, we were obliged to remain at anchor the whole week; but in the morning of the 15th it shifted to the west-south-west, and permitted us to continue our voyage.

On nearing Cape Cole, the wind gradually freshened, and at noon obliged me to take in two reefs in the top-sails. At six o'clock we passed the Anholt Reef, upon which was an American ship, that had left Elsineur some time before us. We saw her cut away her main-mast; yet I doubt her having been able to get off this dangerous range of rocks, extending several miles out to sea.*

On the 16th, at six in the morning, we passed the Skaw light; but could not perceive it, from the weather being foggy. I supposed myself, however, to be out of the Cattegat.

As it is well known, that a hold becomes foul in a tight ship sooner than in a leaky one, I ordered ours to be freshened twice a week, by pouring in clear water from the sea, and pumping it out, after it had remained twelve hours.

On the 17th the two ships came in sight of the high land of Drommels, and on the 18th encountered a violent storm. At one in the afternoon the wind blew so strong, and the sea ran so high, that the rolling of my vessel rendered the taking in the sails a most difficult task. While this was doing, the darkness became so great, from the squalls succeeding with rapidity and the rain pouring down in torrents, that we could hardly distinguish one another. Meanwhile, the waves rolled over the deck, and removed or carried away every thing we had not had time to secure from their violence. From the exertions, however, of the crew, but little damage was done, and about four o'clock every thing was comfortably adjusted. During the night we kept lights in different parts of the ship, that we might be seen by the

---

* English miles are every where used in this work.

1803.
Sept.

Nadejda. But this precaution did not prevent our separation; for at day-break, the only ship in sight was a merchantman. Persuaded, however, that nothing unfortunate had happened to our friends, I resolved to continue my course to Falmouth, which was the first appointed place of rendezvous. On the above occasion my marine barometer again showed its excellence; as it had fallen regularly during three days, and at the time of the storm was at 29 inches 3 lines.

19th. At nine o'clock in the evening of the 19th the aurora borealis made its appearance, and continued for the space of half an hour, diminishing by degrees. A few hours earlier in the evening the barometer had risen five lines.

23d. At length, on the 23d, to my great joy we reached the British shores. This was so much the more agreeable to me, as I expected a continuation of fine weather, of which we had been deprived since our entrance into the Cattegat. From the 21st the wind had greatly abated; but the sea was still so high, that, on the pitching of the ship, it often entered my cabin windows. Finding by the lead, that we were on the northern side of Deep Water Bank, I steered straight for the North Foreland. At noon we found ourselves in latitude 51° 58' north, and at eight o'clock were between the Goodwin Sands and the Falls. Though the tide was against us, yet, by means of a fair wind, we soon cleared the danger; and, having past the South Foreland and Warne, we steered for Dungeness.

24th. On the 24th the barometer was at 30 inches $2\frac{1}{2}$ lines, the weather delightful. At six in the morning we came abreast of

Beechy Head, and towards evening reached the Isle of Wight, where we were almost becalmed.

1803.
Sept.

An English frigate, which we met with the next day, informed us, that the storm we had encountered in the North Sea had raged with much violence in the Channel, and that many ships had been dismasted, and others driven on shore. We therefore thought ourselves fortunate in having escaped with the loss of a few trifles not worth mentioning, and a night's rest.

25th.

At ten o'clock in the evening of this day we saw the Eddistone light, and I had resolved to continue my course; but observing another light not far from the Eddistone's, that appeared and disappeared at regular intervals, and not being able to explain this to my satisfaction, after proceeding about six miles further, I thought it prudent to bring-to till day-light.

At break of day, seeing nothing but the Eddistone light-house, and concluding that the other light had been put up for some temporary purpose, I bore away for Falmouth, and at eleven o'clock cast anchor there.

26th.

After mooring the ship, I dispatched an officer to inform the commander of the forts of our arrival, and to inquire if our salutation would be answered by an equal number of guns. Having received a very polite answer in the affirmative, the salute was given, and I went on shore with some of my officers. Though the Nadejda had not arrived; yet, expecting her every hour, I resolved to lose no time, but prepare for sea with all expedition. My decks required to be caulked, in conse-

1803.
Sept.

quence of the storm we had encountered; and, from its being late in the year, I ordered a new set of sails to be bent. I however contrived that all my ship's company should be able to go on shore in turn, to purchase whatever they might want, and amuse themselves in the last European port at which we should touch.

My conjecture respecting the Nadejda was well-founded, for she brought-to alongside of us the third day after our arrival. She had been a greater sufferer than we by the storm, having opened the seams of her sides, so as to render a thorough caulking necessary. I was highly gratified to find that her crew had behaved with the same courage and alacrity as my own; and with this circumstance in our favour we had nothing to wish, but a common run of good fortune during the expedition, to ensure us success. During our stay at Falmouth, I visited every place worthy of remark; but as I am now writing for English readers, I shall omit, as unnecessary, the observations I made, and the description of this part of their coast.

CHAPTER II.

PASSAGE FROM FALMOUTH TO TENERIFFE.

Departure from Falmouth. Remarkable Meteor. Method of preventing Bilgewater. Precautions against Disease. Sublime Appearance of the Peak of Teneriffe from the Sea. Fortunate Escape from a Hurricane. Account of the Towns of Laguna and Santa Cruz, in the Island of Teneriffe. Bad Anchorage of the Bay of Santa Cruz. A Mummy, supposed to have been embalmed by the ancient Inhabitants of Teneriffe, given to our Ambassador.

We had for several days been ready for sea, but were detained by our ambassador's visit to London. Upon his return, on the afternoon of the 5th of October, both ships got under way, and about midnight were under full sail in the Atlantic.

The next day we had easterly winds and cold weather. Observing in the morning much bilge-water in every part of the ship, I gave orders that the hold should be filled regularly every day with sea-water mixt with burnt lime, and then pumped out; and that the hatchways should be taken off, whenever the weather permitted. This I found to be the best method of prevention.

All the way from the Lizard Point we had a fair wind blowing fresh; but it much abated on the 10th. We had observed for several days a number of petrels; and on this day our decks

1803.
October.
were covered with small birds, blown by the south-east winds from the Continent. They were so feeble, that the cats on board caught a great number of them. At eleven o'clock I took some distances between the sun and moon, and an altitude for our chronometers; and I found by the former, that we were, at noon, in 13° 55' west longitude;* and by the latter, in 13° 28', our latitude being 38° 44' north. In the evening, we saw to the south-west a very remarkable meteor. It passed almost horizontally over a quarter of the sky, and disappeared under a cloud, leaving a track behind, which remained for the space of ten minutes in a very luminous state.

17th.
The wet and gloomy weather, which had continued with little or no intermission since our departure from Falmouth, on the 17th cleared up. Our ship's crew were not the only beings that rejoiced at the circumstance; for we were surrounded by a number of sharks, who, playing round the ship, apparently testified by their gambols their delight at the change. During the continuance of the bad weather I would not permit the decks to be washed; but ordered them to be scraped every day, charcoal in stoves to be kept burning below, and, where the air had not a free circulation, warm vinegar to be sprinkled. This method of cleaning ships in cold climates is much preferable to frequent washings, which, from the decks not drying quickly, is sometimes productive of disease.

Nearing the tropic, I ordered our winter clothes to be stowed away; a jacket and a pair of trowsers for each man, in case of

---

* The longitude is reckoned from Greenwich.

damp and chilly nights, excepted. By this measure we gained between decks a great deal of room. I also laid it down as a rule not to be departed from, that, during our stay in warm climates, a third of the crew should in turn wash themselves every morning from head to foot with sea-water.

On the 18th we had a light breeze from the north-west, and fine weather. At noon I found myself in 30° 8′ north latitude, and 15° 14′ west longitude; and as we were only eight miles to the southward and thirteen to the eastward of our reckoning the day before, I concluded the current was not very strong. At three o'clock we saw, from the mast-head, the islands called the Salvages, to the north-west; and as the weather now became warm, I gave orders that, till our arrival in a colder climate, grog should be served out instead of brandy; a change which our sailors did not much relish, from being accustomed to what they called *the solid stuff*.

On the 19th, as soon as it was light, the island of Teneriffe was descried, forty-five miles to the south-west. The clouds hanging over it prevented our distinguishing the Peak till seven o'clock, when this celebrated mountain, with its snow-crowned summit, showed itself in all its splendour. The majestic height of this enormous mass, raising its huge head from out of the bosom, as it were, of the vast expanse of waters, struck me with force for the first time, and impressed my mind with sublime emotions towards the Creator. On my formerly passing the island, the haziness of the weather had prevented me from beholding this wonderful spectacle.

1803.
October.

Early in the morning of this day, a large ship was perceived at a distance; and about five o'clock in the afternoon she came up with us, and hoisted a French flag. We also hoisted our ensign, and spoke to her. She proved to be the French privateer, L'Egyptienne; who, taking us for English merchantmen, had, in idea, made sure of both ships as prizes: on finding, however, her mistake, she sheered off without annoying us.

On taking the bearings of the north point of the island, it was found that our chronometers went perfectly right, and that our reckoning was to the westward eighty-one miles. During the last twenty-four hours, the current was nine miles to the eastward and eight to the southward.

20th. At day-break of the 20th we bore for the harbour of Santa Cruz, and about noon anchored there, with the assistance of the captain of the port, who came on board my ship in the offing. As soon as we were moored, I went on shore with captain Krusenstern, to pay my respects to the governor-general, the Marquis de la Casa Caghigal, who received us, I am sorry to say, with a politeness very different from what characterizes the nobility of Spain. In the course of the day the privateer that spoke with us yesterday, and a Spanish brig of war, entered the harbour. The brig brought orders from the court of Spain, that, in case of our arrival at Teneriffe, every attention and assistance should be given to us; and the politeness of the governor rose in consequence of it. An American brig also came to an anchor; and by her we learned that, in not making the island of Madeira, we had had a most fortunate escape; as, about the time we should have been there, a hurricane had taken place; and of so tremendous a nature, that many small houses were torn from their foundations, and nearly all the ships in the roads driven on shore, or dashed to pieces on the rocks. The American herself would have been inevitably lost upon the Lock Rocks, against which she was hastening, but for a sudden squall from the shore, that snatched her out of the jaws of death, by driving her forcibly to sea. We thus had reason to bless the contrary winds, that hindered us from reaching a place at which we had intended to touch, and which might have proved the termination of our voyage.

Our principal view, in touching at Teneriffe, was to furnish ourselves with fresh provisions and wine; and we applied for this purpose to Mr. Armstrong, to whom captain Krusenstern had a letter of recommendation. With the utmost alacrity, he dispatched his servants about the country to purchase what we wanted; and in the mean time did every thing in his power to render our stay on shore agreeable. His wife, a beautiful and well-educated woman, by her musical accomplishments, captivating manners, and anxiety to please, cheered those hours which, from the unsociable and reserved life of the Spaniards of Teneriffe, would otherwise have dragged heavily on.

Though Laguna has been denominated the metropolis of the island of Teneriffe, Santa Cruz is in reality the chief or government city, from the governor-general of the Canary Islands residing in it, and from trade there being in a much more flourishing state. The buildings of this town are principally of stone; and, by being situated on the declivity of a hill, afford a very pleasing prospect from the sea, and can easily be kept clean.

1803.
October.

The bay of Santa Cruz is defended by three forts, St. Pedro, St. Raphael, and St. Christoval; a cannon-shot from which last had the unfortunate chance of taking off an arm from the ever-to-be-regretted Nelson, in his well-known attack upon the island, in the year 1797.

From the accounts I could gather, the population of Santa Cruz does not much exceed five thousand souls. The lower class of its inhabitants are so very poor, that many of them have no other bed-chamber than the street, no other covering than the sacks they use for their daily labour, and no other food for subsistence than stinking fish. Of the higher class I can say but little: judging, however, from their solitary life, and their not having a single public place of amusement, or a decent garden (except a small inclosure that hardly deserves the name), to which to retire for change of air during the extreme heat of summer; I must join in the common opinion of foreigners residing on the island, that, a few comforts excepted, their life is scarcely more enviable than that of the poor.

This town can always furnish ships with fresh provisions, excellent water, and plenty of live stock, fruits, and other vegetables. All these articles, however, are excessively dear, wine excepted; for a pipe of which I paid only ninety Spanish dollars. As a specimen of their dearness, I shall mention, that a small sheep cost us seven dollars, a middling-sized pumpkin, a dollar, and a fowl, half a dollar. But the most mortifying circumstance is, that there is no regular market in the town: every thing that is wanted must accordingly be sent for into the country. This was so great an inconvenience, that, but for the assistance of Mr. Armstrong, we should have been detained here for a considerable period, and probably have gone at last with half the articles only which this truly obliging gentleman had the goodness to purchase for us.

The bay of Santa Cruz is not a safe anchoring place, especially in winter; from its being open to the south-east, a quarter from which the wind sometimes blows with great violence. To this may be added, that it has in many places a rocky bottom, and abounds so much with lost anchors and warps, that it is necessary to buoy up the cables to prevent their chafing: we found three small casks to each of our cables to be sufficient for the purpose. The best anchorage here is reckoned to be in from thirty-five to eighteen fathoms. The Spaniards commonly moor their ships with two anchors each way; but this I think too much, especially if the anchors and cables are good: however, it is adviseable to have all the ship's anchors in readiness, particularly in the concluding months of the year. We were moored south-south-east and north-north-west, having Fort Christoval north 81° 30' west; South Fort, south 55° 30' west; and St. Raphael, north 5° east: and the only damage we sustained was the loss of a warp, which we could not heave up when we unmoored.

To come into the bay, you must sail close in shore, after passing round the north-east part of the island; and you should endeavour to get bottom as soon as possible: for which purpose a heavy lead with fifty fathoms of line should be in readiness. The shore here is very high, and so deceiving, that when

1803.
October.

I thought myself four leagues from it, I afterwards found by my run that I had been mistaken by nearly half that distance.

During our stay here, the Peak was so constantly over-clouded, that we could only see it twice distinctly. The summit was then covered with snow; but this is not the case, we were informed, in the months of June and July.

I had promised myself much pleasure from the observatory of the town, of which the governor had the goodness to permit us a free use; but my expectations in this respect were disappointed. The craziness of the building not permitting us to use the quicksilver artificial horizon, we were obliged to make all our observations on board; and from 172 altitudes taken between eight and nine o'clock in the morning, it appeared that my chronometer No. 50 had lost 14″; that Pennington's had gained 2′ 9″ since the 1st of September, and No. 136 lost 3′ 32″ since the 18th of July.

The latitude of our anchoring place, according to the different meridian altitudes, appeared to be 28° 26′ 36″ north. The variation of the compass, 15° 22′ west.

Upon our departure, Mrs. Armstrong presented me with a small but curious and perfect collection of conchs and shells, which she had received from Jamaica. I also procured several pieces of the lava of the Peak, amongst which were some that consisted entirely of sulphur. Our ambassador was still more fortunate; he was presented with a complete human body, like a mummy, and two dried legs, in perfect preservation: from which it would appear, either that the ancient inhabitants of the island were acquainted with the art of embalming, or that the part of the mountain where they buried their dead must have possessed properties capable of preserving animal substances from decay.

Mr. Berg, a midshipman of my vessel, having visited Lagona, gave me his observations upon that town, from which I made the following extract. "The road from Santa Cruz to Lagona is so mountainous, that asses and mules are the only mode of conveyance. The town consists of about a hundred houses, which, a few excepted, are extremely poor, three monasteries, and two convents."* Mr. Berg visited the monastery of St. Augustine, and found it richly endowed. Speaking of his journey, he says, that it was almost a continued scene of poverty. The environs of the town, however, were truly beautiful and picturesque.

---

* Mr. Lansdorff says that it contains only two convents of monks and two of nuns.

CHAPTER III.

PASSAGE FROM TENERIFFE TO THE ISLAND OF ST. CATHARINE.

Departure from Teneriffe. Precautions for Health on entering the warm Latitudes. Amusements of the Crew. Make the Island of St. Antony, one of the Cape de Verd Islands. Variation of the Chronometers. Impolicy of passing through the Cape de Verd Islands in going to the Cape of Good Hope. Rejoicings on Crossing the Line. Importance of attending to the Sea Currents. Seek in vain for the Island of Ascension. Cape Frio. Island of Alvaredo. Singular Peril of the two Ships. Arrival and Stay at St. Catharine. Account of that Island, its Productions, and Inhabitants.

1803.
October.
27th. WHILST we were getting under way, on the 27th of October, the governor with his suite came on board to take a formal leave of us. Upon his quitting the Nadejda, captain Krusenstern fired a salute, which was returned by an equal number of guns from the castle. He then came on board the Neva, where I bade him farewell by three cheers from the shrouds, which I had previously manned for that purpose. This ceremony over, the two ships set sail with a light breeze.

30th. Having passed the Canary Islands, the change of the atmosphere was very perceptible: from the 30th the air became so close and thick, that every one on board felt himself heavy and indolent. From this circumstance I thought proper to order some lemon-juice, (of which a sufficient quantity had been taken on board at Santa Cruz,) to be mixed with the grog served out to the crew; and I occasionally changed this beverage for Teneriffe wine. It may easily be imagined that we exposed ourselves as little as possible to the scorching heat of the sun, to which the whole of my people were strangers; none of them having ever before quitted the North Sea. By way of precaution against this inconvenience, an awning was spread, and strict injunctions given that no one should appear upon deck without a hat or cap, or sleep out of his birth; well aware, that many of the crew, finding themselves too warm below, would prefer lying upon deck, notwithstanding the danger of sleeping in the open air. These injunctions must have appeared rather severe to men, hardy by nature, and little accustomed to any scrupulous care of their health. In other respects, their situation was not to be complained of. From the trade-winds blowing moderately, they had so little to do, that I seldom heard them move, unless when walking the deck for exercise, or upon the appearance of some curious object which they were unacquainted with. The grampus, benita, and dolphin, were our constant companions; and the last of these was an universal favourite, especially when in chase of the flying-fish. My people had a further source of amusement, and of a most rational kind. I had provided for them a copy of the Voyages both of Anson and Cook; which, in leisure hours, were read to them by such of their comrades, in turn, as were best qualified for the office. In providing these books, I had not only their amusement, but the benefit of the expedition in view; and both purposes were probably answered. Certain, however, it is, that they crowded round the reader, on these occasions, with eager curiosity.

1803.
Nov.
6th.

At five o'clock in the morning of the 6th of November we saw the island of St. Antony, one of the Cape de Verd islands, twenty miles to the southward. Bringing the middle of it to bear south half east, I took some altitudes for the regulation of my chronometers, by which the longitude appeared as follows: by the chronometer No. 50, 25° 11'; by Pennington's, 25° 45'; and by that of No. 136, 26° 23'. Finding the last-mentioned to vary the least, I altered the rate of the other two; so that, for the future, No. 50, instead of gaining 0" 63, might be considered as losing 2" 87; and Pennington's as gaining 10" 83, instead of 4" 96. The variation of Pennington's chronometer might be accounted for by its having been taken on shore at Teneriffe; but the acceleration of No. 50, as it had never been moved, baffled all my inquiries as to the cause; and though the alteration of the rates may appear a bold measure, I felt myself warranted in it, both by my observations, and by comparing the journals of my chronometers, to which I scrupulously attended every day.

10th.

Having nothing further to do with the Cape de Verd Islands, we shaped a southerly course, in retiring from the shore; but the wind from the south-east was so light, that the Neva could not pass the whole group till the 10th, when we were in 13° 53' latitude north, and 27° 13' west longitude.

If nothing is wanted from these islands, it is better to pass them to the westward, and not venture nearer than ten or twelve miles from the island of St. Antony; as it often happens that the wind blows fresh at sea, whilst a perfect calm prevails near the shore. Some ships, in their way to the Cape of Good

Hope, pass to the eastward of the islands of St. Antony, St. Lucia, and St. Vincent; while others attempt a passage through the group: but these last often regret the folly of their enterprise. It is true, that if it succeed, the voyage is shortened by 150 miles; but considering the risk, from variable winds, calms, and currents, it is certainly a very impolitic step. A proof of this I witnessed in the year 1797, when the Raisonnable man-of-war, in convoying some East-Indiamen, was induced by one of the East-India captains to attempt a passage amongst the islands; but, after twelve hours labour, we were obliged, from some of the above causes, to desist, and were glad to get back, to resume our former course.

On the 16th, being in latitude 6° north and longitude 21° 8' west, we lost the north-east trade-wind, and had variable winds in its stead. This change was accompanied with squalls, and with thunder, lightning, and rain. The rain was indeed so heavy and continual, that, as a security against damp, I ordered the ship to be fumigated with oil of vitriol, and stoves of live charcoal to be hung between decks. The same unfavourable weather prevailed till we reached the latitude of 1° 34' north, and the longitude of 22° 57' west, where we received the south-east trade-wind, and it cleared up.

During the last nine days we had suffered greatly from the inclemency of the weather. The rain, however, had its advantages, as it furnished us with about thirty casks of good water for washing and making spruce-beer, the essence of which I had obtained in England.

1803.
Nov.

It will not be deemed astonishing, that during this period we saw nothing near us, except a tropic bird, and some dolphins and benitas.

26th.

By observation on the 26th, we were in 10′ south, and in 24° 9′ west. As soon as I was sure of our being on the point of passing the line, I put the ship about; and coming up with captain Krusenstern, complimented him upon our arrival in the southern hemisphere with three cheers. I shall detain the reader a moment by describing our feelings on this occasion; for which I shall, no doubt, be pardoned, when I mention that we were the first Russian navigators that had ever crossed the equator.

27th.

The ceremony of salutation only served as a prelude to the commemoration, on the next day, of the most important epoch of our lives. We commenced with the performance of prayers by our chaplain. This solemnity over, I assembled the whole of my crew, officers and men, upon the quarter-deck; and, congratulating them on the honour they had acquired, by being the first of their nation who had passed under the line, I ordered a bumper of Teneriffe to be served round; and, with hearts softened by the recollection of our native land, and dilated with joy at the hitherto successful course of our voyage, we pledged one another to the health and long life of our Imperial Master and his august family. The glee of my ship's crew was great, but it was afterwards not a little heightened by the excellent feast I had ordered them; consisting of soup made of portable cakes, ducks, potatoes, and plum-pudding, with a bottle of porter to every three men, and plenty of Teneriffe wine. During our own dinner in the cabin, the Imperial ensign was hoisted, and the whole of our guns discharged; and "Success to the Russian flag," in repeated bumpers, was re-echoed from the cabin to the fore-castle. Never, I believe, did a ship of any nation pass under the line with so few sour faces; nor do I think any seaman who reads this account, will deny that our dinner was infinitely preferable to the best ducking my men could have undergone.* Our evening passed as merrily as our dinner; and every man retired to his birth, without a thought but what tended to the prosperity of his country, and the happiness of the dear objects he had left there.

Amongst the many different things deserving the attention of navigators, the sea-currents are not the least important. I am indeed firmly persuaded, that attention to this subject may lead to useful discoveries. I accordingly made it a rule to keep a journal of the daily difference between the ship's course by reckoning and observation, and shall give my opinion on this point as often as an opportunity occurs in the progress of my narrative. From the Canary Islands to the latitude of 6° north, where the variable winds took place, the motion of the sea was towards the south-west quarter; it then took a north-east direction as far as 1° 34′ north, when we received the south-east trade; and then again to the westward, in which it continued till we passed the equator. On calculating the variation of the current, from all the above-mentioned tendencies of the sea, it

---

* This custom of ducking on crossing the line ought to be discontinued, on account of the disorderly proceedings to which it often gives rise, and the injury which the health sometimes suffers by it.

appears that the Neva, in her run from Teneriffe to the line, was driven by it about sixty miles to the southward, and nearly the same distance to the westward.

After having passed the equator, the south-east trade freshened by degrees, and, as we proceeded, veered a little to the east, which was favourable to our course.

On the 5th of December, when in latitude 16° 30′ south, and longitude 31° 18′ west, the wind shifted to the north-east. In the morning I took some lunar distances, by which the longitude was found to be 30° 38′, differing forty miles from the chronometers; but as it is impossible to depend upon observations of this kind to the nicety of a few miles, I conceive our situation in the chart to be nearly right.

Captain Krusenstern came on board the Neva to-day, to dine with me, and recommended our going in search of the island of Ascension. I readily consented to this, as we had the best opportunity in the world of resolving a point of such consequence to mariners, with hardly any loss of time to ourselves. The two ships therefore steered accordingly.

We continued this search till the 9th; but finding that all our attempts would be vain, or at least that the island does not exist in or about the latitude of 20° 30′ and between the longitude of 30° and 37°, we resumed our former course. As the wind was perfectly favourable, I ordered all the casks on board to be prepared for fresh water, being determined to have as much of this useful commodity with me as possible. I also took precautions in time to preserve the health of my people when they should arrive at the Brazils: amongst other regulations, I ordered the watch-officers to take strict care that no one under their command should dispose of any thing belonging to him; and, as a greater security against this, that the baggage should be registered and given in charge to the petty officers; for I knew that the Brazilians were very apt to make the common men drunk, and then buy of them clothes and other useful articles.

The northerly winds had now blown fresh, and, for nearly a week, the ships had made a rapid progress. On the 11th, being surrounded with butterflies of every kind, and finding myself in the evening in fifty-five fathoms water, with bottom of shells, coral, and pebble-stones, I expected to fall in with Cape Frio the next morning; in which I was not mistaken. We saw it at five o'clock to the westward, about thirty miles distant. We were then in forty fathoms, with sandy and oozy ground. On approaching the shore I hove out a dredge, but caught only some very small shell-fish, resembling crabs. They were about the fifth or sixth of an inch long, and very quick in their motions. There was such a quantity of these curious animals, that when the decks were washed, every bucket of water contained from five to ten. We were also surrounded by dolphins, one of which we caught, that measured four foot in length. Having been brought alive on the quarter-deck, I saw it change colour eight times before it died. Some of the hues were extremely beautiful.

Our voyage from the equator to this place was shortened in some measure, by the current assisting us sixty-two miles

1803.
Dec.

to the southward, and seventy-four to the westward: its direction during the south-east trade, or till we arrived at the latitude of 15° south, was to the south-west, when it changed to the north-east.

13th. On the 13th we had southerly wind and fine weather. Being all the day in sight of Cape Frio, I could easily adjust my chronometers, of which I found No. 50 and No. 136 to the eastward of the true longitude; and especially the last, which had lost seventy miles, if we allow Cape Frio to be in 41° 43′ west. By the azimuth of yesterday and to-day the variation of the compass was 4° 35′ east.

14th. In the night of the 14th we lost sight of shore, and at noon, by observation, were in latitude 24° 14′ south, and in longitude 42° 17′ west, by No. 50, which had been regulated by the bearings of Cape Frio.

16th. Reckoning ourselves, on the 16th, near the island of St. Catharine, we bent our cables; and about eight o'clock in the evening brought-to, with an intention of keeping in thirty fathoms water all night.

17th. At four in the evening of the next day, we saw a small island to the south-south-west; shortly after, another was perceptible to the west-south-west; and about half after eight, the whole shore was completely in sight. Thinking that we were to the southward of the island of Alvaredo, I altered my course to the north-west; and sailed along shore at about seven miles distance, having twenty-five, twenty-three, and twenty-two fathoms water, with pebble and fine sand and broken shells. At ten the weather became hazy, and did not allow us to take the meridian altitude. This deprived us of the only means we had of ascertaining our situation; and as we had no charts of this place, except lord Anson's, upon which we could not rely, we resolved to continue along shore till the next day, in the hope of a pilot, or of good weather for observation.

Though the air on the 18th was clearer than on the preceding day, we could not distinctly see the shore till noon, when my ship's latitude, by observation, was 26° 59' south. While making my observations, I discovered a small brig to the south-west, and went in pursuit of her; but after a run of about eight miles, finding I was getting too near the land, I gave up the chase. At three o'clock, captain Krusenstern came up with me, and proposed surveying the coast to the southward, previously to our going into harbour. We had hardly formed this resolution, when we were becalmed. The clouds began to gather fast about us, and thunder was heard to the southward. Deeming this a prognostic of bad weather, our plan of survey was of course abandoned, and we shortened sail as quickly as possible. At four o'clock a heavy squall, with rain, came on; and the weather growing worse and worse, I was obliged to take in all my sails, except the main-top-sail, which was closely reefed, and the fore-sail and mizen. At ten we were in a situation of the utmost peril. The wind blew strong, the sea ran extremely high, and the darkness was so great that our ships could not see each other: in consequence, we had nearly run foul of the Nadejda. The vessels were on the point of coming in contact when I was called upon deck.

1803.
Dec.

Seeing the danger, I instantly brailed the fore-sail, and kept my wind as near as possible: the Nadejda at the same time hoisted her fore-top-mast stay-sail, and bore away; and thus, providentially, no damage ensued. Though the wind abated about midnight, its strength was still so great, that we did not again 20th. catch sight of shore till the 20th; on which day, at noon, we found ourselves exactly where we had been forty-eight hours before. At two in the afternoon, I took some lunar distances, by which the longitude was found to be 48° 20'. At the same time my chronometers gave:

Pennington	-	-	-	-	48°	4' west.
No. 50	-	-	-	-	47	31
No. 136	-	-	-	-	46	33

At four a pilot came on board, and confirmed my conjecture, that one of the islands in sight was Alvaredo. Of this I should not have entertained a doubt, if I had not found this island placed in some charts to the southward of St. Catharine. By advice of the pilot we remained in the offing till sun-rise the 21st. next morning, when we made for the shore, and at six o'clock in the afternoon came to anchor off the castle of Santa Cruz. Our passage into the harbour was between the islands of Alvaredo and Gallos. From the account given by La Perouse of this passage, I expected to have found it very difficult; instead of which, it proved one of the easiest I had ever attempted. I crossed the whole breadth of it, and no where found less than twenty-one fathoms of water, over a bottom of clay. I also sent my jolly-boat to sound; and it reported fourteen fathoms close to the breakers of the island of Gallos, and eleven fathoms near the Alvaredo, dark muddy ground in both places. To reach the harbour, you must pass between the above-mentioned islands; and then, keeping the depth of five fathoms, if the ship be large, steer south-south-west and south-west. In entering this passage, we once had four-and-a-half fathoms only; but on hauling to the westward, the water instantly deepened. From the island of Alvaredo the depth gradually decreases, and about the castle of Ponta Grossa no more than five fathoms are to be found. From thence it again increases to six fathoms, and continues at this depth to the harbour of Santa Cruz.

When we anchored, the bearing of the Ponta Grossa was north 71° east; Ratondoos, south 10° east; Santa Cruz, north 15° west; and the north-west end of Alvaredo, north 37° east. On our approaching the castle of Santa Cruz, Portuguese flags were hoisted on all the forts; and soon after an officer, (an elderly gentleman,) came on board, to inquire who we were, and to what place we were bound. I was very much amused at the astonishment expressed by him, when he heard that we were Russians, and were going round Cape Horn. He asked me a thousand childish questions; and would probably have remained long on board, had he not been obliged to give in his report to the governor.

We had no intention of making a longer stay here than was sufficient for taking in water and provisions: and, while this was doing, we meant, for the refreshment of our people, to have permitted them to amuse themselves as often as possible on shore: but an unforeseen circumstance not only prevented this, but

1804. Feb.

prepared for them a work of much labour and time. On overhauling the riggings, our main and fore-masts were found so rotten as to be unfit for service. It was therefore necessary to replace them: and, notwithstanding the utmost diligence on our part, and the kindness of the governor, to whose assistance we were highly indebted, this was the business of a month. The trees of which the masts were to be made, were felled at the distance of about two miles only; but, from the unfavourable nature of the ground, and the want of proper instruments, the conveyance from thence to the beach was tedious and difficult: it occupied at least seven days.

The tree we used for our masts was the red olio, the trunk of which is so tall and straight, that it will furnish a mast for a first-rate man-of-war, without having a joint in it. The wood, though not so light and pliable as fir, is much stronger. As a counterbalance to the inconvenience of its weight, I ordered our new masts to be shortened four feet. There are two other sorts of olio, the black, and the white, but neither of them is fit for spars, the black being too heavy, and the white too brittle.

Feb. 1st.

On the first of February the work was completed, and I had two of the best possible masts. On this day we should have sailed, but for the desire expressed by the governor, and other gentlemen of the island, to see our ships. Our departure was in consequence postponed for two days.

During our stay at this island we were all busily employed. Dr. Horner, the astronomer, of the Nadejda, established his observatory in the castle of Santa Cruz, and regulated my chronometers. Their rate of going had again varied: No. 136, which before had only lost 9" 4 per day, had now lost 24" 28; and Pennington's, instead of gaining 10" 62 daily, had gained only 9" 37. I knew not how to account for so extraordinary a variation as that of No. 136; but Dr. Horner was positive as to the fact, which made me the less regret the not having had time to take observations myself. By Mr. Horner's observations, the latitude of the observatory was 27° 22' north, and the longitude 48° west.

1804. Feb.

As the whole of the trade with the Portuguese colonies is restricted to the being carried on through Rio de Janeiro, I shall detain the reader for a few minutes, whilst I attempt (though it demands a far abler pen than mine) to give some idea of a place, which, on account of that restriction, is as yet but little known.

The luxuriant verdure and rich fertility, which this favoured isle presents to the view, form a singular contrast with the surrounding element. Observing every where on the shore, woods of orange and lemon-trees; hills crowned with fruit-trees; valleys, plains, and fields interspersed with odoriferous plants, and beautiful flowers, which seem to spring up almost spontaneously; the eye becomes enchanted with the prospect. The air is soft and fresh, and while the smell is delighted with the perfumes that embalm it, the ear, in silent rapture, listens to the warbling of numerous birds, which seem to have selected this beautiful spot for their habitation. The senses, in short, are all gratified; every thing we see, hear, or feel, opens the heart to the sweetest sensations. These charming shores might be called Nature's own paradise; for so lavish has she been of her bounties, that she has favoured them with an eternal spring. We read in fairy tales, of enchanted gardens, guarded by serpents and other venemous monsters; and a knowledge of this island might lead one to give credit to such wonders; for no place on the globe, perhaps, has a greater quantity or variety of such reptiles. In some places, both here and in other parts of the Brazils, it is said, they are so numerous, that the postillions to Rio de Janeiro are obliged to gallop their horses full speed to escape them, as they lie across the road. The inhabitants pretend to have a cure for their stings: I would not, however, advise any rash intruder on the domains of these animals, to confide in this pretence, or to cease practising the utmost wariness. I was astonished that our gentlemen, several of whom went in pursuit of butterflies (and the most beautiful in the world are found here), never met with an accident. In supplying my ship with water, which must be fetched from the woods, I employed Portuguese, instead of my own men, from a sense of the danger.

The island of St. Catharine was originally peopled by deserters from the neighbouring settlements; but its population has considerably increased, many European families having settled in it. By the governor's account, the population amounts, at present, to 10,142 souls, of which about 4000 are negroes. The condition of this unfortunate race, in this island, is less wretched than that of their brethren in the West Indies, or in any European colony I have yet visited. Nearly the whole of them have been converted to Christianity by their Portuguese masters, and have already a black St. Benedict to apply to, in cases of emergency.* The military force of the island consists of a regiment of regulars, amounting to about 1000 men, and 3000 militia. The regulars are, in time of peace, so divided, that whilst one half are on duty, the rest may live at home and cultivate their grounds.

The residence of the governor of St. Catharine is in the town of Nostra Señora del Destero. It is close to the water-side, on that part of the isle, which is separated from the main land by a channel of about two hundred fathoms. The town has a good number of inhabitants. Fresh provisions of every kind, excellent water, and plenty of European and Indian corn, as well as sugar, coffee, and rum, may be obtained there; and with this further advantage, that many of the articles are of a moderate price, as will appear by the following list:

	Raices.†
A large hog	8000
A middling one	4000
A sucking pig	1000
A bullock	7000
A fowl	320
A duck	480
A bunch of onions	60
A thousand lemons	1000
A pound of brown sugar	75

---

* Mr. Lansdorff, in his description of Nostra Señora del Destero, says, that the slaves there are very barbarously used. I doubt not that instances are to be found of brutal treatment, but they are exceptions to the general rule.

† Seven hundred and fifty raices make a Spanish dollar.

1804.
Feb.

	Raices.
Fifty-eight pumpkins	3480
A turkey	480
A bunch of bananas	60
A hundred and forty-four pounds of rice	4000
A hundred and forty-four pounds of wheat	1600
An alkera, or seventy-two pounds of Indian corn	640
A roba, or thirty-two pounds of coffee	1600
A medina, or four bottles of rum	320
An alkera of maniock	480

Though this part of the Brazils produces cotton, coffee, rice, timber, and many other valuable objects of commerce, it is, generally speaking, extremely poor, from the prohibition of foreign trade. If, instead of being obliged to carry their merchandise to Rio de Janeiro, a free commerce with Europe were permitted, the inhabitants would soon improve and enrich themselves; since, with all the disadvantages of the above restrictions, many of them live in comfort. What then might not be expected from proper encouragement? The Portuguese government must be aware of the advantages to be derived from the trade of this colony, and its unjust preference of Rio de Janeiro is a problem very difficult to solve.

I am ignorant whether there are any of the sea-snakes upon this coast, that are found upon that of Coromandel; but there are alligators here. We caught a young one, and sent it on board the Nadejda to the naturalists, who have preserved the skin. Although this little monster was scarcely a yard long, his scales were not to be penetrated even by a large harpoon;

and, but for the dexterity of one of my sailors, who contrived to slip a rope under his belly, we should not have been able to have caught him.

1804.
Feb.

It would be a waste of time to describe that wonderful little insect, the fire-fly, as many accurate descriptions of it already exist. But I cannot avoid adding my testimony to what has been said of its astonishing splendour, by observing, that, by way of experiment, I have several times read with no other light than what was reflected from a number of these insects placed upon the table.

The port and town of Nostra Señora del Destero is fortified all round, as may be seen in the chart; but scarcely any of the batteries were in order, while in many of them the guns were lying either on planks or on the ground.

The inhabitants of St. Catharine are civil and hospitable. La Perouse was right in saying, that they are in general honest and disinterested, though there are individuals amongst them not quite deserving of that character. The mast-maker, for example, claimed a thousand dollars for our two masts, though the general opinion was, that half that sum would have been an ample compensation. This may be deemed a trifling circumstance; but I think it right to mention it, that future navigators may be led to take the same precautions here as they do in Europe, of settling the price before-hand, of what they mean to purchase.

I should be chargeable with ingratitude, were I to omit

1804.
Feb.

paying a large tribute of acknowledgment to the governor of this island, Don Francisco Shever de Courado, for his truly kind and hospitable conduct to us during the whole of our stay. To this gentleman's perfect acquaintance with this part of the world, we were also indebted for much information relative to the whole of the Brazil coast.

Living on shore during the greatest part of our stay here, I was a spectator of the manner in which the inhabitants of this island, both masters and slaves, spend their Christmas holidays. The customs of the masters, differing but little from the practice of the Catholics of Europe, scarcely attracted my attention. This was not the case with the negroes, who, being divided into parties, according to their casts, afforded me much entertainment by their whimsical national dances, in which were introduced actions and gestures characteristic of the manner of their conducting themselves in battle. This innocent amusement of dancing continued for a fortnight without intermission. I was at a loss which to admire most, their unwearied spirits, or their decent behaviour. This festival reflected, I thought, the highest honour on the humanity of the masters; and its policy also was visible in the sobriety and decorum of the slaves; qualities rarely to be met with in that class of people in other colonies. The last of these merry-making days was concluded by a kind of comedy, played before the governor, by negroes expressly chosen for the purpose; at the termination of which, one of the actors thanked him, in the name of his countrymen, for the happiness they had enjoyed under his administration during the preceding year.

The native Americans here are so shy, that no intercourse takes place between them and the Portuguese; I therefore saw very little of them. The governor told me, that they mistake the negroes for monkeys, and kill them, whenever they meet them alone. It seems hardly credible, that human beings should exist so lost to reason, as not to distinguish creatures of their own species from brutes; and I cannot help regarding the account as a story purposely fabricated to keep the slaves from running away.*

The principal food of the inhabitants of this island is maniock, a root which is sedulously cultivated in every part of the settlement. It is very nourishing, and makes much whiter bread than our flour, but harder, and not quite so palatable.

The ships that touch here, to take in provisions, or to undergo repair, should prefer our place of anchorage, to that of Bon Port; or else should anchor nearer the town, as, independently of an excellent bottom, they will be immediately within reach of every thing they may want. Not aware of our own advantageous situation in this respect, we had previously ordered what we wanted from Nostra Señora del Destero.

There are two watering places, one near the island of Atomeri, and the other at St. Michael. The last is the most convenient; but as it was at too great a distance from us, we watered at the first, where, from an over-abundant confidence in the honesty of the inhabitants, we lost two of our casks,

---

* See Lansdorff's Voyage, page 42, English translation.

1804.
Feb.

having left them on shore over-night without a guard. During our stay we had fine weather till the middle of January, when it became so warm, that it was scarcely supportable: the thermometer, however, only rose to 84°.

North-east winds prevail on this coast during half the year; with, however, occasional southerly breezes, that continue for forty-eight hours, and are accompanied with rain. On our arrival, we had few or none of these breezes, though they often afterwards interrupted our course. The ebb and flow of this place are very inconsiderable, unless when the wind blows strong. The ebb comes from the south, and the flow from the north-east quarter. The rise of water was generally observed to be about three feet, but during the last full moon it rose to five feet.

I shall conclude these remarks, with observing, that I cannot agree with those who are of opinion that the climate of St. Catharine is unhealthy. Our crews were at work from morning till night, constantly exposed to the sun, at that time nearly in its zenith; notwithstanding which, they continued in perfect health. On our arrival, I must allow, that we had from three to six upon the sick list, who complained of a pain in their bowels, and a slight ague; but these symptoms passed off in a few days. I was, however, particularly attentive to the circumstance of health. I allowed my ship's company tea for breakfast, and for their common beverage a very weak grog. I also took care, that they did not drink much of the water that was newly brought on board; deeming it a prudent step that they should accustom themselves to it by degrees.

Harbour of
St. CATHERINE.
1804

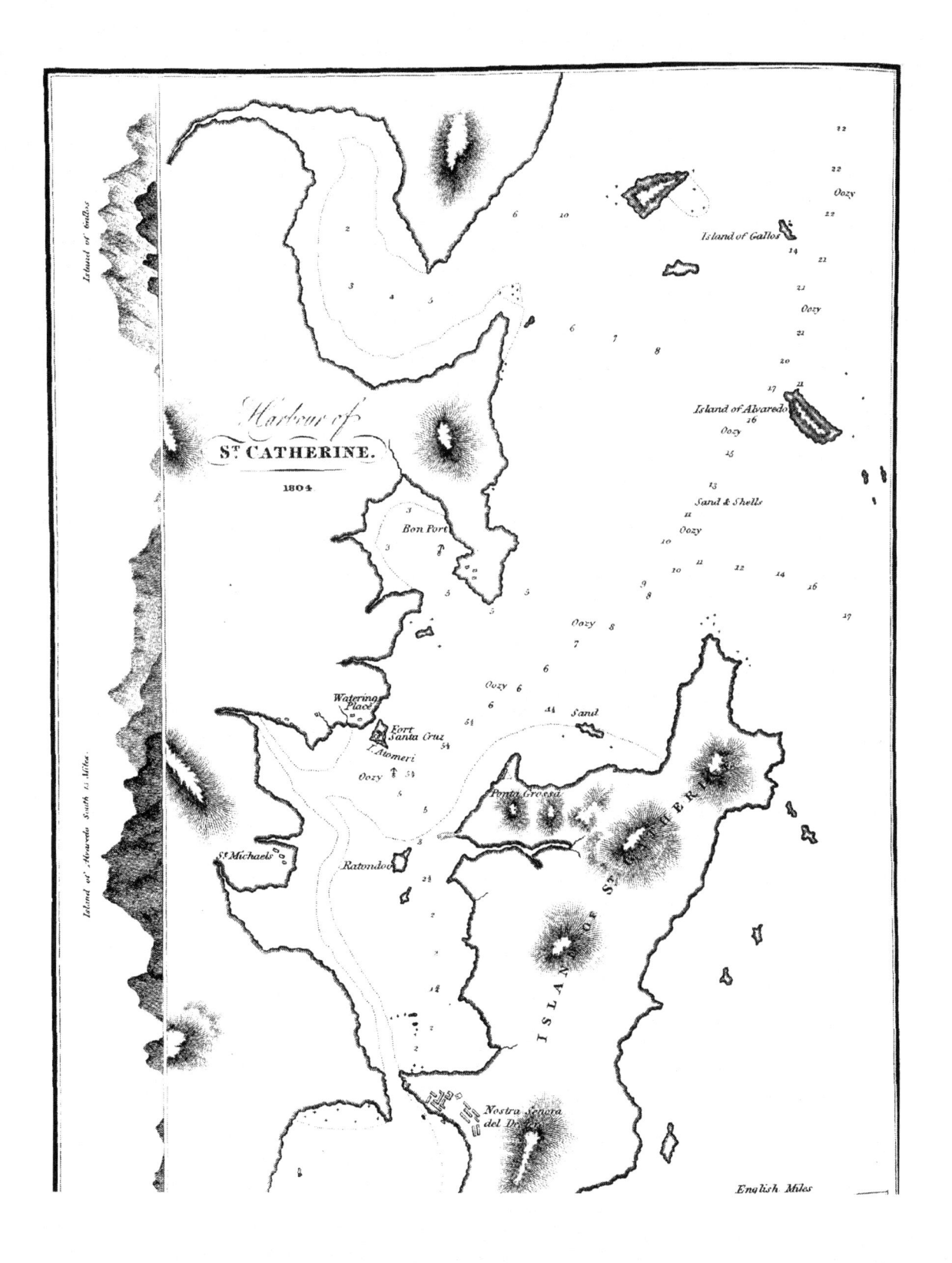

CHAPTER IV.

PASSAGE FROM THE ISLAND OF ST. CATHARINE TO EASTER ISLAND.

Departure from St. Catharine. Danger of the Neva from striking upon the Body of a dead Whale. Change of Climate, and bad Weather. Perceive Staten Land. Currents. Supposed Difficulty of passing Cape Horn erroneous. Advice to Navigators doubling that Cape. The Neva and Nadejda separate in a Fog. The Neva proceeds alone for Easter Island. Arrival there. Survey of the Coasts. Account of the Inhabitants. Latitude and Population of the Island different from what Captain Cook makes them.

On the 4th of February, at two o'clock in the afternoon, the two ships were again under way, and, with the wind at south-east, shaped their course between the islands of Alvaredo and St. Catharine. On nearing the north end of the last-mentioned island, the wind freshened so much, as to oblige us to take in two reefs in the top-sails. Notwithstanding the delay occasioned by this, we were in open sea by six in the evening. The passage by which we came out of the harbour was equally good with that by which we had come into it. Being apprehensive of squally weather from the east, I kept near the shore. The water, however, was never less than five fathoms, and it gradually deepened till we had fifteen fathoms, with at first sandy, and afterwards muddy bottom. At seven o'clock all the small islands on the coast were to the westward.

1804.
Feb.
4th.

1804.
Feb.

11th. For the first two days, we had the wind at south-east; it then went round to the north, and settling at last in the north-east quarter, the ship's velocity was so great, that on the 11th we were in latitude 38° 19′ south, and longitude 50° 47′ west. On passing the mouth of the river De la Plata, we were opposed by pretty strong currents to the north-east; but having expected this, we shaped our course to the south-west, more than would otherwise have been necessary.

12th. On the 12th we had a south-west wind, with squalls. This was disagreeable to us, not only on account of the delay it occasioned, but from the weather becoming extremely cold. In the course of the day, we saw some grampusses and albatrosses; one of the latter of which was black, except the belly and wings, which were white.

18th. On the 18th we were in 45° 29′ south and 58° 32′ west, which was twenty-three miles to the eastward of the lunar observation, which I took in the evening. During the night we struck upon the body of a dead whale, and had nearly lost our masts by the shock.

19th. Some storm-birds made their appearance the next day; but as our barometer stood high, I placed little faith in the prognostic. At four o'clock in the afternoon we sounded, and had seventy fathoms water, and at eight fifty, with fine sandy bottom.

We now advanced so rapidly to the southward, that I could perceive every day the change of climate. Already the cold had increased to a degree of uncomfortableness; but we resolved to inure ourselves to it, as it was probable, before the ships doubled Cape Horn, we should have ice floating round us. During the course of the 22d, whales of a middling size played round our vessel. One in particular followed us closely for some time. We were much amused with their traverses as they pursued backward and forward the floating heaps of sea-weeds that passed us from the latitude of 40°.

Early in the morning of the 25th, Staten Land appeared; but as the weather was extremely hazy, its shore could not be clearly distinguished. On sounding, at nine o'clock, we had seventy-five fathoms, with bottom of fine sand, gravel stones, and coral. At eleven, bearings of Cape John were taken, by which it appeared that our chronometers, No. 136 and No. 50, were sixty-one miles to the eastward of the true longitude. We steered east-by-south till three in the afternoon, when, the wind shifting to the north-west, we altered our course to south-east. At six we passed through a space of smooth water, which, as the sea was much agitated on both sides of it, was no doubt the effect of two contrary currents. We had the greater reason to remark this smooth expanse, from seeing no more of the masses of weeds, which had been continually passing since our arrival in latitude 40°, and by which the two ships had been completely surrounded in the morning.

I allowed my people, from this day, either tea or essence of malt,* for breakfast. I also ordered pumpkins and onions to be

---

* Essence of malt, dissolved in hot water, affords a wholesome beverage, and is an excellent antiscorbutic.

1804.
Feb.

boiled with their salt meat, and plenty of portable soup to be served up with their pea-soup. I had no doubt that such wholesome and nourishing food, together with warm clothing, with which we were well provided, would prevent many of the diseases of which former navigators have so generally complained.

I can give no other information respecting the currents that prevail in this quarter, than that they were constantly varying. By one in particular, we had gained, as was proved by our reckoning when we came in sight of Staten Land, twenty-five miles eastward. On our leaving St. Catharine, it tended, during the first three days, to the south-east, and when we were opposite the mouth of the river De la Plata, to the north-east; after that it bore to the southward, and at last to the northward, as far as Cape John.

We had hardly entered the Southern Ocean, when we were again incommoded by contrary winds and bad weather. On the 26th the south-west blew in squalls, and was so strong the next day, that we were obliged to reduce ourselves to the storm stay-sails. On the 28th it abated a little, but continued squally till the next day, when we had a second storm, from the violence of which we lost both our gangways, and should have parted with all our boats, had it not again abated towards noon.

26th.

28th.

Our situation during the last three days was extremely distressing. Assailed by cold and rain, by strong winds, and a heavy sea, we had another enemy to contend with, in the hail, which fell during the whole time, and was driven against us with such force, that no one on board was able to face it.

On the 1st of March, the wind had considerably subsided, but the weather continued foul till the next day, when it cleared up, with a northerly breeze. We were then, by observation, in latitude 59° 2' south, and longitude 63° 45' west. On the 3d, in the evening, the wind shifted to the westward, and blew moderately.

For a fortnight from the last-mentioned day we had contrary winds, or calms, except during the 11th and 14th; when easterly and northerly breezes sprung up, and gave us a very handsome run. On the 14th, I narrowly escaped having my arm shattered by the bursting of a gun, with which I was shooting at the albatrosses; happily the bursting took place near the muzzle, and I received no injury. On the 15th also, the weather was fine, and a floating mass of sea-weeds, resembling those we had before seen on the Patagonian coast, again passed us. These were probably blown by the northerly winds from Terra del Fuego.

The calms which succeeded on the 18th and 19th, did us some good; as, the weather being fine, we had an opportunity of drying our clothes. On the 20th we had a fair wind, and the next day found ourselves, by observation, in 51° 33' south, and 93° 29' west. We now congratulated ourselves on having passed round Cape Horn, as our latitude was fifty miles to the northward of Cape Victoria, or of the northernmost point of the Straits of Magellan. A more important source of self-congra-

1804.
March.

tulation to me, was, that since our departure from Russia to this place, a single man on board my ship had not been seriously ill. Many navigators dread the passage round Cape Horn; but, in my opinion, it resembles that of all other promontories in high latitudes; and from what we ourselves experienced, it would appear as if the same variable weather prevailed at this southern point of America, during the worst months of winter, as in Europe. If lord Anson suffered here from tempestuous weather, the same misfortune might have happened to him, in any other place. I am persuaded, that, on consulting the journals of different ships of the United States, which now so often go by this track to the north-west coast of America, more successful voyages will be found, than unsuccessful ones. The only serious objection to the passage, in my opinion, is the desolate nature of the shores of this Cape, where, if a ship should be in want of masts, or repairs, no assistance can be obtained. It is true, there are harbours in the neighbourhood of Terra del Fuego; but we are not yet well enough acquainted with their true situation, for a damaged vessel to go in search of them.

In captain Blay of the British navy, we have another instance of a navigator, who met with such rough weather here, that, after having been tossed about by contrary winds for several weeks, he was obliged at last to bear away for the Cape of Good Hope. These accidental circumstances do not, however, prove the place to be dangerous. I might as well assert the banks of the British Channel to be dangerous, because I found myself, on one occasion, in such a situation there, that, for the space of a month, the ship I was in was only able three days to carry close-reefed top-sails; during the rest of that period, we were obliged to remain under the storm stay-sails only.

1804.
March.

The barometer off Cape Horn does not rise so high, in good weather, as in our northern climates of the same latitude, while in bad weather it sinks much lower. When the wind was at south-west, our barometer commonly stood at 28 inches, 6 or 7 lines; the weather was then often squally, with hail, snow, and rain. This state of the barometer, however, though the weather was foggy, sometimes foretold a change of wind from south-west to north-west; for as soon as the mercury rose a few lines higher, the sky cleared, and the wind veered to south-east, and at last got round to the northward.

The chief inconveniences of this place, are the coldness of the weather, the violence with which the hail and snow fall during the squalls, and the extreme dampness of the atmosphere. Whoever has passed the North Cape in Europe, in the winter season, will understand the nature of the difficulties he has to encounter here. Introductory to bad weather, heavy dews generally take place, both morning and evening.

Some navigators have observed, that there are always strong westerly currents about the Cape; for instance, lord Anson mentions, in his journal, that he was driven by them to the eastward with great force, till he reached the latitude of the Straits of Magellan, in the Southern Ocean. Nothing of the kind, however, happened to us; as, by lunar observations of the 31st of March and of the 3d of April, it appeared, that in the run from Staten Land to Cape Victoria, which was the business of twenty-

1804.
March.
four days, we were only forty miles to the eastward of our reckoning.* We perceived, too, that the current was different at different times, tending to the south, the west, and the north, as well as to the east. From these circumstances I conclude, that the terrible dangers ascribed to Cape Horn, have their existence only in the fertile imagination of former voyagers, who, in my opinion, in relating the wonders they have seen, have displayed more eloquence than veracity.

The opinions are various, as to the best time for going round Cape Horn, and at what distance it may be most advantageous to take the passage. I am acquainted with several persons, who have doubled this Cape four times, and who recommend the month of December or January, as the best season for the purpose. Of these, some prefer Le Maire's Straits; and others, sailing to the eastward of Staten Land, and then, if the wind should permit, to steer directly for the Cape, under an idea, that the winds vary more near the shore of Terra del Fuego, than further to the southward. On the other hand, I have heard some masters of vessels in the whale-fishery affirm, that the end of April or the beginning of May was the best period, assigning as a reason, that the Spaniards, when they have to make this passage, never leave the river Plata till the middle of March. On viewing these contradictory opinions, I determined to be governed by my own judgment, as circumstances might arise, and the event proved that I was right in this. The result of my expe-

---

* Captain Krusenstern says, that he was driven three degrees and a half to the eastward by the current; a circumstance I can no otherwise account for, than by supposing, that I allowed more for the heave of the sea than he did.

rience is, that, except in particular cases, Staten Land should be left to the westward, and, having passed it, that the latitude of 58° 30' should be gained as soon as possible: the longitude should then be increased to 80° or 82°, and the course shaped to the northward. If the south-west winds should have set in, I would rather keep to the southward, as far as 60° or 61°, and there ply to windward, waiting for a favourable change, than lessen my latitude, without considerably increasing the longitude. I would also advise keeping the ship full seven points from the wind, when she is lying to westward (in case of a scanty fair wind), to enable her the more easily to cut through the westerly swell, very prevalent in these parts. This advice, to steer so far westward, is not given merely on account of the westerly currents, which, as I have before mentioned, I did not find very strong, but that the most might be made of the south-west and westerly winds, for advancing afterwards to the northward.

On many of the English charts, a small island is laid down in latitude 56°, and longitude 62°; but I have reason to think no island exists there, as we were nearly in those bearings in the course of the voyage, and could perceive no signs of land. My opinion is the same of another island, bearing the name of Penice du Dosa, and laid down in 46° 30' south, and 58° 15' west.

But to proceed: On the 24th we had a strong wind at east-north-east, and hazy weather, with drizzling rains. In the afternoon a thick fog came on, and continued till night, which proved extremely dark. Though I was under few sails, my vessel was unfortunately separated from our friend the Nadejda before morning. Every endeavour was in vain used to regain sight of

1804.
March.
her. At length, despairing of success, I resolved to proceed without her, and bear for Easter Island. It is needless to describe our feelings on thus losing our companions;—they may easily be imagined, when it is considered, that we were now left to struggle alone, with the many various accidents that might assail us. Separated by immense seas, from every civilized part of the globe, we had no succour to expect, on any trying occasion, but what our own fortitude, and the special protection of the Divine Providence, now doubly invoked, might afford.

28th.
On the 28th, the wind from the south-west blew hard during the night, and it came on with so tremendous a squall, that I certainly should have lost my fore-mast, but for the alacrity of my people in taking in the sails. Towards morning the clouds dropped so low, that I apprehended a storm. The sun, however, appeared about noon, and in the evening the weather improved. During the two last days we had been accompanied by two black petrels, that greatly resembled Buffon's *briseur d'oss*, the wings excepted, which were much shorter. These birds always run a considerable distance on the surface of the water, before they take flight.

31st.
On the 31st at noon, we found ourselves in latitude 39° 20' south, and longitude 98° 42' west. This longitude was 1° 51' to the west of that given by the lunar observation of the day. Since our parting from the Nadejda, I had regulated my ship's course, so as to pass a little to the westward of the place where Marchand had seen some birds, which, as he says in his journal, were never known to fly far from shore; and, during the last two days, we had steered in the line in which that navigator thought

some land might be discovered; but we saw nothing to confirm this opinion.

1804.
March.

From the 1st to the 13th of April, though the weather continued unsettled, the wind blew less strong, and squalls were less frequent. On the 13th I found myself in latitude 29° 45′ south, and longitude 104° 49′ west: the correctness of our longitude could be relied on, from its near accord with the lunar observation, which was 104° 33′. On this day I ordered the forge to be brought upon deck, and the work to commence, of manufacturing axes, knives, large nails, and chisels, for the inhabitants of the South Sea Islands.

April 13th.

The cables had been bent to all my anchors, and I had been perfectly prepared for an anchorage for several days; and at eleven in the morning of the 16th we saw Easter Island before us, in conformity to what our lunar observations had given us reason to expect. At noon we found ourselves in latitude 27° 13′ south, and, from thirteen altitudes, by No. 50, in 109° 44′; by No. 1841, 110° 12′; by No. 136, 108° 59′; and by Pennington, 108° 34′ west longitude. The shore, at that time, was about thirty miles distant; by which I found that the first-mentioned chronometer was thirty miles to the westward, the second sixty-five to the westward, the third eight to the eastward, and the last thirty-three to the eastward. From noon we steered west-by-north, and at five o'clock neared the eastern side of the island; but as the weather was both squally and hazy, towards evening I reefed my top-sails, and stood out to sea for the night. A great number of small gray gulls had indicated the proximity of the island some time before it was descried.

16th.

1804.
April.
17th.

Early in the morning of the next day, we were twelve miles to the eastward of the shore; and at eight, with the wind at north-west, we approached the southern point, which is remarkable for two large rocks, one of which so strikingly resembles a ship, with her main-top gallant-sail set, that, upon first perceiving it, one of my people mistook it for the Nadejda.

The eastern part of Easter Island is very pleasant. It is covered with verdure, and many spots of it appeared to be planted with bananas. Towards the middle stood two large black statues, one twice the size of the other; yet it appeared as if both were intended to form but one monument, as they were contiguous to each other, and inclosed within the same mound. The south side of the island is craggy and steep, composed of a stone, resembling slate or lime-stone, lying in horizontal strata, the upper surface covered with grass.

After getting round the south point, I steered towards the west side of the island; and when at the distance of about three miles, I recognised Cook's Bay, against the shores of which a heavy swell broke. Not far from the beach we observed four statues, three of which were very tall; the other appeared to have been broken down, so as to have lost half its height. They bore a great resemblance to the monuments described by La Perouse, in the voyage in which this navigator so unfortunately perished.

I had intended at first to anchor in Cook's Bay; but the weather being unsettled, I was apprehensive of westerly winds, which would have rendered it very unsafe. As we had seen nothing of the Nadejda since our separation, I resolved to wait at this island a few days, in the hope of her rejoining us, and to take a slight survey of the place. Accordingly, on the 18th, we again ranged along the eastern side of the island, and found it as pleasant as it appeared the day before. The middle of it is much lower than its extremities; and a few huts are dispersed here and there amongst the fruit-trees, of which, however, there were no great plenty. We kept so near the coast, that we could easily distinguish the natives following the ship along the beach. They were entirely naked, and of a dark copper colour. In coasting it this time, we observed five monuments. The first, which consisted of four statues, presented itself to view as soon as we had passed the south end of the island: the second had three: the third was the one we had seen the day before; and at no great distance from the eastern point stood the fourth and fifth. The neighbourhood of the two last-mentioned monuments contained a greater number of habitations, and seemed better cultivated, than any other spot we had yet seen. We also observed numerous heaps of stone, covered with something white at the top; respecting which, I could form no satisfactory conjecture.

Though the wind was at north-west, the surf broke rather heavily against the shore, along the whole extent of which I could not discover a single anchorage. At sun-set the wind died away, and left us nine miles to the northward of the east point. During the day, we were surrounded by flying-fish and different sea-birds.

On the 19th we had light breezes and a heavy swell from

1804.
April.

the south-west. At day-light we took our course along the northern shore. I at first proposed passing it as near as possible, but was prevented doing so, by the frequent calms and rain; the ship, however, was never further distant than five miles, so that we could clearly distinguish all the points and remarkable places. This side of the island appeared to be but thinly inhabited. I saw four monuments: the first of which consisted of one statue only; the second and third of two each; and the fourth of three. On our approaching nearer, fires were lighted in different places by the inhabitants, and were kept burning till sun-set. We supposed these to be signals of invitation on shore; but as no good landing-place was to be found, I continued lying to westward. In the mean time my jolly-boat, which had been dispatched to try the current, returned, but discovered nothing worthy of remark.

20th. On the 20th the weather was so unsettled, that I could not prosecute my survey along the northern side of the island, and therefore attempted that of the west, though with no greater success, from being becalmed.

21st. The next morning the weather was so squally, that I could not reach Cook's Bay till eight o'clock. I wished to have dropped anchor there, but the heavy south-west swell prevented me. Determined, however, to leave some indication on the island, by which the Nadejda, in case of her touching there, might trace us, I dispatched lieutenant Powalishin in the jolly-boat, with knives, small pieces of iron, empty bottles, and some printed linens. His orders were, to go as near the shore as the surf would permit, and distribute the above-mentioned articles to the natives, who, without doubt, would swim off to him. At the same time, I recommended him to examine the bay and try the soundings, but without attempting to land. At two in the afternoon he returned, and brought some plantains, bananas, sweet potatoes, yams, and sugar-cane. Every thing being thus executed according to my wish, I only waited to get another view of the north side of the island; and, having succeeded in this, at six o'clock we set sail for the Marquesas, with the satisfaction of having surveyed one of the most curious spots in the world.

1804.
April.

Easter Island was descried by us bearing west-north-west, at the distance of forty miles; and, had the weather been clear, it might have been perceived at sixty. It first appeared to lie low, with a high rock to the right. When we had advanced about ten miles nearer, this rock disappeared, and two small elevations were perceived to the left, which afterwards joined the main land in sight. We sailed round this island, at a very short distance, but could no where discover a safe anchoring place. The shores are rocky and steep, excepting a small bay on the east side, near the south point, and another bay on the north side, not far from the north point. Cook's Bay, where the jolly-boat sounded, is certainly the best place to anchor at; though that is by no means safe when the south-west winds blow; as the swell is then so great, that the heaviest anchors would give way, especially as ships must lie close in shore. We had sixty fathoms, stony bottom, at the distance of a mile and a quarter from the shore. Lieutenant Powalishin found ten fathoms at one and a half cable length, sixteen fathoms at three cables, and twenty-three at four cables. Thus, according to the

1804. April.

opinion of La Perouse, who says that the best anchorage is in twenty-four fathoms, ships should bring-to at five cables length from the beach.

Vessels may come into this bay from the southward or from the northward, according to the wind, and the anchorage cannot be mistaken, on account of the sandy beach opposite to it; all the rest of the shore being rocky. Bringing the sandy beach to bear east-by-south, or east, and losing sight of the two rocks that lie near the south point, you will be in the depth La Perouse recommends, with sandy bottom.

It appeared to me that the inhabitants of this island are not so poor in provisions, as former navigators have asserted them to be. If they have no animals, as is said, they are nevertheless plentifully supplied with substitutes, which, if not so substantial, are at least equally nourishing. Their houses, though greatly inferior to ours, appear to be sufficiently commodious for a people living in a state of nature; they resemble, in form, our long-boats turned upside down. Some of them stand separately, and others two or three together. The door was of a conical form; but I did not observe any windows. Every house was planted round with bananas and sugar-canes.

The shore is encompassed by monuments, very correctly described by La Perouse. They are built of stone, with a rude representation, on the top of each figure, of a human head surmounted with a cylinder.

From the many fires, regularly lighted about nine o'clock,

it may be inferred, that victuals are prepared here in the open air, and that nine o'clock is the accustomed hour for a general meal.

That the inhabitants of this island should have no fresh water, as is related by some navigators, is to me a matter of surprise; because, during the rainy season, they might easily supply themselves with it in tanks, so common throughout the West India islands: but, if it be true, as La Perouse informs us, that they drink sea-water, like the Albatrosses of Cape Horn, they have no need of this article.

When lying-to, near Cook's Bay, we saw a great number of people; who, on perceiving our boat, swam off to meet it, expressing their joy with a loud noise, and pointing out with their hands the best place for landing. Finding, however, that the boat did not intend to land, thirty of them forced themselves through a very heavy surf, and joined it. Mr. Powalishin uttered, repeatedly, the word *teéo* (friend), and made signs that they should come to him, one at a time. To the first of his visitors he gave a sealed bottle, with a letter in it to captain Krusenstern, requesting, by signs, that it might be delivered to a ship as large as ours, if such should arrive there. Afterwards he distributed among them knives, Russian copper money, strung upon wire, to be worn round the neck, some pieces of printed linen, and lastly several mustard bottles, with small pieces of wood fastened to them, upon which the name of our ship was written. The knives were received with great eagerness by the islanders; and I was very sorry that I sent so few, as an old islander of sixty, who came after the rest, and presented Mr. Powalishin with a bag made of grass, filled with sweet potatoes, solicited one in the most earnest manner: there were, however, none left, and he only received some copper ear-rings, and a few other trifles; but with these the poor old man was so satisfied, that he left with Mr. Powalishin all he had, including the rush-mat; which he used as a support in swimming.

To judge from the behaviour of this man, he must have seen Europeans before. He was the only one who had long hair on the head, and a bushy brown beard; the rest were all cropped, and beardless. When they were desired to go to the ship, they expressed by signs, that it was too far; which proves, as also do the rush-mats, which every one had to assist him in swimming, that the boats seen by La Perouse, do not at present exist on the island.

Lieutenant Powalishin thinks that there were about 500 persons on shore near him, including children. Being very busy with his visitors, he did not observe if there were any women amongst them; but he saw that many of them had a kind of short cloak, or piece of cloth, suspended from the shoulders, and scarcely covering the thighs. Amongst the crowd were some, who waved constantly square pieces of white and striped cloth, of the size of a pocket-handkerchief. From what he, and all who were with him in the boat observed; it appears that these islanders are stoutly built, and tall, some of them being six feet, and of a colour resembling a sun-burnt European. Those that swam to him had their faces and hands tatooed, which was all that was remarkable in their appearance.

From the description which Mr. Powalishin gave me of what he saw, I know not how to reconcile myself to the tremendous large ears mentioned by Mr. Forster, who represents them as hanging down upon the shoulders, and having holes perforated in them, through which five fingers may be thrust. Mr. Powalishin assured me, that this was not the case with those of the islanders who visited him, whose ears were no longer than ours. If, therefore, any of this long-eared race still remained on the island, they did not, in this instance, make their appearance; probably, however, the fashion of expanding the ears here, is now at an end.

Our boat was so near the shore, that the houses and monuments of the bay were distinctly seen. The monuments were built of stone, and appeared to be about thirteen feet high, a fourth part of which height was taken up by the cylinder placed on the head of each figure.

I cannot well judge of the handicraft of these islanders; but the bag and mat of the old man are deserving of notice. The first, which was fifteen inches long and ten wide, was made of hard grass, in a very masterly manner. The second, which was four feet and a half long, and fifteen inches and a half broad, consisted of sugar-cane, platted over with rushes; and, in point of workmanship, was scarcely inferior to any thing of the kind made in Europe.

Captain Cook places Easter Island in latitude 27° 5′ 36″ south, and longitude 109° 46′ 20″ west; but, by my observations, the middle of it proved to be 27° 9′ 23″ south, and 109° 25′ 20″ west.

1804.
April.
On the 13th and 15th of the present month I took thirty lunar distances, and brought the calculation by our chronometers to the time of our making land. I know not how to account for this difference of latitude, unless by supposing that this celebrated navigator calculated his to some point lying to the northward of the middle of the island. His estimate also of the population of the island, which he says is from six to seven hundred, appears to me a little strange. When I consider the number of persons that assembled in the bay on the approach of our boat, and the many habitations which I observed round the coast, I think, I may safely assert, that the island contains at least fifteen hundred inhabitants.

During our stay here, we found the variation of the compass to be 6° 12′ east.

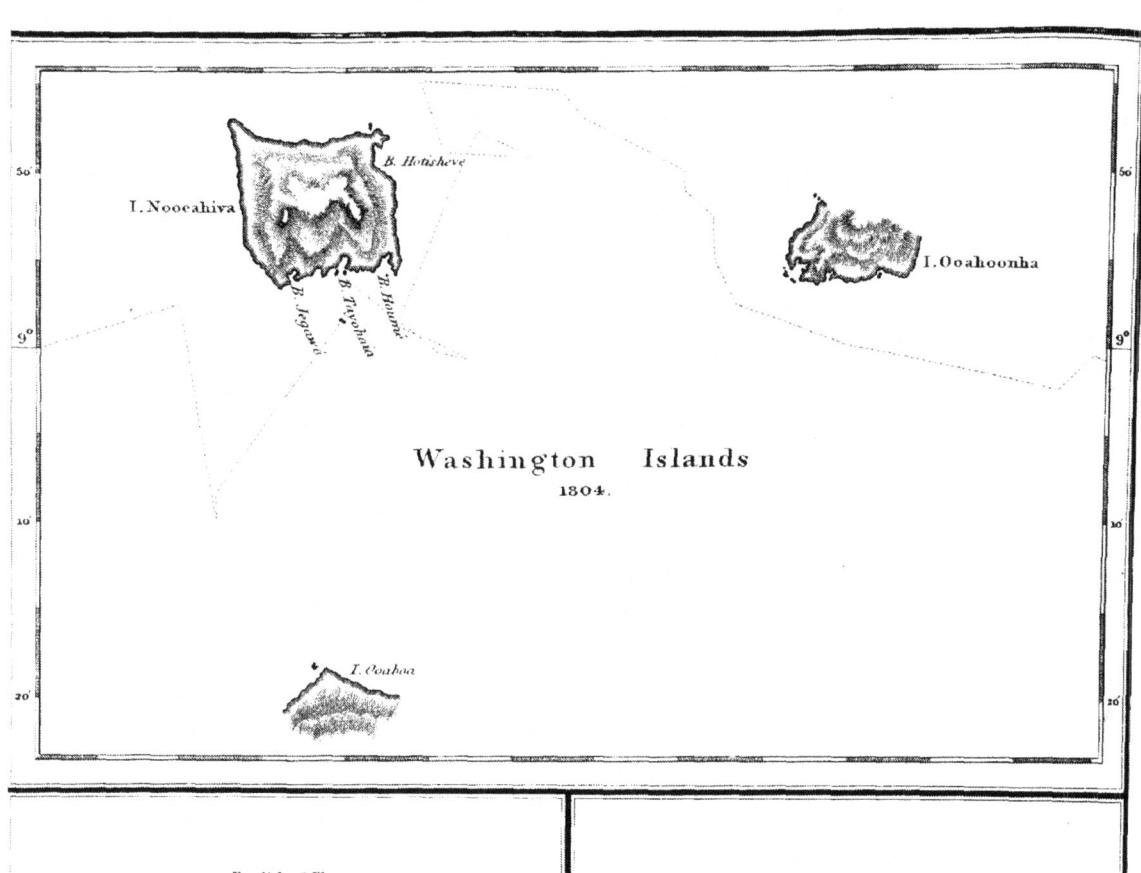

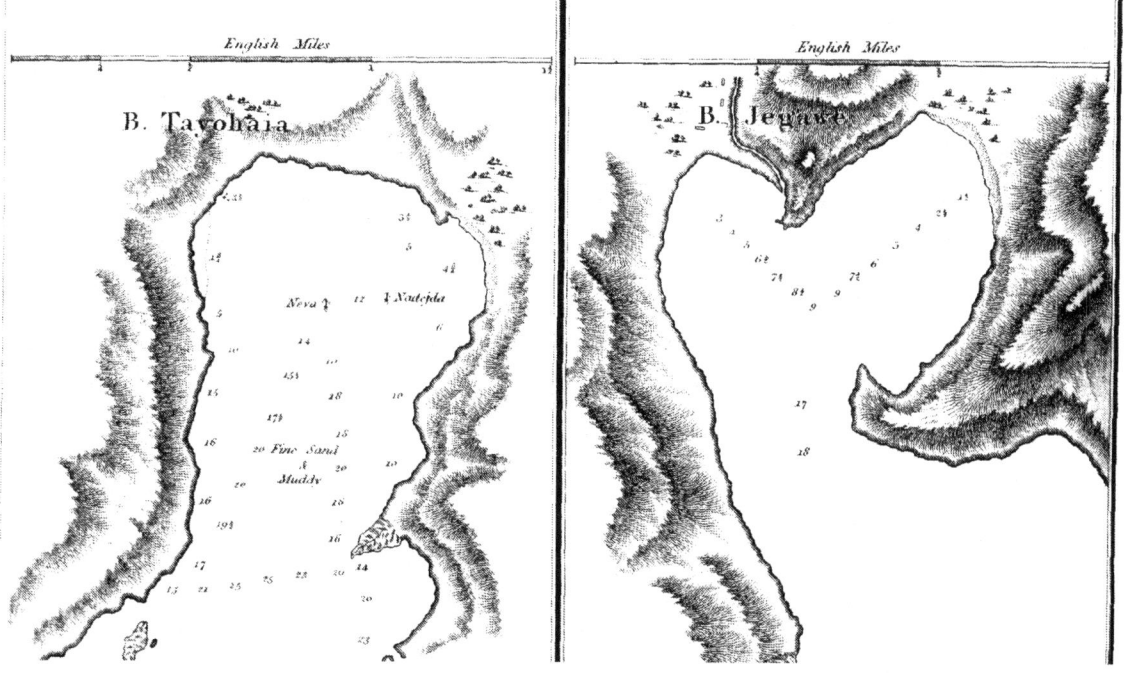

Washington Islands
1804.

I. Nooeahiva
B. Hotisheve
B. Jegare
B. Tayohaia
B. Haumi
I. Ooahoonha
I. Ooahoa

B. Tayohaia — English Miles
Neva · Nadejda
Fine Sand & Muddy

B. Jegawe — English Miles

CHAPTER V.

PASSAGE FROM EASTER ISLAND TO WASHINGTON ISLANDS.

Departure of the Neva from Easter Island. State of the Winds. Make the Marquesas. Take a Survey of this Group. Visited by Canoes from the Island of Noocahiva, one of the Washington Islands. The two Ships meet. Anchor in the Bay of Tayohaia. Receive a Visit from the King of the Bay. Attempts of the Women to gain Admittance on Board. Traffic for Provisions. Further Visits of the King, with some of his Relations. Trick played us by His Majesty. Misunderstanding with the Inhabitants. Visit the King, with Captain Krusenstern. Palace. Burying-ground. A Grappling stolen from one of our Boats. The King dines on Board the Neva. The Neva visited by the Queen. Excursion to Jegawé Bay. Excellent Anchorage there. Prepare for Departure from Noocahiva. Further Account of the Religion, Government, and Customs of the Inhabitants.

1804.
April.

WE left Easter Island, as I have observed above, on the 26th of April, at six o'clock in the evening. We were not many miles from the shore, when a south-east wind began to blow. From its regular and temperate nature for a while, we thought we had reached the trade-winds, but we soon discovered our mistake; for it shifted the next day, and continued variable till the 30th, when a north-easter sprung up, and lasted till we reached the Marquesas. It seems that in this part of the world, the south-east trade does not stretch so far from the equator, as on the east side of America.

Nothing remarkable happened to us during this passage. It

1804.
April.

was tranquil, and my people had an opportunity of rest from the fatigues they had undergone off Cape Horn. We were accompanied by the tropic birds and benitas; the last were sometimes caught with a hook and line, and furnished the crew with an agreeable fresh meal.

May.
6th.

Concluding, by my observations, that, on the 6th of May, which was Easter Sunday, we were near the Marquesas, I ordered a dinner of fresh provisions for my ship's company, with half a bottle of Teneriffe wine to each man. This so elated them, that, towards evening, they sung and danced as merrily as if they had been among their relatives and friends in Russia. I mention this to show, that, though we had experienced many hardships since our departure from Europe, our spirits were not broken, and we knew, upon occasion, how to enjoy ourselves. Expecting that the Marquesas would be in sight the next morning, I thought proper, at sun-set, to bring-to for the night.

7th.

As soon as it was day, the island of Fatoohiva (Magdalena) was seen to the westward, at the distance of thirty miles, resembling in appearance three hills. About thirteen miles to the eastward of this island, is a flat long rock, of which ships should be extremely wary, as it lies almost on a level with the surface of the water. On passing Fatoohiva, the island of Motane (St. Pedro) appeared first, and then, in succession, Towata (St^a. Christina), Hoivahova (La Dominica), and Fatoohoo (Hood's island). This last is the most remarkable of the cluster: its height is very considerable, and it looks like a stupendous solid rock.

At noon we found ourselves a-breast of the island of Motane, in latitude, by observation, 10° south. On some maps this island appears smaller than that of Fatoohoo, whereas it is double the size.

1804.
May.

I steered to the eastward of this group of islands, to survey them more minutely, and draw a chart from the survey. They are all lofty and steep, except the Towata, which has a more level appearance than the rest. At seven o'clock we passed the island of Fatoohoo, and steered to the west, till we found ourselves between it and the island of Ouahoonha (Riou's), one of the Washington cluster, when I brought-to for the night.

In the morning of the 8th we neared the island of Ouahoonha: and I had intended to survey it all round; but the unsettled state of the weather prevented me, and I was obliged to bear for the island of Noocahiva (sir H. Martin's), another of the Washington cluster; which, when we were a-breast of the rocks, off the north-west point of Ouahoonha, was in sight. The island of Ouahoonha is also high and hilly: on the south-west side of it, we perceived many small bays, fit for landing boats; but there is only one that will admit ships, which is situated close to the south point, in latitude, by our observation, 8° 56'. It appears, however, to be considerably exposed to the southerly winds. This bay is remarkable for two small islands, one of which is high and rocky; the other level, and covered with grass. Though we passed the shore at the distance of about four miles, we were not so fortunate as to see a single human being come off to welcome us; which greatly surprised me, as lieutenant Graves says, in his journal, that the inhabitants came on board his ship very readily, and behaved with much civility. From this circum-

8th.

1804.
May.

stance, I thought it not unlikely, that some navigators, passing this way before us, had treated them in an unfriendly manner, and made them afraid of showing themselves to vessels arriving off their shores; and, as the wind in the afternoon was in a quarter that would enable me to reach the north part of Noocahiva, about six o'clock, with disappointed feelings, I tacked for that purpose.

The night proved squally, and we were once in the course of it in danger of being driven on the shore of Noocahiva, but a sudden gust from the land fortunately saved us. In the morning, a canoe with eight persons made for the ship, from the east side of this island; and, when at a short distance from us, one of the company sounded a large conch, while another waved a piece of white cloth. Thinking these to be tokens of friendship, I ordered, in return, a white handkerchief to be waved, and a white flag hoisted. My guests climbed the ship's sides, with the assistance of a rope that was thrown to them from deck, and behaved in as free and amicable a manner as if they had lived amongst us all their lives. Our curiosity did not in the least interrupt their singing, dancing, and other wild testimonies of joy, on receiving the different presents we made them, and especially the knives, which they called *cohe*. Observing that four more canoes were hurrying from the shore, I ordered our present visitors to leave us; and in a moment they all jumped overboard, one after another. As soon as the new visitors arrived, those who left us made a most tumultuous noise; and, displaying our presents, vociferated, repeatedly, the word *cuanna*. In one of the new canoes, which was rowed by fifteen men, was the chief, who held a long stick, to which was fastened a bunch of bananas, a piece of white cloth manufactured on the island, and a square fan. Being under sail, I did not like to be surrounded by too many of these savages, and I therefore signified that a few only were to come on board. The chief, as soon as he comprehended my orders, jumped out of his canoe into the water, and climbed up the ship with astonishing alacrity. As soon as he was on the quarter-deck, he sat himself down, and presented me with the bunch of bananas, and the cloth that had been fastened to the stick. I was going to put on his head a cap of striped stuff; but he refused the honour, and begged a knife, which was given him with a pair of ear-rings, made of two copeks, which is the smallest Russian copper money. One of my officers made him a present of a small looking-glass, which delighted him so much, that I thought he would have lost his senses. Our new guests behaved with the same familiarity as the preceding ones. They were all perfectly honest in the exchange of articles, and so docile, that no one left the ship without asking my permission. I showed them fowls and pigs; the fowls they called *moa*, and the pigs *boaga*, intimating by signs that there were plenty of both on shore; but, from their surprise at the sight of our sheep and goats, I inferred that they had never till then seen such animals.

We steered all the morning of the 9th to the southward, in the hope of reaching the bay of Tayohaia towards evening; but at noon we were becalmed, and gave up the idea of being at anchor before night.

During the night, the rain was so heavy, that a dozen casks

1804.
May.
10th.

might have been filled in a very short time. At day-break we reached the south end of Noocahiva; but as the wind blew from the south-west, we tacked about. The bay, from which the canoes had come out the day before, is situated on the east side of the island, and is pretty large. The islanders did all they could to persuade us to stop in this quarter; but, as it was completely exposed to the easterly winds, I could not comply with their request. At eight in the morning the wind shifted to the north-east; and, as the weather cleared up a little, I made for the shore: and at nine, to our equal joy and surprise, a jolly-boat was seen coming to us from the Nadejda. Having been separated nearly seven weeks from our friends, the pleasure we felt, on hearing they were all in good health and spirits, can hardly be expressed.

At noon we entered the long-desired bay of Taiohaia; but, the wind failing, we were obliged to warp the ship to the anchoring place. While this was doing, I went on board the Nadejda to pay my respects to captain Krusenstern, with whom I found the king of the bay and a great number of islanders, who were entirely naked. His majesty differed in no respect from his subjects, except that his body was more punctured or tatooed. I had the good fortune to please the king at first sight; he called me *Too*, and promised to pay me a visit as soon as possible. There were also on board the Nadejda a Frenchman and an Englishman, who, having resided several years in these islands, were extremely useful to us, as will be seen hereafter.

Returning on board my ship, I found the king already

arrived, with presents of fruit. There were also many islanders swimming round the vessel with fruit, which they wished to dispose of: there were women amongst them; but it was signified to them, that I had resolved to admit none of their sex on board till the ship should be ready for sea, and at sun-set they swam back with the rest.

1804. May.

The next day, as soon as it was light, we were surrounded by a still greater multitude of these people. There were now a hundred females at least; and they practised all the arts of lewd expression and gesture, to gain admission on board. It was with difficulty I could get my crew to obey the orders I had given on this subject. Amongst these females were some not more than ten years of age. But youth, it seems, is here no test of innocence; these infants, as I may call them, rivalled their mothers in the wantonness of their motions and the arts of allurement.

About seven o'clock the traffic for cocoa-nuts, bread-fruit, bananas, and different articles of curiosity, began, and was continued briskly till noon. Of the three first commodities, I obtained a considerable quantity, at a cheap rate, giving only, for seven nuts, and a bunch of bananas and bread-fruit, a piece of an old iron hoop, not more than five inches long. At eight o'clock two canoes arrived, with the king in one, and his uncle in the other. They brought with them four pigs, which they wished to exchange for two of our English sheep; but finding me averse to this, the canoes took them back on their return. I offered, as a present to the king, some axes, knives, and other articles; but he would only take a striped cap, observing, as he

1804.
May.
refused the rest, that such precious things could not be accepted, till he had something to give me in return. He immediately sent on shore his canoe, which soon returned with fifty cocoa-nuts, for which, in addition to what I had before given, I made a present to the uncle of an axe and three knives. While this was going on, another of his majesty's relations came on board, and exchanged a large pig, for a cock and hen.

The king, during his stay, took such a liking to the large looking-glass in the cabin, that he could scarcely leave it for a moment; and as he stood before it, he made the most ridiculous distortions. For a green parrot which I had, he offered two large pigs; but I refused to part with it. However, to keep his majesty in good humour, I gave him a quantity of sugar, of which I knew he was extremely fond. Soon after breakfast, to my great surprise, our royal guest leaped overboard, without saying a word to any one, and swam on shore. This strange method of taking leave disconcerted me, and made me a little suspicious; but, being assured by our interpreter, Roberts, that it was agreeable to the custom of the country, my suspicions vanished. We observed, that of the immense number of people swimming round our vessel, not one paid the least attention to their king as he passed them, but continued what they were doing, uninterrupted by his presence. His attendants remained on board some time after his departure, and begged to be shaved, having been told by one of their countrymen, that the operation was much easier and more pleasant with a razor, than with their shells.

At one o'clock I put a *taboo*, or prohibition, upon further commercial intercourse for the present, by hoisting out a red flag, as it was our hour of dinner. The moment the islanders understood, from our interpreter (the Englishman of whom I have just spoken) what was meant, they retired to a short distance from the ship; but their noise was as tumultuous as ever.

As soon as dinner was over, the taboo was taken off, and the traffic began again. We had as yet no reason to complain of misconduct on the part of the islanders. Whenever any thing was purchased, it was hoisted on board, and a piece of iron hoop (our common payment), fastened to the end of the rope, was let down in return. Some of these traders were occasionally admitted into the ship; but on receiving payment, they in general instantly jumped overboard, seemingly the happiest beings in the world.

We moored the ship to-day; and, as the weather was warm, I called the islanders to our assistance. This produced great joy amongst them; and the capstern was manned in an instant. After the business was over, I made each a present of an iron nail; and they departed, as before, perfectly happy.

To my great satisfaction, Roberts was induced to stay on board and attend the ship during her continuance at these islands.

On the 12th we were again awaked in the morning by the noise of the swimmers; but their number was so small, in comparison with that of the day before, that only fifty cocoa-nuts, and a few other trifles were purchased. About noon the king

1804.
May

paid us another visit, accompanied by his brother, and exchanged four cocks, which he brought with him, for one of ours, whose crowing had particularly pleased him. The brother also had taken a liking to one of our ducks, and offered a middling-size pig for her, promising at the same time another, not quite so large, for a drake. This exchange was not only advantageous, but very gratifying to me, as it might be the means of introducing into the island a useful domestic bird, unknown there before. During this visit, a circumstance took place of a serio-comic nature. One of my midshipmen, in examining the oar of a canoe that I had purchased, happened to let it fall, and it struck against the head of the king, who was sitting on the deck. His majesty immediately fell down, and began to make the most extraordinary wry faces, as if in great pain. The accident mortified me so much, that I reprimanded the young man a little severely for his carelessness. He was himself considerably alarmed; and, in apologizing, presented the king with a small piece of iron. This changed the scene; his majesty burst into a loud laugh, and expressed by signs, how cleverly he had deceived us, and that he was not in the least hurt. This scene over, the king went on shore in high spirits, and I was myself not a little pleased that the accident terminated as it did.

In the afternoon, captain Krusenstern came to see me, and in the course of conversation informed me, that the king had also brought him in the morning a pig; but as on his coming on board, the officers being at dinner, there was nobody to receive him on deck, he was so much displeased, that he ordered the pig to be taken back again. Though this circumstance appeared to us of a trifling nature, it had nearly been productive of serious consequences. One of the savages, returning on shore, reported that the king was in irons on board the Nadejda, for refusing to part with a pig. The bay was instantly in commotion; and our launch, which was then watering on shore, was surrounded by a host of savages, who threatened, if their chief was not immediately released, to put Roberts, who was attending the launch, to death. Though the poor fellow did all he could to convince them of the falsehood of the story, he certainly would have been cruelly treated, had not his majesty opportunely made his appearance, and assured the throng that he had received no insult or injury. This conduct of the islanders was a little grating to us; but we showed no resentment, considering them as uneducated children of Nature, who suffered their passions to run away with their judgment, and force to carry it over reason.

Notwithstanding these tumultuous symptoms, I ordered the launch to be dispatched again the next morning for water; and I proposed to captain Krusenstern our paying a visit to the king. At eight o'clock we set out, thirty in number, with Roberts for our guide. Our way at first was along the beach, and then through a grove of cocoa-nut and bread-fruit trees. Having passed some poor cottages, we reached the house of the king's brother, where we stopped for a while to repose ourselves. The multitude that followed from curiosity, crowded upon us continually; but a word occasionally from Roberts, was sufficient to make them keep at a proper distance. As we proceeded, there were many springs of water on the way, and the path being narrow, we were wet and dirty before we reached the place of destination. Arriving at the king's abode, we made a proper

1804.
May.

disposition of our armed force, and then entered a building resembling a summer-house. The foundation was of stone. The sides were constructed with poles, placed horizontally one upon another, some of which were moveable, to admit air and light. The roof, which was covered with leaves of the bread-fruit tree, had only one slope. The front of the building had a door in the middle, about five feet high and three broad.

The inside of this edifice was divided lengthwise into two parts, by means of a large piece of wood, like a beam or rafter, placed on the floor. The division furthest from the entrance was covered with mats, spread upon clean dry grass, and answered the purpose of bed-chamber and drawing-room.

The walls of the building were hung on the inside with several domestic utensils, made of the calabash; and with stone axes, pikes, clubs, and other instruments of war. In one corner of the room was a curious sort of drum, made of the hollowed trunk of a tree, and covered with the skin of the shark.

Adjoining to this habitation was a small store-room, the entrance of which was from within, and so narrow and low, that it was difficult to creep through it. There was also another tolerably large building or room, apart from the house, where his majesty, on particular festivals, takes his meals.

On our entrance, we were received by the king and queen with great politeness: several of the royal family were present, and in particular the king's daughter-in-law, called the Goddess of the Bay. I questioned this goddess, by means of Roberts, concerning the customs and manners of the country, and found that she felt her consequence in its full extent.

Having distributed scissars, knives, looking-glasses, and other trifles amongst this royal group, we departed, to proceed to the house of our interpreter, and were introduced, on the way, to the king's grand-child, who is respected as a divinity by the islanders. The infant was exhibited by his uncle, who stood within the inclosure of the house. I expressed a desire that his little highness might be brought to me; but understanding that he was under the law of taboo, which would not permit him to leave the inclosure, I approached him, and presented him with a piece of white cloth. The royal family had accompanied us to this place, as well as the multitude; but of the latter, no one dared to pass within the prohibited boundary.

Our walk to the habitation of Roberts was extremely pleasant, as it extended along an eminence, from whence we had a beautiful view of our ships in the bay, and the plantations of the natives in the valleys. Though the house was not so large as many we had passed, it was well adorned on the outside with different kinds of fruit-trees, which afforded us, after our fatigue, a very acceptable repast. Being refreshed, we visited a burying-ground, which, I must confess, was by no means equal to my expectation. It contained but a few wooden statues, rudely carved, while cocoa-nut shells were strewed in such abundance on the ground, that we were greatly incommoded by them. Roberts informed us, that sacrifices to the dead consisted here of cocoa-nuts; and I observed one quite fresh, on the head of a statue, that was erected over a grave. I observed also the

1804.
May.

remains of a dead body, exposed on a simple board, supported by poles, under a roof of leaves. A considerable period must have elapsed since the body was placed there, as the skeleton only remained. The most pleasing sight in the burying-ground was a kind of monument lately erected to one of their deceased priests. It was constructed in a very handsome manner, was ornamented exteriorly with green leaves of the cocoa-nut tree, and had an altar within, of by no means a savage appearance.

Having satisfied our curiosity in this melancholy place, we returned to our ship by a road, on which stood many houses; but they all so nearly resembled the king's, though some were larger, that it is not necessary to describe them. The crowd that accompanied us during our stay on shore offered us various articles in the way of exchange, and behaved in so fair and friendly a manner, that I thought these islanders incapable of dishonesty. My ideas, however, were soon changed; for, on arriving at the boats, I found that one of our grapplings had been cut away under water, and carried off in so dextrous a manner, that neither the quarter-master nor the bargemen could conceive how it had disappeared. In this wily business they must have employed the knives we had distributed among them; showing us thereby that they well knew how preferable our instruments, made of iron, were to theirs, made of stone or shells.

Soon after my arrival on board, the king returned my visit, and brought with him a pig, and a stone axe, in exchange for two of my iron axes. As we were just going to dinner, I invited his majesty to partake of it. Of our several dishes he preferred that of pancakes with honey, which he relished so much, that the whole of what was served up was dispatched in an instant. His relish of the pancakes was no matter of surprise to me, being aware that savages in general, like children, are fond of sweet things the first time of tasting them; but when I saw him drink port wine, glass for glass, with us, I own I was astonished: he afterwards, however, felt the effects of it in their full force.

1804.
May.

The next morning, I received from the queen a message, that if I would send my boat on shore, she would come with some of her relations to see me; adding, that a taboo being imposed on her, she was forbidden to go into a canoe, or to swim. I complied with this agreeable request immediately; and about noon I had the pleasure of seeing the queen, her daughter, and the Goddess of the Bay in my cabin. They remained with us a considerable time, and were regaled with tea, sweetmeats, and other delicacies. Our presents of knives, scissars, and looking-glasses, however, pleased them most, and especially the Goddess of the Bay, who was so enchanted with her reception, that she appeared unwilling to leave the ship. Our royal guests, on this occasion, were dressed in yellow cloth made of the bark of a particular tree, and had their bodies smeared with oil of cocoa-nut, mixed with a kind of yellow paint, which affected our olfactory nerves in no very agreeable way: but this could no more be dispensed with by a Marquesan woman, when full-dressed, than rouge and eau de Cologne by an European lady of fashion. The handsomest of my party was certainly the Goddess, whose name was Anataena. She was a daughter of the king of another bay in the island, called Houmé, and owed her title of divinity to her marriage. These personages having left us, I granted to other females the long desired permission to visit the ship and satisfy their curiosity.

14th.

1804.
May.

Finding that there was no possibility of providing ourselves here with a greater quantity of live stock than we had already obtained, captain Krusenstern and I, with some officers of both ships, repaired to Jegawé Bay, which was about three miles and a half to the westward of our station. On our landing, we were surrounded by men and women, with fruit and other commodities for sale; and in a very short time sixty bunches of bananas were in our possession. After visiting the king, and breakfasting at his house, we proceeded in search of what was the main object of our excursion. We were, however, disappointed: the natives would sell us nothing but fruit and vegetables, though plenty of hogs and fowls were seen about their houses; and towards evening we returned to our ships.

The bay of Jegawé is a very safe place for anchoring; it forms a small bason, defended from all the winds, and ships may lie there quite close to the shore, especially on the south side, which renders it an admirable place for such as may be in want of thorough repair. The entrance is rather narrow; but as its depth does not exceed eighteen fathoms, and the bottom is good, you may warp in with ease, when you cannot sail in. To a small river of fresh water there, I gave the name of the Little Neva, the banks of which abound with inhabitants, who are able to supply vessels with a sufficiency both of fruit and hogs, though to us they would spare none of the last-mentioned article.

16th.

From the difficulty of further augmenting our live stock, we began on the 16th to prepare for sea. I rewarded Roberts for his services, with linen, pieces of iron, and other articles that were useful to him in his present situation. I also left with him a quantity of garden seeds, which he promised to cultivate. Gunpowder was the only thing I refused him; for it was a law with me, not to suffer a single grain of this dangerous commodity to be given to the islanders. As this was to be the last day of our stay, I ordered, at night, some rockets to be let off, the appearance of which terrified the natives extremely. They verily believed that we had the power of sending up stars, and that these luminaries, after disappearing in the sky, returned to us to be sent up again.

1804.
May.

Though in my narrative of events as they occurred, I have exhibited, perhaps, no very imperfect view, either of the islands we are quitting, or their inhabitants; it may not be amiss to add a few particulars, to render the picture more complete.

The old Marquesa islands, the names of which I have already given in their place, are five in number. They extend, by the observations I made, from 138° 18' to 138° 55' west longitude, and from 9° 25' to 10° 30' south latitude.

The new Marquesas are in like manner five in number; and are called by their inhabitants, Ooaboa, which is Trevannion's island; Ooahoonha, which is Riou's; Noocahiva, which is Martin's; and Hiaoo and Fatooda, which are Roberts's. The first three occupy about thirty-five miles in latitude, and forty in longitude; they were discovered in 1791, by Mr. Ingram of the United States, in his voyage to America for furs, and were named by him after the immortal Washington. Having stopped only at the island of Noocahiva, I can say nothing of the rest,

1804.
May.

except that they are high and craggy. It struck me, however, as singular, that none of them should have a conical elevation, but should all rise out of the sea almost perpendicularly. The island of Noocahiva, in my opinion, is the largest of the whole group. Having passed almost round it, I can venture to say, that there is no danger in sailing quite close to its shores. On the east side, which is high, and of no very pleasing aspect, is seen the bay called Hotisheve, which appeared to me to be open to the easterly winds, which in this part of the world blow almost continually. To the south are three bays: the first, called Houmé, is situated towards the south-east point; the second, Jegawé, at the south-west point, with an excellent anchorage, as I have before observed; and the third, Tayohaia, about midway between the other two. This last has also a good anchorage, but, being surrounded by high lands, is subject to strong squalls, against which a vessel should be on its guard when at anchor, and should take care to be always well moored. In coming in, and going out, anchors and boats should be ready to assist, in case of a change of wind, or a calm. When the islets of Mitao and Mootonoeé, that lie at the mouth of the bay, so near the shore as to be scarcely distinguished at a distance, and which I placed, by my observations, at 139° 40' west, and 8° 56' south, are in sight, steer for the first, and double it when at the distance of forty fathoms, where you will find twenty-seven fathoms of water. In coming out, the ship should be kept close to the eastern shore, on account of the winds, which at sea blow always from the eastward. The best anchorage in this bay, with regard to the currents, is under the south-east point, in twelve fathoms. From lying rather close to the other shore, I was obliged to work at my cables every day, as the ship was continually turning round. However, this is the surest side, if the ship should have parted with her anchors in a squall from the mountains, as happened here once to an American; because she may then run out to sea, under her stay-sails only, with ease. Though the watering place is by no means convenient in the bay of Tayohaia, yet, with the assistance of the natives, a launch may be completed in less than two hours, as the casks need only to be thrown into the water, to be filled, and the islanders are expeditious in cutting fire-wood on the beach: for this trouble, a small piece of iron, per man, is a satisfactory recompense. It is necessary, however, while the work is going on, that one or two of the ship's crew, armed with muskets, should attend, otherwise many things may be lost; for the islanders have no scruple in this respect, and will even knock off the iron hoops from the casks, while in the act of rolling them along the surf. A single discharge from a musket is, however, sufficient to terrify the most daring.

Our short stay at this island, and our ignorance of the language of its native inhabitants, would have rendered our information very incomplete, but for the fortunate circumstance of our meeting with Roberts, who seemed to have been sent providentially to our assistance. This personage was a run-away English sailor, and had long resided on the island. He had married one of the king's relations, and was treated, in consequence, with great respect by his new countrymen, whose language he appears to speak with fluency. From this Englishman I received many of the particulars I am about to relate.

Noocahiva, like all the other islands of this group, is governed by a number of chiefs, each of whom is independent of the rest, having a separate district, and different subjects. These chiefs, or kings, are almost always at war with each other. Though their kingly dignity is, to outward appearance, more fictitious than real, they enjoy great privileges. They have large domains, and are in high respect with the people. In a fruitful season, they have a right to a fourth part of the produce of the lands of their subjects; and in other seasons, an apportionment according to circumstances. Their dignity descends to them by hereditary succession. They can carry on war without consulting their people, and have sometimes a happy mode of making peace: for example, After war had raged for a long time, both by sea and land, between the chiefs of the bay of Tayohaia and two other neighbouring bays, the brother of the king of Tayohaia married the daughter of one, and his son the daughter of the other of the two chiefs; and the consequence was a suspension of hostilities by sea; with this condition, that if both princesses should finish their days in harmony and happiness with their husbands, perpetual peace by land, as well as by sea, should thenceforward prevail between the three nations. How happy would it be for humanity, how much innocent blood would be spared, if all the princes of the world would, by similar alliances, introduce the reign of peace! But, alas! royal ties are in general no secure pledge of tranquillity to the respective nations.

I have hitherto said nothing of established laws or established religion; and it appeared to me, as if neither had existence in the country. With individuals, as with chiefs, the law of right seemed to be the law of strength; and even violence, theft, and murder, had no punishment but what personal revenge might dictate. As to religion, though there are priests amongst them, we never perceived the least signs of worship. When any person dies, the corpse is immediately washed, and exposed on a plank in the middle of the house, and his relations and friends assemble to mourn over him; on which occasion they weep bitterly, and scratch their bodies with sharp bones, or shells. Sometimes this attendance on the dead is a scene of crying and laughing alternately; these different emotions immediately following each other, as I have often witnessed, in savages. For instance, on my firing a gun, though it terrified them almost to death, a burst of laughter almost instantaneously succeeded their fright. The ceremony of washing and weeping being over, the body is carried to the burying-ground, where it is exposed on a wooden platform, and left to waste away in the open air. In war, the bodies of the dead are always buried, for fear of their falling into the hands of the enemy; nothing being so humiliating to a Marquesan, as to see a scull of one of his party tied to the foot of an individual of an adverse party, who shows his triumph in this manner, if he obtains one in any way.

The most barbarous honours are paid here to priests, on their decease. Roberts assured me, that, on the death of a priest, three men must be sacrificed; two of whom are hung up in the burying-ground, while the third is cut to pieces, and eaten by visitors; all but the head, which is placed upon one of the idols. When the flesh of the first two are wasted away, the bones that remain are burnt. The custom of the country requires, that the men destined for sacrifice should belong to some neigh-

1804.
May.

bouring nation, and accordingly they are generally stolen. This occasions a war of six, and sometimes of twelve, months: its duration, however, depends upon the nearest relation of the deceased priest; who, as soon as he is acquainted with his death, retires to a place of taboo; and, till he chooses to come out, the blood of the two parties does not cease to flow. During his retirement, he is furnished with every thing he may require, human flesh not excepted.

Former voyagers have asserted, that the Marquesan men and women have no individual attachments, but cohabit promiscuously, as inclination may dictate. This, however, is a mistake: the marriage state is held nearly as sacred among them as it is among any uncivilized people It is true indeed, fathers sometimes offered us their daughters, and husbands their wives; but this proceeded from their ardent desire of possessing iron, or other European articles, which, in their estimation, are above all price. This out of the question, jealousy is so prevalent with the men, that upon the smallest suspicion of infidelity, they punish their wives with severity. Though there is no law here against adultery, any more than against any other crime, there is a custom so generally sanctioned respecting it, that it on some occasions supplies the place of law: which is, that if a husband knows his wife to have been unfaithful to him, he may endeavour to seduce the wife of the adulterer, and avenge his own wrong by possessing her. The only ceremony relating to marriage that takes place in the Marquesa islands, is this: If a young man falls in love with a girl, and his love is returned, he endeavours to get possession of her person; or, failing in this, goes immediately and claims her of her parents; and, if they consent, he takes up his abode with them. The young lovers live together for a while, on the most intimate footing; and if, at the termination of that period, they still are attached to each other, the marriage is concluded, by their quitting the paternal house, and removing to one of their own.

In rich families, every woman has two husbands; of whom one may be called the assistant husband. This last, when the other is at home, is nothing more than the head servant of the house; but, in case of absence, exercises all the rights of matrimony, and is also obliged to attend his lady wherever she goes. It happens sometimes, that the subordinate partner is chosen after marriage; but in general two men present themselves to the same woman, who, if she approves their addresses, appoints one for the real husband, and the other as his auxiliary: the auxiliary is generally poor, but handsome and well-made.

It is no disgrace here, if a woman be brought to bed on the very day of her marriage; the child is still legitimate: indeed there is no such thing known as illegitimacy. Divorces take place with as little ceremony as the nuptial rites are performed.

A man may take another wife, and a woman another husband, whenever they find it mutually convenient to do so. Though near relations are forbidden to marry, it sometimes happens, that a father lives with his daughter, and a brother with his sister. Some years ago an instance occurred of a mother cohabiting with her son, but it was regarded with horror; which shows that, even among savages, the rights of maternity are respected above all others. On the birth of a child, the ceremony is observed of cutting off the navel-string; and till it is performed, nobody can come in or go out of the house in which the child is. All prohibitions are signified here by the word taboo; which is divided into the king's taboo and the taboo of the priests, and is very strictly observed by the commonalty: the powerful, however, sometimes violate it.

Every inhabitant of the island may possess property by succession, or in any other way. There are rich and poor here. The rich have plantations, houses, and canoes; the poor have nothing, and pass their days like others of the same station in the rest of the world. All the houses are built alike, and resemble summer bowers, as I have before observed in describing the king's habitation. I admired the cleanliness of the interior of these small houses. The opulent have separate buildings for their dining-rooms, on particular occasions of feasting, which the women are not permitted to enter; and so strict is the prohibition, that they dare not even pass near them. The selfish gluttony of the men, who would deprive the other sex of the pleasure of eating pork, I believe, is the origin of this custom.

Besides a magazine for provisions, the rich have small gardens, or rather enclosures, round their houses, planted with trees, of the bark of which a sort of cloth is made. The magazines are merely deep holes dug in the ground, and covered with leaves, clay, and sand. There are no kitchens to the houses. The food is prepared in any spot near the habitation, in the open air, in the same manner as in other islands in these seas, and which many navigators have described.

My endeavours to ascertain with accuracy the population of the island were fruitless: from comparing, however, Roberts's account with what I could observe myself, I judged that the south side of it contained about four thousand inhabitants.

The natives are a handsome and well-made people; the men especially, who are tall and strong-limbed. The commonalty are of a dark complexion, with straight black hair. The nobility are much fairer.

Tatooing is so much in fashion here, that there is not an individual without some marks of it. Many were covered all over with different figures, some of which displayed much taste. The king, however, surpassed all his subjects in this kind of embellishment. His body was so completely figured, that scarcely the smallest spot of the natural colour of his skin could be perceived. To be thus perfectly tatooed, is a business of great expense; the masters of the art expecting to be paid handsomely for their work. The practice of tatooing appeared to me very ridiculous at first; but when accustomed to it, those who had the most figures I thought the most comely. It is astonishing that women, who are in all countries so fond of beautifying their persons, do not tatoo themselves here; except with a few lines on the lips, round the perforation in the ears, and on the hands.

There is hardly any clothing worn by these people. The men have sometimes a sort of towel round the waist, but in general they go quite naked. Mr. Langsdorff has said, that circumcision is universal among them. So far from this being the case,

1804.
May.

I observed instances of the prepuce being drawn forward over the glans and tied with a string, the ends of which hung down about four inches. To this string much value seemed to be attached; for it happened that the king's brother, in coming on board my ship, had the misfortune to lose it, and his anxiety upon the occasion was extreme. As he stepped on the gangway, he eagerly covered the untied part with his hands, and made earnest signs for a piece of rope-yarn; till he had received which, and restored the part to its previous state, he appeared as if incapable of moving from the spot where the accident happened.

The women are more decent, as to clothing, than the men. When full-dressed, they are wrapped in a kind of cloth of their own making, which is fastened round the waist, and then folded over the shoulders, so as to leave one only or both breasts uncovered. In general, however, nothing is hidden but the part which nature forbids them to expose; and so tenacious are they of the covering to this part, that the most salacious will not consent to take it off.

The men wear their hair in different forms. Some cut it quite close, and shave a little space upwards from behind; others shave half the head lengthwise, leaving the hair long on the other half; and others again shave off all the hair, except a tuft on each side, which is twisted into the shape of horns. Some daub themselves over with yellow paint only, and others with cocoa-nut oil and yellow paint mixed. They all wear ear-rings and necklaces. The necklaces are made of shells or wood, and sometimes of the teeth of swine, or the porpoise: those made of wood are embellished with a handsome red pea. The women tie up their long hair in knots, and, on ceremonious occasions, besmear themselves like the men.

The food of these islanders consists chiefly of fish, swine, cocoa-nuts, plantains, bananas, bread-fruit, tarro-root, and sugar-cane. The last is rather a scarce article; as also is pork, which seldom makes its appearance but on occasions of festivity. Both sexes eat their meals together, except when public dinners are given in the dining-rooms, where women dare not appear, for reasons which I have before assigned.

In case of a bad harvest the poor suffer dreadfully, as they never lay up a sufficient stock of provisions to prevent the horrors of famine. A few years ago, numbers of them were obliged to roam among the mountains in search of what they could find, leaving their wives and children at home dying with hunger. Roberts told me, that in the bay of Tayohaia only, four hundred perished on this occasion. In these times of dearth, every one was in danger, he said, of losing his life; not only for want of nourishment, but from the violence of one stronger than himself, who may seize and devour him.

Considering the mild temper of the inhabitants of this island, it is difficult to believe that they are cannibals. Roberts, however, assured me, that the bodies of the prisoners taken in war were eaten, all but the sculls, which were preserved for trophies. We purchased several of these sculls, paying a knife for each; but neither their wearing them as trophies, nor offering them for sale, proves cannibalism: like other savages, they may cut off

1804.
May.

the heads of their vanquished enemies, without the idea occurring to them of eating their flesh.

The Marquesans carry on war both by sea and land. Their arms consist of heavy clubs, spears, and an instrument in the form of a small oar. The clubs are four feet nine inches long, with a broad and flat upper end, which is generally carved with different figures. The length of the oar is six feet, and the spears are from eleven to thirteen feet. Besides these formidable weapons, the islanders are expert in throwing stones from slings made of the fibres of the cocoa-nut. Though not deficient in courage, they never fight openly. They are very much afraid of fire-arms, the destructive power of which they learned some time since from an American ship, from which a shot was fired that killed one of the royal family, whilst he was swimming about with a great many others of his countrymen. The circumstance was this: One of the islanders threw a bread-fruit on board, which struck the captain, who was walking on the quarter-deck. The sentinel, seeing this, instantly discharged his musket, and, missing the guilty person, unfortunately shot a brother of the king. This has produced such an effect, that the sight alone of fire-arms is sufficient to keep the whole island in awe.

The simplicity of this people is astonishing. Their actions seem the result of instinct, rather than of common sense; which makes them often commit faults, ruinous even to themselves. Theft is so common amongst them, that hardly any thing is safe in their houses, especially in time of scarcity. Roberts assured me, that the island would abound with swine, if the young ones were not stolen, and then eaten to prevent detection. I can easily credit this propensity to thieving, when I recollect, that the king's brother himself stole a piece of sugar from me, and, being accused of the crime, endeavoured, in the most barefaced manner, to persuade me that it was committed by a duck which I had given him, and which was then under his arm.

It is proved by facts that ignorance is the mother of superstition. It will therefore excite no astonishment that the inhabitants of Noocahiva should possess this quality in the highest degree. Every one here is persuaded, that the soul of a grandfather is transmitted by Nature into the body of his grandchildren; and that, if an unfruitful wife were to place herself under the corpse of her deceased grandfather, she would be sure to become pregnant. It is also a current opinion, that there are individuals on the island who can cure the effects of the strongest poison, by simply rubbing the sides of the patient with their hands, which is supposed to make the poison come out from under the ribs. But the belief in evil spirits has the greatest weight, and is carried to the greatest absurdity amongst them; for it is imagined, that these spirits come sometimes into houses, and by whistling, and other more tremendous noises, demand pork and cava or ava, which, being placed in the middle of the room and covered, are immediately devoured by them. Surely these instances prove how insignificant, in its natural state, is the human understanding.

I saw none of the war-canoes of this place, and can therefore say nothing respecting them; but the common canoe is long and narrow, the bottom made out of a single tree, and fastened

1804.
May.

to the sides, by inserting a piece of small twine through numerous holes. The head resembles that of a galley, and to the stern a crooked piece of wood is fixed, through which runs the sheet of a triangular sail, made of matting. These narrow boats are well balanced by three long poles laid across, to the ends of which, on one side, is fastened a piece of wood.

The island of Noocahiva produces all the necessaries of life. It has excellent fresh water, and in such abundance, that it flows down in cascades from different elevations, greatly tending to beautify in many places the views of the coast. The climate is so salubrious that, by Roberts's account, many live here to the age of a hundred years. I saw myself the king's mother, who was about eighty, and did not yet think herself very old.

Having had but little leisure for minute inquiries respecting the vegetable kingdom in this part of the globe, I shall content myself with describing the few articles only that came within my observation.

TREES.

Toomoomey, or Bread-fruit-tree. The branches of this tree spread out widely, and the leaves resemble those of the fig-tree, but are of a larger size, and of a deeper green. Its fruit is of an oblong figure, measuring lengthwise from five inches and a half to six inches and a half, and breadthwise from four to five inches; it is of a light green colour, but turns black after two or three days keeping. This useful tree, I was told, bears fruit here three times in the year. The first and the best crop, called by the natives mainooé, ripens about our January. The second, which is the poorest, about the middle of June; and the third, about September. From the bark, a sort of thick brown cloth is made, which is sometimes dyed yellow.

Toomooehee, or Cocoa-nut-tree: too well known in Europe, to require a description.

Maeeca, or Plantains. There are many sorts of this tree here; the fruit of some of which is nine inches long, and seven and a half round.

Toomooishee. A kind of Chestnut-tree, that bears fruit in the months of May and November.

Timanoo. A firm strong tree, growing sometimes to nine feet in circumference. It is only used for building war-canoes, and is forbidden to be cut for any other purpose.

Toomoomyee. Of this tree the common canoes are made.

Kenai. A soft tree, used for small canoes, and other unimportant works: it takes root as easily as our willow.

Pooadea. This is the largest tree on the island. Its trunk, I was told, measures in some instances thirty feet in circumference: the branches, which are only allowed to be cut for religious ceremonies, spread wide, and are well adapted to give shade to burying-grounds.

Cogoo. This tree is used for fire-wood. It bears a black

1804.
May.
berry, which is mixed with a certain odoriferous root, and used for painting the skin yellow.

Toar. A tree of which all the implements of war are made, on account of its hardness.

Fow. A tree of a middling size, from the bark of the branches of which threads for fishing-lines and nets are made.

Eooty. From the bark of this tree, the best cloth is made. The manner of manufacturing it is similar to that which has been described by several navigators, as practised in the Sandwich Islands.

Eama. The fruit of this tree answers the purpose of candles. It resembles small chestnuts, which, when peeled, stuck one upon another on a stick, and set on fire, burn in succession, and give an excellent light.

Hiaba. A large tree, the bark of which is used for making short pieces of cloth, such as the islanders sometimes tie round the waist.

Foa. This tree produces a very handsome fruit, pieces of which being strung together, are used, on festivals, as wreaths for the head, and ornaments for the neck.

ROOTS.

Taoo. A sort of yam. Its leaves may answer the purpose of brocoli, which it resembles in taste.

Carpé. This root is about three feet long. The greater part of it grows out of the ground. It takes twelve months to ripen, and is made into puddings, or prepared like yams.

Hoé. A kind of wild potatoe, which has a bitter taste, and affords but little nourishment. It is only used by the islanders in times of famine.

Titou. A root that grows wild in the fields, and resembles our turnip.

Togoogoo. A root of the size of a cocoa-nut without its husk: when boiled, it turns to a sort of pudding.

There is only one species of salad herb on the island, that is calculated for the table. It is called *emahé,* and considerably resembles our field-mustard.

Knowing from experience how necessary the language of a country is to a person who travels in it, especially where no assistance can be obtained, except what some lucky chance may present, as, for instance, our interpreter Roberts; I endeavoured to collect as many words and sentences of the language of this island as possible, which I shall give in the Appendix, in the hope of their being useful to future navigators.

During our stay at Tayohaia, I could make no observations on shore: however, having taken a great many lunar distances the day before our arrival at the island of Noocahiva, we were enabled to lay down with great precision the island of Motané.

1804.
May.

From thence we took bearings of all the other islands as they came in sight, and found their latitude and longitude to be as follows:

	Lat. S.	Long. W.
East end of the island of Fatoohiva	10° 28'	138° 18'
South end of Motané	10 0	138 30
East end of Touata	9 59	138 45
East end of Hoivahova	9 45	138 26½
South end of Ooahoona	8 56	139 12
The entrance of the bay of Tayohaia	8 56	139 40
North end of Ooaboa	9 19	139 40½
The middle of Fatoohoo	9 27	138 31

The variation of the compass, according to different azimuths, was 6° east.

CHAPTER VI.

PASSAGE FROM THE WASHINGTON ISLANDS TO THE SANDWICH ISLANDS.

Nautical Difficulties on leaving Noocahiva. Search in vain for an unknown Land, seen by Marchand. Surprise of my Crew at the Sight of a Shark which we caught. Make the Island of Owyhee. The Nadejda leaves us to proceed to Camchatca. Anchor in the Bay of Carocacoa. Traffic with the Inhabitants. Reason for refusing to admit Women on Board. Excursion on Shore with the Chief of the Bay. Habitations. Temples. Visited by Mr. Young, who governs the Island in the Absence of the King. Village of Tavaroa. Leave Owyhee. Island of Otooway. Visited by its King. Island of Onihoo

At five o'clock in the morning of the 17th, we unmoored, and about nine got under way. The wind was in so unsettled a state, that it flew round the compass, and obliged me to warp out of the bay; which would have been effected with ease, but for the necessity I was under of bringing-to again, to assist the Nadejda, who, by keeping under sail, instead of warping, had drifted too near the shore. This accident prevented our being out to sea till night.

The king remained on board with me till it was dark. He was very facetious upon the visit the ladies had made me, observing repeatedly how uncommonly satisfied they had been

1804.
May.

with our treatment, and especially the Goddess, round whose neck I had tied a piece of gold twist.

During our warping out of the harbour, one of the warps gave way, and immediately the king sent his canoe on shore for a diver, to assist us in recovering it. This was by no means necessary, as we could easily have found it with our grapplings; but the king's intentions were so friendly, that I did not oppose them; and, in recompence, I gave both him and the diver some pieces of iron, which pleased his majesty so much that he left the ship in high glee; though he took no leave of us, but jumped overboard, as in every preceding instance, and swam to the shore.

At ten o'clock we hove-to in the offing, to hoist in our boats, and wait for the Nadejda, who had been obliged to remain at anchor all night.

18th. Early in the morning of the 18th the wind blew at east-south-east, and the weather was so squally, that we were obliged to be constantly employed about our sails: this was the only inconvenience we had to suffer, as we then stood almost in the middle between the islands of Ooaboa and Noocahiva. At nine o'clock we saw our friend the Nadejda, who had brought-to under the shore, to hoist in her boats. Having joined her, we doubled the south-west end of Noocahiva; and I intended to have steered to the northward, under the idea of ascertaining the position of the cape I had seen on the 8th instant, on the north side of the island; but observing captain Krusenstern to bear away to the west-south-west, I abandoned my design. I had the satisfaction, however, of determining the latitude of the south-west end of Noocahiva, which I found to be 8° 59' south. 1804. May.

Before our departure from Tayohaia, it had been settled that the two vessels should steer west-south-west, to the distance of three degrees, at least; in order to ascertain the supposed existence of an unknown land, mentioned in Marchand's Voyage.

On the 19th we had easterly wind and fine weather, and at eight o'clock in the evening had made the proposed distance to the westward; but seeing no appearance of land, we tacked, and took a direct course to the Sandwich Islands. Having been destitute of fresh meat since we left St. Catharine, I ordered cocoa-nuts and bananas to be distributed amongst the ship's company every day, and essence of malt to be used at breakfast. 19th.

On the 26th we crossed the equator; and at noon, by observation, were in 56' north, and 146° 12' west. This day was remarkable for our catching a shark. My people, who had never seen a fish of this kind, out of the water, were very much struck at its appearance. A Tartar, one of the crew, swore it was the devil, and advised our throwing it overboard again. I ordered it, however, to be cut up, and some of the best pieces to be cooked for dinner; and, to my great satisfaction, I found that every one on board but myself was pleased with his meal. 26th.

On the 3d of June the wind settled to the north-east, and the weather, which had been changeable for the last four days, became so fine, that we had nothing to wish for, but a speedy arrival at the Sandwich Islands. We were a little surprised at June. 3d.

1804.
June.

not finding the usual south-east trade-wind. We had, however, in its stead, light breezes from the north-east, that completely answered our purpose. I observed, that, after having crossed the line, the weather was colder, by several degrees, than we had found it in the southern hemisphere; and to this I attributed our not seeing either birds or fish of any kind, which, in similar climates, had always followed us in great quantities.

8th.   At nine o'clock in the morning of the 8th, we descried the island of Owyhee to the north-west; and at noon the east end of it bore from us, by the compass, north 3° west, twenty miles distant. By observation, we were in latitude 19° 10' north, and in longitude, by the chronometer, No. 136, 153° 51', and by No. 50, 154° 5' west; by which it appeared, that the first was sixty, and the last forty-six miles to the eastward of the true longitude. This, however, was but a trifle in comparison of our ship's reckoning, which was found to be 5° 39' to the eastward.

At two o'clock in the afternoon we were so near the shore, that we could distinguish the habitations, which were numerous, and some of them charmingly situated. We were visited here by six canoes, containing two or three men each. These persons accosted us with as much familiarity, as if we had been acquainted with them for years. On coming on deck, they shook hands with every one they saw, repeating the word, *how-lo-lo*, meaning, as I conceived, *how do you do*. They brought us, however, no fresh provisions; and it seemed as if the sole object of their visit was to inquire who we were. Having satisfied their curiosity, they left us, and we proceeded in our course; but the weather becoming thick and rainy about sun-set, we determined to keep in good offings for the night.

At day-light we approached the shore; and at eleven o'clock saw the south-west end of the island, which appeared like two eminences rising beyond the south point, which is low compared with the adjacent land. We passed the south point about noon, and brought-to, to wait for some canoes that were paddling towards us. Two of these came alongside of the Nadejda, and proposed exchanging a large hog, they had brought with them, for some woollen cloth; but finding their wish could not be complied with, they carried the hog back, refusing every other article that was offered for it. At four in the afternoon we sailed along the shore, to induce other canoes to come out with fresh provisions, of which both ships were much in want, but especially the Nadejda, whose officers had subsisted on salt meat alone for some time; but, unfortunately, not a soul appeared till late in the evening, when we were obliged to steer off shore. From the observation of this day, the south point of the island was 18° 35' north.

The light breezes, which prevailed during the whole of the next day, would not permit us to get near the shore. At noon we brought the south point of the island to bear north 79° east, and by observation were in latitude 18° 58' north. Towards evening, captain Krusenstern took leave of me, intending to sail for Camchatca in the night. I urged him to stop a few days longer to refresh himself, but I could not prevail; and a favourable wind from the east springing up about eight o'clock, he shaped his course accordingly, and departed.

1804.
June.
11th.

Having found, by experience, that nothing could be obtained by cruizing round the coast, I determined, on the 11th, to come to anchor, and for that purpose steered for the bay of Caracacoa.

On drawing near the shore, a canoe came along-side from a village called Pereerooa, not far from the south-west point. In this canoe were an Englishman, of the name of Johns, and a native, who called himself George Kernick. This native spoke the English language remarkably well, having been seven years in England, whither, he said, he had been carried by captain Paget. My first questions related to the present state of Owyhee, as to provisions; and I was glad to find, that, though the king and all the nobles were then on the island of Wahoo, in consequence of a war with the inhabitants of Otooway, I might be sure of procuring all sorts of refreshments, and on reasonable terms. He added that, during the king's absence, the island was governed by an Englishman of the name of Young, who would no doubt come on board to pay his respects, the moment our arrival should be known to him. Soon after the first canoe left us, three others of a similar description came off, and brought with them three small pigs, which I purchased for eight yards of common Russian cloth.

In the mean time the wind shifted a-head, and obliged us to tack. At noon, having the bay of Caracacoa north 15° east, about ten miles distant, we found ourselves, by observation, in 19° 17′ 8″ north. Soon after, the wind, inclining again a little to the westward, allowed me to steer for the anchorage; which, however, I could not have fetched, but for a strong current to the northward, that, it is said, always prevails here. Sailing quite close in shore, we had two boats towing a-head, and we kept the ship by the wind till five o'clock, when, having passed the south point of the bay, we dropped anchor in seventeen fathoms; the south point bearing south, and the north point north 80° west. Before night the ship was moored north-north-east and south-south-west, with three quarters of a cable each way. The decreasing depth of water as we entered the bay, was forty, thirty-five, twenty-eight, twenty-two, and seventeen fathoms, over a bottom of sand and shells.

1804.
June.

From the accounts of former navigators, I expected to have been surrounded by the natives as soon as the ship had dropped anchor; but to our good fortune, not an individual was seen till after sun-set; which, I found, was owing to the taboo. I call it good fortune, because we were enabled to secure the ship without molestation. Just before dark, a company of about a hundred young women made their appearance in the water, swimming towards our vessel, and exhibiting, as they approached us, the most unequivocal tokens of pleasure, not doubting of admittance. It was with a degree of regret that I felt myself obliged to give a damp to their joy: but I was too firm in the resolution I had formed, not to permit licentious intercourse on board, to be won from it, by any allurements or entreaties, by any expression of joy or of sorrow; and this troop of nymphs were compelled to return with an affront offered to their charms, which they had never experienced before, perhaps, from any European ship.

The next morning, believing the taboo to be still in force, I was preparing to go on shore; when I found the vessel sur-

12th.

1804.
June.

rounded by canoes, furnished with different articles for sale. In consequence, I altered my intention, and commenced the necessary and important business of traffic. As none of the canoes brought any live stock, I was induced to ask the reason; and was given to understand, that Mr. Young had forbidden any pigs to be sold to ships that might arrive, without his express permission. As it was uncertain when this important personage might be at the bay, I dispatched Mr. Johns, an Englishman, who had engaged to remain with me as interpreter, to the chief of the bay, to inform him, that if I could not be supplied with fresh provision here, I should put to sea in the night, to seek this commodity in some more hospitable place. My message had the desired effect. The chief came shortly after on board, and presented me with two middling-sized hogs, and a considerable quantity of different sorts of vegetables. I paid him great attention, and presented him in return with three bottles of rum, two axes, and an adz; which pleased him so much, that he promised to supply me daily with such necessaries as I might want during my stay. In the mean time the general trade had been carried on so briskly, that by noon, not only the officers, but the men, were possessed of a variety of articles, many of which, though pleased with them for the moment, they afterwards threw away as useless and cumbersome. Though the islanders took knives and small looking-glasses in exchange for their goods, they always gave the preference to our printed and common coarse linens, while pieces of iron hoop, of which we had a great number, were held by them in no estimation. As a compliment, I invited the chief of the bay to dine with us; and I had the satisfaction of observing the keen appetite with which he honoured our repast, and the handsome manner in which he afterwards paid his respects to the bottle, filling his glass alternately with Port wine and brandy, till he became so inebriated, that it was with difficulty we could get him out of the ship.

As night approached, the vessel was again surrounded by the female troop, who had so kindly offered us their company the preceding evening, and who now seemed resolved upon intrusion, if not admitted freely to our society. But I made known to them the impossibility of their succeeding in their attempt; and I requested also the interference of the chief, who gave orders that all his people, male and female, should in future leave the ship at sun-set. In consequence of this injunction, we found ourselves generally alone, as soon as our ensign was lowered; and it must be confessed, that, after the noise and bustle of the day, which were hardly supportable, this change of scene was very agreeable to us. The cause of my peremptoriness as to these female visitors, was the fear of their introducing among my crew a certain disease, which, I had been given to understand, was very prevalent in the Sandwich Islands; and certainly the persons of several of the inhabitants, of both sexes, bore evident marks of its ravages. In spite of Mr. Young's prohibition, we purchased during the day two large hogs, two smaller ones, two goats, ten fowls, and cocoa-nuts, sweet potatoes, tarro-root, and sugar-cane, in abundance.

In the morning of the 13th, we were again surrounded by canoes. About noon the chief brought us four large hogs, one of which he gave me as a present, while for the others I was obliged to pay a bar and a half of iron. I offered him several other articles by way of exchange; but he refused them all, signifying that these animals belonged to the king, who had given directions that they should be sold for bar-iron only. Besides these, we purchased, in the course of the morning, twelve more small ones, and as many fowls.

In the afternoon, I informed the chief of my intention of paying him a visit on shore, with some of my officers. He seemed much pleased, and immediately left us, to prepare for our reception. In the mean time our long-boat was armed, and towards evening we left the ship. The surf was so heavy at the village of Caracacoa, that we were obliged to land at a place called Vainoonohala, where we were met by the chief, who informed me, that he had enjoined taboo on the people every where around. The consequence of this was, that, during our stay on shore, no one dared to quit his house; and our walk, which would otherwise have been rendered disagreeable by the crowd, proved to be extremely pleasant.

After passing some poor cottages, we came to a grove of cocoa-nut trees, many of which we observed had marks of shot; and we afterwards learned, that these trees had been struck by the guns from the English ships, after the unfortunate affray in which captain Cook lost his life.

On quitting this grove, we proceeded along the beach; but the surf was so great, that we were completely wet before we reached Caracacoa. The chief had gone by another road, alleging, that he could not with propriety pass in front of a temple, which we should see on our way. The first object we met with, deserving of notice, was a large building, in which a schooner that had belonged to captain Vancouver, was kept. Here the chief joined us, and, after showing us his double canoe, that was on the stocks, but not yet finished, conducted us first to his own house, and afterwards to the palace of the king. This palace differed from the common habitations of the island in size only. It consisted of six distinct huts, erected near a tolerably large pond of stagnated water. The first hut we entered, constituted the king's dining-room, the second his drawing-room, the third and fourth the apartments of his women, while the last two served for kitchens. These huts, which were all alike, were constructed of poles, and covered with leaves. In some of them, the door was the only means of admitting light, while others had two small windows for the purpose; one near the corner, in front, and the other near the same corner, in the side of the hut. They are all erected upon a sort of pavement of stone, and are enclosed. I know not in what state the palace is kept during the king's residence in it, but when we saw it, it was uncommonly filthy: it is, however, held by the natives in such high veneration, that no one presumes to enter it, with any covering on his body, except the *maro*, which is merely a piece of cloth tied round the waist. Our chief, on entering it, took off his hat, his shoes, and the great coat we had given him, though none of the natives were present.

From the palace we went to the royal temple, which is a small hut, fenced round with paling. Before the entrance stands a statue of a middling size, and further on to the left six large idols are seen. We were not permitted to enter this holy place, in which, we were told, his majesty takes his meals during the taboo days. Near to this was another enclosed spot, containing dif-

1804.
June.

ferent idols: but the chief, who was our guide, spoke English so indifferently, that we could scarcely understand a word of what he said respecting it. On approaching the great temple, called by the natives *Heavoo*, not *Morai*, as some navigators have said, the chief refused to follow us, signifying that, as he was not of the first nobility of the island, he could not with propriety enter it. This was rather mortifying to us, as we might stand in need of his assistance: he was not, however, to be persuaded, and we were obliged to proceed alone. This temple is merely a piece of ground, enclosed chiefly with wooden rails, but here and there with stones, and of the form of an oblong square, the extent of which is about fifty yards by thirty. On the side towards the mountains is a group of fifteen idols, which were wrapped in cloth from the waist downwards; and before them a platform, made of poles, is erected, called the place of sacrifice, on which we saw a roasted pig, and some plantains and cocoa-nuts. On the side to the right of the group of fifteen, are two other statues; further on, on the same side, is an altar with three more; and on the opposite side another group of three, one of which is in a state of great decay. On the side towards the sea stands a small cottage, which is also in a ruinous state. The several groups of figures were arranged so as to form within the enclosure a sort of semicircle. During our research we were joined by the chief priest of the temple, who informed us, that the fifteen statues wrapped in cloth, represented the gods of war; the two to the right of the place of sacrifice, the gods of spring; those on the opposite side, the guardians of autumn; and that the altar was dedicated to the god of joy, before which the islanders dance and sing on festivals appointed by their religion.

These temples were by no means calculated to excite in the mind of a stranger religious veneration. They are suffered to remain in so neglected and filthy a condition, that, were it not for the statues, they might be taken rather for hog-sties than places of worship. The statues, meanwhile, are carved in the rudest manner: the heads of some of them are a great deal larger than the body. Some are without tongues, while others have tongues of a frightful size. Some again bear huge blocks of wood on their heads, and have mouths reaching from ear to ear.

In coming out of this place, we leaped over a low stone fence; while the priest came out by a narrow opening; observing, that to do as we did, would be a crime in him punishable with death. There are many laws of this nature, which strangers should be careful of observing; though transgressions are not so strictly punished in them as in the natives.

From the temple we returned to the place where we had landed, by another road, so strewed with loose and rugged stones, that we were every moment in danger of falling. As I passed the different habitations, I could not help observing that hogs and dogs were the constant companions of their masters, with whom they fed, and lived; which occasioned a general filthiness, disgusting to more senses than one. I was surprised at not meeting, during this excursion, with more than three or four bread-fruit trees: the best grounds were covered with a plant, from which, I was told, a good red dye is extracted.

As soon as we had embarked in our boats, the people, who had kept within their houses in consequence of the taboo, ran

1804.
June.

out in crowds, loudly wishing us a good night. On getting on board, I was sorry to find that scarcely any thing had been purchased in our absence.

14th.

In the morning of the 14th the barter for provisions commenced briskly; but on the arrival of the chief of the bay on board it almost instantly ceased. Suspecting this personage to be the cause of the change, I ordered him out of the ship; and I had the satisfaction to find that I was right in my conjecture, for immediately on his departure the traffic was renewed, and I obtained a considerable quantity of live stock. To enhance the price, a report was spread that a large ship had arrived in the bay of Toovyhy, and that Mr. Young was gone to visit her, which was the reason we had not yet seen this gentleman. I however doubted the truth of the report, and it failed of its end.

15th.

The next morning Mr. Young arrived. He expressed much sorrow at not having waited upon us sooner; declaring, at the same time, that he had not been informed till yesterday of our arrival. Concluding that this arose from the intriguing disposition of our chief, I determined to punish his knavery, by not inviting him to our dinner of to-day; which he felt so keenly, that, to make amends, he gave me a large hog, at the same time owning his fault, and promising never to conduct himself towards me in any under-hand manner again. On this promise I forgave him, and we were once more friends.

Mr. Young had brought with him six hogs, two of which he made me a present of, but asked me for the other four a piece and half of canvass, assuring me they belonged to the king, who had set this price upon them. I however declined purchasing them at so exorbitant a rate, and they were sent on shore.

In the afternoon we made a party to go to the village of Tavaroa, to see the memorable spot where Europe had been deprived of her most celebrated navigator, captain Cook. We landed at the very rock on which this truly great man lost his life; and were afterwards shown the part of a mountain where his body had been burned. This mountain has several excavations, in which the bones of the dead are deposited; and one in particular is said to contain the precious remains of the kings of the island, down to the last deceased Tyreboo.

Tavaroa bears much resemblance to the other villages which I saw in the island: it has a mean appearance, and contains nine heavoos, which we could not enter on account of the absence of the priests: they differed, however, from the great heavoo in no respect but the size. They were dedicated to different deities, and belonged to the different chiefs of the country, who were then in the army with the king.

After walking about for a while, we stopped to pay our respects to an old lady, the sister of the great chief of Tavaroa. She was about ninety years of age, and perfectly blind. On Mr. Young's introducing me, she took my hand, and would have kissed it, if I would have permitted the condescension. She was sitting under a large tree, surrounded by a crowd of young people, who seemed to amuse themselves with the oddity of her appearance. She talked chiefly of her attach-

1804.
June.

ment to Europeans, and greatly lamented the death of captain Cook.

The environs of this village exhibit scarcely any signs of verdure. The ground is covered with pieces of lava, which are used here for a fence to the houses. On our return to the ship, we found on board some sailors belonging to the United States; one of whom, during the preceding year, had been on the north-west coast of America. He informed us that the Russian settlement of Archangel, in Sitca, or Norfolk Sound, had been destroyed by the natives; to which I was the more inclined to give credit, from its corresponding with what had appeared in the Hamburgh papers previous to our departure from Europe.

16th.

Having furnished myself with what provisions I wanted, I determined to put to sea; and on the 16th, the ship being unmoored, we set sail at nine in the evening with a landbreeze, which blows pretty regularly in this bay. On inspecting our two cables, we found them both very much chafed, though the anchors had been let go on a clean sandy bottom. From this circumstance, I would recommend ships to bring-to a little further from the place where we anchored, towards the precipice, where a soft bottom was found by our soundings; and it might be prudent to buoy up the cables even there.

We had not been long under way, before the wind fell: however, I was determined rather to tow the ship out, than to anchor again, especially as the night promised to be calm. On clearing the bay, we had a few light breezes, but they soon died away, which obliged us to tow hard, with all the boats a-head, to keep out of danger. In the morning I dismissed Mr. Johns, my interpreter, after having recompensed him for the services he had rendered us, and given him a few trifling presents for his chief, who had sent me a pig a few days before, and had further intended me the honour of a visit, but had been prevented by the sudden death of his wife. For Mr. Young's civilities, when he left us the preceding evening, I filled his canoe with biscuits, porter, brandy, and wine.

At day-break of the 17th, we found ourselves about six miles from the bay, and at noon had an observation in latitude 19° 34′ 49″ north. The north end of Carracacoa bore south 67° east, and the west point of the island was north 6° west. At six in the afternoon a breeze sprung up, with which we reached the western point of Owyhee. We should now have distinctly seen the island of Mové, but the weather was so thick and cloudy, that its summits alone were visible. From what we experienced it may be inferred, that beyond the north point of the bay of Carracacoa the current sets to the north-west, though short of that, it runs directly against the point itself. Vessels therefore should be upon their guard when near this place in calm weather.

In the morning of the 18th, the wind blew so strong at north-east, that the ship went at the rate of eight miles and a half an hour. This was a very agreeable change, after the tiresome calm of the two preceding days.

On leaving Carracacoa, I purposed making for the island of

1804. June.

Wahoo, to see the king of Owyhee, who was there with his army. So great indeed was my curiosity on this subject, that to gratify it, I would have sacrificed a few days to the business nearest my heart, that of arriving at Cadiack. Learning, however, that a species of epidemic disease was raging in that island, I relinquished my intention, and took my course for Otooway.

By observation at noon, we found ourselves in latitude 20° 20′ north, and longitude by the chronometers, No. 136 and 50, by which I shall reckon for the future, 157° 42′ west.

19th. On the 19th, at five o'clock in the morning, the island of Otooway appeared to the north-west, and at eight we passed the south end of it. On reaching the bay of Weymea, I brought-to, to wait for four canoes that were paddling towards us. In one of them were five men; the others had only a man in each. They had nothing to sell but a few spears, and a fan of exquisite beauty, made of the feathers of the tropic birds, which I obtained for a small knife.

The wind blew fresh till we came up with the west end of the island, where we were perfectly becalmed; the currents, however, dragging us till night, and forcing us between the islands of Otooway and Onihoo. Meanwhile the king of these islands, whose name was Tamoory, paid us a visit. On entering the ship, he accosted me in English, and presented at the same time several certificates of recommendation, as he supposed, that had been given him by the commanders of the different vessels which had touched at Otooway: but, on inspecting these papers, I found that some of them were by no means in his favour; and I gave him a hint on the subject; and advised him for the future to be more obliging to those of whom he wished to receive testimonials of his honourable conduct, and to treat better European navigators, who prefer at present touching at the island of Owyhee.

On hearing that we had just left that island, he was anxious to know what was doing there. I informed him that the king was at present on the island of Wahoo; and that he would have been at Otooway long ago, but for an epidemic disease, which had spread amongst his troops, and would perhaps oblige him to relinquish his conquests, and return home. This intelligence was extremely gratifying to our royal visitor; who, however, assured me, that, happen what would, he was determined to defend himself to the last; adding, that he had thirty thousand warriors on the island, meaning, probably, all the inhabitants, amongst whom were five Europeans; that he had besides, three six-pounders, forty swivels, a number of muskets, and plenty of powder and ball.

The king was waited on in the vessel by one of his subjects, who carried a small wooden bason, a feather fan, and a towel. The bason was set round with human teeth, which, I was told afterwards, had belonged to his majesty's deceased friends. It was intended for the king to spit in; but he did not appear to make much use of it, for he was continually spitting about the deck without ceremony.

On quitting us, he expressed some displeasure at my not being willing to spare him either bar iron or paint, the last of

1804.
June.

which he very much wanted, to finish a vessel, he said, he was building. He did not, however, refuse to accept of a blanket, and other more trifling articles, of which I made him a present.

During his stay with us, by some accident one of his canoes overset; but it was soon righted again. Things of this kind very frequently happen; but the islanders are so expert in swimming, that no misfortune ensues.

The island of Otooway is high, and, in clear weather, may be seen at a great distance. The shore, on the western side, rises gradually from the water; and, from its numberless habitations, which appear better built than those of the island of Owyhee, presents every where a most beautiful landscape. I am sorry to say, that there is not a single good anchorage round the whole island, except in Weymea Bay, which is also exposed to westerly winds.

The island of Onihoo, with its two small islets or rocks, is situated to the west of Otooway. It produces such an abundance of sweet potatoes, and other esculent roots, that ships may be supplied with them in any quantity.

From the increasing importance of the Sandwich islands, I shall devote a chapter to a further account of them; in which, I trust, will be found some particulars curious and interesting.

CHAPTER VII.

ACCOUNT OF THE SANDWICH ISLANDS.

Government of the Sandwich Islands. Particulars of the Institution of Taboo. Division of Time. Priests. Human Sacrifices. Funereal Customs. Nobility. Customs as to Eating. Advance of the Inhabitants towards Civilisation. Reign of the present King Hamamea. Mr. Young. Cattle. Feathered Tribe. Division of Owyhee into Provinces, Districts, and Farms.

THE Sandwich Islands serve at present as a resort for all ships going to the north-west coast of America, as they can refit there and take in provisions. The islands are divided in two dominions, of which one, consisting of the islands of Otooway, Origoa, and Tagoora, is governed by Tamoory; and the other, including all the islands to the southward, by Hamamea.* Hamamea is said to be a prince of ability and courage. He is so much attached to Europeans, that their ships enter his ports, not only without the least fear, but with a certainty of obtaining, on the best terms, every thing the place they may anchor at is capable of furnishing. By this conduct, he has not only obtained various articles of necessity for his subjects, but has even formed an army, that may be styled, compared with others among the South-Sea islands, invincible. Add to this, that he has upwards

1804. June.

---

* By some navigators he has been called Tomeomeo, Comeomeo, and Toamama, but incorrectly.

1804.
June.

of fifty Europeans in his service; and so great a quantity of small guns, swivels, muskets, and ammunition, supplied by the ships of the United States, that these articles in the island of Owyhee have greatly sunk in value.

The power of the kings is unlimited. The succession to the throne is hereditary, though it is often disputed by the most opulent grandees of the island. Hamamea himself obtained his elevation by violence. On the death of the late king Tyreboo, he contrived first to divide the dominions with the son of the deceased, and afterwards to seize upon the whole himself. Next to the king, the greatest power on the islands vests in the chiefs, or grandees, who are called Nooy Nooy Eiry.

The military force of the country consists of all who are capable of bearing arms. Every man is brought up to war from his infancy, and is obliged, if called upon, to follow his chief wherever he may go. Besides the general army, Hamamea has a body-guard, composed of the best warriors on the island, which is always near his person. He has also several schooners, from ten to twenty tons, built by Europeans, after the plan of captain Vancouver's, and armed with swivels. We saw, however, none of these vessels, as they were all in the expedition with the king.

Here, as in the Marquesas, force reigns instead of laws. The king may take the life of any of his subjects at his pleasure, and the chiefs may do the same with those who are subordinate to them. The grandees generally decide their own quarrels by the strength of their respective adherents; but if one of them should disobey the king, the body-guards are immediately dispatched to put him to death, or to bring him alive to the royal presence. Should it happen, that the chief or grandee on this occasion conceives himself sufficiently powerful, he disputes this despotic mandate, and a war generally ensues between the sovereign and his rebellious subject.

To give the reader some idea of the jurisprudence of this people, I shall furnish him with two incidents that were related to me by Mr. Young, and which had taken place in the island of Owyhee since the period of his arrival there. An islander was condemned to death for eating a cocoa-nut during the taboo. One of the Europeans on the island hearing this, went to the king, and interceded for the life of this man, representing that the crime was of too insignificant a nature to deserve so severe a punishment. The king heard the representation of the stranger without interrupting him; and when he had done, replied, with all imaginable coolness, that, as there was a great difference between the inhabitants of the two countries of Owyhee and Europe, there must of necessity be a difference also as to crimes and punishments: and, without further delay, the poor culprit was deprived of his life.—The other anecdote is of a still more sanguinary nature. The king had given to Mr. Young a piece of land, with several people on it. Of these, one happened to have a quarrel with his wife; and, on their separating, rather than resign to her his child, a beautiful boy, he put him to death. Mr. Young, hearing of this cruelty, immediately went to the king, to demand justice on the offender. But how great was his astonishment, when told by his majesty, that the man was not an offender liable to punishment, since by killing his child,

1804.
June.

he had injured no one but himself! The king however added, that Mr. Young, as master of his own people, might act respecting them in what manner he pleased. From these two instances we may form some judgment of the morals of a country, where the most trivial fault is often punished with death, while the blackest crime is left unnoticed.

The word taboo signifies here, as in the Marquesas, a sacred prohibition. The king may lay a taboo on any thing he pleases; and there are instances in which he is obliged to observe it himself: these are established by religion, and are held by him in the highest veneration. The principal taboo is that called Macahity, which answers to the twelfth month of the year. Besides this, there are four taboos in every month, the eleventh excepted, which has no established taboo. Of these four, the first is called Ohiro, and takes place on the 1st day of the month; the second, Mooharoo, on the 12th; the third, Orepaoo, on the 23d; and the fourth, Ocané, on the 27th. Taboo Ohiro continues three nights and two days, and the other three only two nights and a day. The taboo Macahity is not unlike to our festival of Christmas. It continues a whole month, during which the people amuse themselves with dances, plays, and sham-fights of every kind. The king must open this festival wherever he is. On this occasion, his majesty dresses himself in his richest cloak and helmet, and is paddled in a canoe along the shore, followed sometimes by many of his subjects. He embarks early, and must finish his excursion at sun-rise. The strongest and most expert of the warriors is chosen to receive him on his landing. This warrior watches the royal canoe along the beach; and as soon as the king lands, and has thrown off his cloak, he darts his spear at him, from a distance of about thirty paces, and the king must either catch the spear in his hand, or suffer from it: there is no jesting in the business. Having caught it, he carries it under his arm, with the sharp end downwards, into the temple or heavoo. On his entrance, the assembled multitude begin their sham-fights, and immediately the air is obscured by clouds of spears, made for the occasion with blunted ends. Hamamea has been frequently advised to abolish this ridiculous ceremony, in which he risks his life every year; but to no effect. His answer always is, that he is as able to catch a spear, as any one on the island is to throw it at him. During the Macahity, all punishments are remitted throughout the country; and no person can leave the place in which he commences these holidays, let the affair requiring his absence be ever so important.

The division of time on the Sandwich Islands is this. A year is divided into twelve months, a month into thirty days, and a day into five parts, sun-rise, noon, sun-set, the time between sun-rise and noon, and the time between noon and sun-set. The year begins with our November. The first month of it is called Macaree; the second, Caero; the third, Ocaoorooa; the fourth, Onana; the fifth, Oero; the sixth, Oykeekee; the seventh, Caona; the eighth, Hoyneré; the ninth, Oherenahoo; the tenth, Oherenima; the eleventh, Oytooa; the twelfth, Macahity. The days of the month have all different names, which are these: the first, Oheero; the second, Hoaca; the third, Coohahi; the fourth, Toorooa; the fifth, Toocoroo; the sixth, Coopaoo; the seventh, Oricoocahe; the eighth, Oricoorooha; the ninth, Oricoocoroo; the tenth, Oripaoo; the eleventh, Hoona; the twelfth, Mooharoo; the thirteenth, Hooa; the fourteenth, Oatooa; the fifteenth, Hotoo; the sixteenth, Mahearona; the seventeenth, Tooroo; the eighteenth, Roacoocahé; the nineteenth, Roacoorooha; the twentieth, Roaopaoo; the twenty-first, Orecoocahé; the twenty-second, Orecoorooha; the twenty-third, Orepaoo; the twenty-fourth, Carocoocahé; the twenty-fifth, Carocoorooha; the twenty-sixth, Caropaoo; the twenty-seventh, Ocané; the twenty-eighth, Ronoo; the twenty-ninth, Mowry; the thirtieth, Omoocoo.

The people of the Sandwich Islands believe in good and in evil spirits, in the resurrection of the dead, and a better life in another world. Their heavoos are crowded with idols, representing, as I have before described, the gods of war, peace, joy, &c., to some of whom sacrifices are offered of fruits, pigs, and dogs. The human sacrifice is only practised on prisoners and rebellious subjects, and is therefore more a political than a religious institution. The priests are brought up to the offices of religion from their infancy, and early learn by heart what they have to speak on the days of taboo. A particular sect of these priests pretend to have the power of killing, by means of prayer, any person they choose. They call themselves Coohanaanana, and are the greatest scoundrels imaginable. As soon as their vile praying against any individual is in agitation, the unfortunate being is sure to hear of it, in some way or other; and so great is the superstition which reigns here, that, believing himself the sure victim of malice, he puts an end to his existance, or loses his senses, or withers away till he dies. It is true, the religion of the country permits the relations of the chosen victim to hire some one belonging to this wicked fraternity, to pray against the murderer; but it never happened that these counter prayers had the effect of depriving any individual of the sect, of either his senses or his life.

1804. June.

The ceremony of sacrifice to the gods, of prisoners of war and rebels, was differently related to me by different persons; but in the main points of this horrid business, there was but little variation in the accounts. The mode of death is strangling. If the victim to be sacrificed is a person of note, a certain number of his adherents, from six to twenty, according to his rank, must be strangled with him. On such occasions, a particular platform or place of sacrifice is erected in the great heavoo, and is almost entirely covered with cocoa-nuts, plantains, and yams. When prisoners are sacrificed, after being strangled, they are singed, and then laid on the platform, parallel to each other, with spaces between, their feet directed towards the idols representing the gods of war, before whom these sacrifices are performed. The chief victim is always placed in the middle, and the vacancies, between him and his fellow-victims, are filled up with dogs and pigs, well roasted or baked. In this state, every thing is left till time shall have wasted away the flesh, when the heads of the sacrificed are stuck upon the rails that enclose the heavoos, and the bones deposited in a place constructed for the purpose.

This account I had from the chief priest of Caracacoa Bay. Mr. Young, however, to whom I communicated it, assured me, that no particular platform was erected for the sacrifice; that the victims were simply laid on the ground, with the face downward, their heads towards the idols, and their arms stretched

1804.
June.

out on the back of one another. He told me also, that no singeing took place, nor were there any dogs in this ceremony. He confirmed the circumstance of the heads of the sacrificed being cut off, and fixed on the wooden rails enclosing the heavoo; but said that it commenced immediately after the expiration of ten days, during which the taboo, called Canaca, prevailed. He added, that only the bones of the arms and legs were taken away, to be deposited in a place appointed for the purpose, and that the other parts of the body were reduced to ashes. The reader must judge for himself respecting the contrarieties in these two accounts. I can only surmise, that they might be in some degree owing to the imperfect knowledge my interpreter had of the language of the natives; and it was by him that my conversation with the priest was carried on.

The funerals here vary according to the rank and wealth of the parties. The poor are buried any where along the beach, after being wrapt in a piece of coarse cloth, manufactured in the islands. The rich are dressed in their best apparel, and put into coffins, which are placed in small buildings or cemeteries, where they are permitted to rot in state. When the flesh is gone, the bones are taken away, and deposited elsewhere. If the deceased be a person of great consequence, six of his favourite servants must be put to death, and buried with him. On the death of the king, a scene of horror takes place that is hardly credible. Twelve men are sacrificed; and shortly after the whole island abandons itself for a month to the utmost disorder and licentiousness. During this period, both sexes go entirely naked, and men cohabit with women without any distinction: the woman who should dare to make resistance, would be considered as violating the laws of the country. The same licentiousness is observed on the death of a noble; but it does not extend beyond the domains of the deceased, and is of a much shorter duration, not continuing, as Mr. Young informed me, more than a few days, though attempts are made by the youth of the party to prolong the period. Those who are put to death on the demise of the king, or any great personage, are such as have offered themselves for the purpose during the life of their master; and they are in consequence considered and treated by him as his best friends, since they have sworn to live and die with him. When I reflect upon the horrid nature of this ceremony, I hardly know how to credit its existence amongst a race of men so mild and good as these islanders in general appear to be; but Mr. Young, whose veracity I had no reason to doubt, assured me of the fact.

Their modes of expressing mourning are by scratching the body, cutting off the hair, and pulling out the teeth. On the death of the king, every one in his dominions must pull out a tooth; and if a great man die, those who were subject to him must do the same; so that, if an individual should have lost many masters, he may at last not have a tooth left in his head.*

The inhabitants of the Sandwich Isles are of a middle stature, and of a dark complexion. In the men, the form of the countenance varies; some have even a perfect European face. The

---

* Mr. Langsdorff, who saw among the islanders that came on board the Nadejda many who had lost their front teeth, supposes, erroneously in my opinion, the defect to have arisen from the teeth having been knocked out in battle by the slings.

1804.
June.

women, on the contrary, nearly resemble each other; the face in all being round, the nose small and flattish, and the eyes black. The hair of both sexes is black and strong. The men cut theirs in different forms; but the prevailing fashion at present, is that of a Roman helmet. The women crop theirs close, leaving a ridge, about an inch and-a-half long, sticking up, and extending from side to side on the forehead. This ridge of hair they daub over every afternoon with a sort of pomatum (if I may use the word), made of shells and corals, to give it a yellowish appearance. The men do the same with theirs, colouring only the hair which forms the crest of the helmet. From this practice, we were at first led to suppose the hair of the head to be of two natural colours, for the ridge and the crest retain a portion of the hue they acquire by the frequent daubings. Contrary to the usage of their neighbours (the other islanders of the South Sea), these people neither paint the body nor wear ornaments in the ears. They have, however, bracelets on their arms, made of bone.

The women ornament their heads with wreaths of flowers, or worsted threads, of different colours, raveled out of European stuffs. They commonly wrap themselves in a long piece of cloth, of the manufacture of the country; and in cold weather cover the body with broader pieces of it, several times doubled The rich and poor are in common dressed alike; but, on particular occasions, the rich put on their feather cloaks, which, with their helmets and fans, form a dress that must be admired every where.

These people are extremely fond of the European dress, and

receive with pleasure, old shirts, jackets, and trowsers. We parted here with all our rags, in exchange for provisions, and other articles, of which we were in want.

1804.
June.

They have been described by former navigators as thieves and swindlers; I have, however, nothing of the kind to allege against them. During our stay in Caracoa Bay, we were surrounded by them every day, and did not lose a single thing. They are certainly very difficult in bargaining, and know how to keep up the price of whatever they have to sell; and, if it happened that we purchased any thing at a dear rate, it was immediately known to the whole throng, and the article could not be obtained afterwards cheaper. They would even let a day or two pass, in the hopes of bringing us to their terms: but aware of this, and unbending as themselves, we generally obtained what was wanted reasonably. Iron, which was considered formerly as of the greatest value here, is now little regarded, unless in bars. Our rusty hoops, which were deemed so precious on the island of Noocahiva, availed us nothing.

The island of Owyhee has undergone, within the last ten years, a very considerable change. Every thing at present is dear, on account of the many American ships, which, in navigating these seas, always touch at the Sandwich Islands for refreshments. In the course of a twelvemonth, the bay of Caracacooa has been visited by no less than eighteen different vessels.

The provisions I obtained for my ship were at the following rates:—For four large hogs, I gave a piece of thin canvass; for

1804.
June.

three others, a bar and a half of iron; for a middling-sized one, two iron axes; for a small one, a single iron axe; for a sucking-pig, a piece of printed linen, measuring nearly three yards, but cut in two, lengthwise. The same for six or eight bunches of sweet potatoes, or a hundred weight of yams; and, lastly, a small knife for a fowl.

I cannot say that the houses of Owyhee pleased me so much as those of Noocahiva. They resemble our wooden barns, with this difference, that the sides are lower, and the roofs higher, in proportion. The furniture of these dwellings consists of mats, which are spread on the floor, and some domestic utensils, made of the calabash, or of wood, which are hung up out of the reach of the different animals, which are here the constant companions of their masters. The rich have separate huts, for the several purposes of sleeping, cooking, eating, &c., as I have mentioned before. They are rather larger than the huts of the poor, and have stone foundations: they are also railed round; but the railing is so bad, that dogs and swine can get in with ease.

The food of the islanders consists of pork, dog's flesh, fish, fowls, cocoa-nuts, sweet potatoes, bananas, tarro-root, yams, &c. They sometimes eat their fish raw; but they bake almost every thing else, their fruits excepted. I was told that the women were forbidden to eat pork, cocoa-nuts, and bananas.

Animals are not slaughtered here, but stifled, by tying a strong cord tight over the muzzle. The flesh is afterwards barbecued or baked, in holes made in the earth. This method of cooking is too well known to require explanation. I must observe, however, that the meat so dressed was excellent, even preferable, I thought, to ours by roasting.

The nobility here are not permitted to borrow, or take any fire from one of the commonalty; but must provide it themselves, or obtain it from their equals. I am not sure, whether commoners may make use of the fire of the nobles; but I was given to understand that this sometimes happened. I was puzzling myself to discover the cause of this curious custom, when an old priest told me, that the nobility were considered as too great, to use any thing not belonging particularly to themselves; which, if true, is surely ridiculous enough.

The women are forbidden, when in their houses, to eat in company with men, and even to enter the eating-room during meals. The men, on the contrary, may enter the rooms in which the women dine, but must not partake of any thing. When in the fields, or at sea, both sexes may eat together, and may use the same vessels, the calabash excepted, in which each sex has its own tarro dainty.

The inhabitants of the Sandwich Isles take salt with their food, and are excessively fond of salted meat. Among their articles of provision, is one made of tarro-flour into small balls, which, by being put into fresh or salt water, is converted into a pudding. It is very nourishing, and will keep for a long time.

The marriage tie is here, as in other islands of the Pacific Ocean, very lax: a man and woman live together as long as they please, and may, at any time, separate, and make choice of other partners. A man may, in reality, have as many wives as he is able to maintain: in general, however, the king has three, and the nobles two, while the common people content themselves with one. It might be supposed that jealousy would be a feeling scarcely known to these islanders; whereas, in fact, it is extremely prevalent; though with regard to their wives they allow to Europeans great freedom, which, as I have before stated, proceeds from interest.

The Sandwich Islands are inhabited by a race of men who are not deficient in talents. They are extremely attached to European customs. Some speak English tolerably well, and almost all attempt to pronounce a few words of the language, however indifferently they may succeed; as, for instance, *nypo* for a knife, *how lo, lo,* for how do you do? and *cabeca*, for a cabbage. They are fond of travelling; many offered me their services, and would have given all they had, to have been taken on board as sailors. Ships of the United States often take them to sea, and find them in a short time very useful.

I am of opinion, that these islands will not long remain in their present barbarous state. They have made great advances towards civilisation since the period of their discovery, and especially during the reign of the present king. They are so situated, that with a little systematic industry they might soon enrich themselves. They produce an abundance of timber, some of which is fit for the construction of small vessels. The sugar-cane also thrives here; the cultivation of which would alone yield a tolerable revenue, if sugar and rum were made of it; and the more so, as the use of these articles is already known to the savages of the north-west coast of America, and becomes daily of more importance there. The principal inconvenience is the want of a good harbour.* There are, however, a number of bays, which are in no respect worse than the bay of Teneriffe, or that of the island of Madeira.

The inhabitants are very ingenious in fabricating their cloth, as well as in colouring it. I was astonished at their skill, when I saw the instruments by which it was effected. Their cloth greatly surpasses that made by the inhabitants of Noocahiva; who, I am persuaded, would part with their most costly things in exchange for this, as it would be deemed by them, excellent article.

I shall here introduce a brief history of the reign of the present king, Hamamea.

On the death of the late king, Tyreboo, great troubles ensued in the island of Owyhee, the consequence of which was, that his dominions were divided between Kiauva, his son, and an ambitious relation, of the name of Hamamea. As war still raged between Owyhee and the islands to the northward of it, Vahoo, Moreky, Renay, and Mové, which had Haykery for their king; Hamamea, after settling affairs at home, proceeded, in the year 1791, against these islands. Having an army of eight thousand men, and two thousand canoes, he soon

---

* Mr. Okeen, whom I shall mention hereafter, informed me, that the island of Wahoo has a very fine harbour.

1804.
June.

subdued his enemy, so far as to take from him all his possessions, except Vahoo. In the year following, when this conqueror was about to terminate, as he supposed, a war so successfully begun, he received information, that his own dominions were in danger from Kiauva. This unexpected news enraged him so much, that, in his fury, he knocked out several of his own teeth. He returned immediately to Owyhee; while Haykery, who had retained only the island of Vahoo, on hearing that Mové was abandoned by his enemy, took possession again of that, and all the other islands he had lost.

Hamamea, landing in the bay of Towyhy, found Kiauva there, who, not expecting this rencounter, retired into the interior. Hamamea followed him. Many battles were fought, with various success; when, at last, the conqueror of Mové completely defeated his adversary by a stratagem. He gave out that he was going to construct a new heavoo, or temple, to his gods; and, on that account, ordered hostilities to be suspended. The enemy, believing him sincere, relaxed in his operations, which Hamamea observing, attacked him suddenly with all his forces, and completely routed him. Kiauva, however, saved himself by flight; but many of his chiefs were taken prisoners and sacrificed.

During the taboo of Macahity, no war could be carried on; but as soon as it ceased, Hamamea, forming his army into two divisions, gave the command of one to his chief captain, Tyana, and put himself at the head of the other. Kiauva, in the mean time, had been by no means dilatory. He collected what forces he could, and was determined to defend himself to the last. Nothing, however, could withstand the courage and resolution of his adversary. Tyana on one side, and Hamamea on the other, carried death and destruction every where. This unfortunate war continued till the year 1793; when Kiauva, dejected by his frequent misfortunes, and deserted by almost all his chiefs, delivered himself up to the mercy of his enemy. His life, after that, was of short duration. Hamamea ordered him to be brought to Towyhy, where he was massacred, with nearly all his principal followers. On the death of this last branch of the Tyreboo family, Hamamea became sovereign master of the whole island of Owyhee.

Such was the situation of affairs when captain Vancouver arrived. Hearing of the implacability of the islanders, he did all he could to soften their ferocity and render them less savage; and he thought he had, in some degree, succeeded; but, on his departure, as soon as his ships were out of sight, the monster Discord began again to rear her head. A report was spread, that the inhabitants of the island of Mové had stolen some people from Owyhee, and had sacrificed them on a certain occasion; and the wrath of Hamamea was again kindled, and he resolved on vengeance. It is probable, that, finding himself strong and in condition for war, he was himself the author of this report, meaning to take advantage of it to conquer his neighbours.

Haykery was, it seems, now dead, and his son and successor, Tryshepoor, was quarreling with the king of Otooway, his uncle, who had advanced pretensions to the dominions of his deceased brother. Hamamea, hearing of these dissensions, ordered his warriors to get ready, and, with a reinforcement of three brass

1804.
June.
cannons, and eight Europeans with muskets, he set out against his enemy, in the schooner presented to him by captain Vancouver, which was armed with swivels.

The three cannon belonged formerly to a schooner of the United States, called the Fair American, which had been seized upon, in the year 1791, by the islanders, and all her crew murdered, except one, a Mr. Davis, who still resides here, and shares the king's favour with Mr. Young. The war, thus renewed, was first directed against Mové; but, as neither that island nor the others had the same means of defending themselves, they were in a short time all taken, as before, except Vahoo, where king Tryshepoor himself resided. In the next year, 1795, Vahoo was also taken; and in this affair, Hamamea's chief captain, Tyana, ignominiously lost his life, fighting against his sovereign. The circumstances were these. When Hamamea set out on his expedition against Vahoo, Tyana was to proceed by sea, to join him with the rest of the army; instead, however, of joining the king, he went over to the enemy. Hamamea had waited a long time for the forces under Tyana, believing them to be still afloat; when he received information of the treachery of his favourite. An unexpected circumstance like this, might have overwhelmed a common mind, but it produced upon Hamamea a very different effect. This brave warrior attacked both his enemies without delay, and, by his courage and the rapidity of his motions, vanquished them both. Mr. Young told me, that he was himself in this expedition, and saw Tyana fall, pierced by a spear. The body of this rebel, and those of many of his associates, were sacrificed in the usual manner, and their heads stuck on the palings of the heavoo.

In 1796, Hamamea was called home by the rebellion of Tyana's brother, Namotahy, and he remained a whole year at Owyhee; but his ambition would not let him rest, and he again returned to Vahoo, where he is at present, to forward the necessary preparations for a war he had planned against the island of Otooway.

1804.
June.

By Mr. Young's account, the forces of Hamamea consist now of about seven thousand natives and fifty Europeans. He has six hundred muskets, eight guns, carrying a ball of four pounds, one, carrying a ball of six, and five, carrying a ball of three pounds; forty swivels, and six small mortars, with a sufficiency of powder, shot, and ball.

His navy is as formidable as his army. Exclusive of a great number of war-canoes, it consists of twenty-one schooners, from ten to twenty tons, some of which are armed with swivels, and commanded by Europeans.*

With such an armament, he certainly would have reduced Otooway last spring, if a disease, as I have mentioned in my narrative, had not spread amongst his troops, and destroyed the flower of his army. When we left the bay of Caracacoa, it was the general opinion there, that he would postpone the expedition against the island of Otooway, and return home; where his

---

* We were told on our arrival at Canton, by an American captain, that he afterwards obtained, in exchange for a schooner, an American ship of twenty guns, called Lilly Bird, which had been run ashore, and could not be got off by the crew; and that in this ship, which the natives contrived to set afloat, the king sailed to Otooway, and conquered the island.

1804.
June.

presence was very much required, as his long absence, with the whole of the chiefs, had occasioned such languor and inactivity amongst the common people, that the produce of Owyhee was not half what it used to be, when the king and his nobles resided in it. I am confident, that in taking his chiefs with him to the war, and leaving Mr. Young to preside over the island in his absence, Hamamea was governed more by policy than necessity.

This Mr. Young was formerly boatswain of a merchant-vessel belonging to the United States. He says of himself, that happening to be on shore when his ship sailed out of the bay, he was detained on some false pretext by the inhabitants, and that he has continued with them from that time, which was in the year 1791. He has recommended himself successfully both to the people and the king. The latter he has accompanied in several of his wars, and appears to enjoy his full confidence. He has also acquired a handsome landed property, and some hundreds of Spanish dollars, the value of which is very well known in this island.

Owyhee is the largest of the Sandwich Islands, and is remarkable for containing one of the highest mountains in the world, Mount Roi. Considering the quantity of lava, and other volcanic substances, that are found every where in this island, it would seem as if it had formerly been subject to eruptions in more places than one; though there is only one mountain at present, called Tavoorapery, where they occasionally happen. I was told, indeed, that three years ago Mount Macaoora, by a sudden burst, did much mischief, but had since that time been perfectly quiet.

Though the coast of Owyhee does not give to the eye much promise of abundance, except in some few scattered spots, and is inhabited chiefly on account of its fishery, and the trade with European ships, the interior is very fertile, and furnishes a variety of excellent fruits and vegetables. What is of still greater importance, the island abounds also with swine, the flesh of which is delicious, and with goats and fowls, which are both delicate and cheap.

Some cattle, which captain Vancouver left in this island, have very much multiplied. It is a pity they have been permitted to run wild; though this has probably been the cause of their increasing so fast. It is said, that some time ago a herd came down from the mountains, and committed great ravages in the plantations in the valleys. A body of armed men was sent to drive them away; and in effecting it, four lives were lost. This determined the king to breed some of these animals in a domesticated state; and I saw a very handsome cow and calf, in an enclosure set apart for the purpose.

Before the introduction of different animals by Europeans, there were swine only on this island, and a small species of rat. This last animal is so numerous, that the inhabitants are obliged to hang up every thing, that it might not be destroyed by them. The king has lately received a couple of horses, that were brought out to him by a ship of the United States, and I understand that he has been promised a stallion and a mare from Spanish America.

There are but few species of birds in the island, and of those the fowl is the only domestic one. The wild tribe consists of a small gray goose; woodcocks; hawks; little gray birds, with a bill like that of our parrot, and red feathers under the belly, of which the most beautiful cloaks and helmets are made; two other species, that resemble our linnet, and some small birds, of no rarity.

The coast of Owyhee abounds in fish, many of which are proper for salting. Amongst the rest is a flying-fish, which is caught in considerable quantities, and is sometimes more than a foot long.

I am told, that the island is perfectly free from all sorts of venemous reptiles. There is but one species of lizard, which is the hairy one; it lives about the houses, and, though very ugly, is highly revered by the natives.

Owyhee is divided into six provinces, the first of which is called Cona; the second, Cohola; the third, Hamacooa; the fourth, Hidoos; the fifth, Poona; and the sixth, Kau. They are governed by the Nooy Nooy Eiry, or grandees, of the island. These provinces are again divided into Hopooas, or districts, which are in the disposition of the second sort of nobility, called Pekynery Eiry. The hopooas, or districts, are subdivided into farms, which are let to different families of the commonalty. These divisions are very useful, in collecting the revenues, which are paid by the farmers to the king and the nobility, in animals of different sorts, in cloth, and in red and yellow feathers.

Though in the account I have given of the Sandwich Islands, many things may strike the reader as extraordinary, I can assure him, that I have recorded no circumstance but what came under my own observation, or was related to me by persons whom I believed to be entitled to credit. For the truth, however, of what I derived from others, I can only thus far answer to the public, that I took all the care I could not to be misled.

In the Appendix, No. II., will be found a small, but, I trust, not ill-chosen vocabulary of the language of these islands. It is given more for curiosity than use, as there are several Europeans there, who may serve as interpreters; and, from the increasing civilisation of the natives, the English language becomes better known to them every day.

I cannot take a final leave of these islands, without acknowledging, that the inhabitants behaved in the most friendly manner to us, during the whole of our intercourse with them. Surrounded by hundreds every day, we never experienced the smallest injustice or injury: on the contrary, we had many proofs of their honesty and hospitality; which shows, at least, how much they have improved since the time of captain Cook.

CHAPTER VIII.

PASSAGE FROM THE SANDWICH ISLANDS TO CADIACK AND SITCA SOUND.

Unfavourable State of the Weather on quitting the Sandwich Islands. Make Cheericoff Island. Pass the Islands of Sithoonack and Toohiduck. Visited by Bidarkas from Cadiack. Danger of the Ship from the Unskilfulness of the Pilot. Anchor in the Harbour of St. Paul. Accept a Proposal of assisting the Commander-in-chief of the Russian Settlements against the Sitcans. Delayed by contrary Winds. Proceed for Sitca. Arrive in Cross Bay. Cautious Conduct of a Sitcan Boat. Visited by Boats from the Company's Ships, the Alexander and Catharine. Find the Commander-in-chief absent. Cautious Conduct of other native Sitcans. Endeavour in vain to take a Boat in which was the Son of our principal Enemy. Skill of the Sitcans in the Use of Fire-Arms. The Commander-in-chief arrives. Curiosities found by him. Aleutian Tents, Hunters, and Dances. Take Possession of a Settlement of the Enemy. Overtures on the Part of the Sitcans. Attack the Sitcans, and are repulsed by them. Fresh Overtures. Flight of the Enemy from their Fort. Horrible Massacre of Infants previous to their Flight. Fort described. Loss sustained by the Russian Party in the Contest with the Sitcans. Sea-Lions killed by our Sportsmen. One of our Fishermen shot. Fabulous Origin of the Sitcan Nation. Eloquence of their Toyons.

1804.
June.
20th.

AT two o'clock in the morning of the 20th of June, the wind settled favourably in the north-east for us to continue our course, and the breeze was so fresh, that by sun-rise we lost sight of Otooway, and thus took leave of the whole of the Sandwich group. We now discovered, that the second cross-tree in our fore-top was cracked, to repair which we were obliged to take in the fore-top sail.

On finding ourselves in 23° 6' north, and 160° 11' west, I ordered the ship to be steered north-west by north, that we might arrive in the longitude of 165° west, when at the latitude of about 30° north. This I deemed necessary, on account of the westerly winds that blow almost continually above the tropic.

After losing sight of Otooway, we had proceeded but a short distance, when the wind veered from the north-east to the point directly opposite, and brought with it such thick weather, that we could hardly see a mile from the ship. The flying-fish left us in the latitude of 25° north, and the cold became very sensible. This sudden change of climate, and perhaps a too free use of fresh pork, produced a relaxation of the bowels in many of my crew, which was speedily remedied, by mixing bark with their brandy, and giving them warm clothing.

On the 27th of June we found ourselves in 36° 24' of north latitude, and 164° 3' of west longitude; and on the 29th passed the parallel, where captains Cook, Dixon, and several other navigators, had observed many signs of land: the weather, however, was too hazy for us to perceive any thing of the kind.

The next day, on reaching 42° 18' north, and 163° 12' west, we met with an amphibious animal, about three feet in length, with a bushy tail and a sharp muzzle. It continued playing round us for more than an hour. We supposed it to be an otter, which never goes far from shore, and conjectured that some unknown

1804.
June.

land must be near: but the weather continuing in the same hazy state, we could not go in search of it.

Though we had scarcely any wind during the whole of the day, the air nevertheless was sharp, especially towards night, when the thermometer fell to forty-five degrees. I am at a loss in what manner to account for the singular climate of this part of the globe, where, in the middle of summer, we met with such cold and disagreeable weather. Perhaps the fogs that prevail do not allow the sun to have its full power there till late in the season, when, by its long duration in the northern hemisphere, the air at length becomes rarefied.

July 3d.

On the 3d of July, when in 48° 20' north, and 160° 41' west, we were surrounded by several kinds of wild duck, and by one species in particular, that seldom flies far from shore.

7th.

On the 7th, reckoning myself to be near Cheericoff Island, I put the ship under easy sail, and had soundings in the night in seventy fathoms, with bottom of mud and gray sand. During the day we passed great flights of wild ducks, and a quantity of sea-leeks, one piece of which being drawn on board, measured seventy-one feet in length.

8th.

On the 8th, at two o'clock in the afternoon, Cheericoff Island was visible, bearing north-east by north, at the distance of about forty miles. It appeared like three distinct hills; but, on approaching nearer, was reduced to one mass, high and steep on the east side, and gently sloping on the west. From the western side of this island, in the direction of south-west, a reef runs out to the distance of three miles, where it terminates in a large flat rock. The weather all day being heavy and thick, I had no observation by which I could determine with sufficient accuracy the position of the place; but about ten o'clock the next morning it cleared up, and we found ourselves at noon in the latitude of 55° 52' north. The east end of the island, by the true compass, then bore south 70° west, distant twenty-seven miles. Its exact position, therefore, must be in 55° 42' 50" of north latitude, and 155° 23' 30" of west longitude. The longitude was determined by two chronometers. This point settled, I made sail, and towards night passed the islands of Sithoonack and Toohidack, quite close.

On the 10th, at one in the morning, we sounded in fifty-five fathoms, white sand mixed with mud, and at two the long-wished-for island of Cadiack appeared, bearing north by east eighteen miles. Many of its high mountains were still covered with snow. At four o'clock we approached the harbour of Three Saints, from which came several leathern canoes, called *bidarkas*, with a Russian in one of them. These were welcome visitors on many accounts, and especially as they brought us a quantity of very excellent fish, an article that was become a great rarity. Encouraged by our success thus far, I hoped before night to make Cape Chiniatskoy; but the wind falling towards evening, we could with difficulty reach the island of Salthidack.

On the 11th, the weather being foggy, we kept under easy sail, in the depth of from forty to twenty fathoms, till six o'clock in the evening; when, conjecturing we had passed the

1804.
July.

island of Oohack, we brought-to. The weather continued in the same state till the afternoon of the next day, when it cleared up, and allowed us to make sail for the harbour of St. Paul, with the wind at south-west.

After doubling Cape Chiniatskoy, we steered west-north-west, till we distinguished the rock called Horboon, for which we shaped a direct course. The pilot, whom I had taken on board from the harbour of Three Saints, insisted upon keeping close to the Horboon; and, by so doing, brought us into considerable danger. When the ship was a-breast of the rock, the wind suddenly shifted to the opposite point of the compass; and, together with the current, drove us against it: fortunately, however, my boats were ready, and we passed it without injury. A calm now took place, accompanied with fog, so that we were obliged to tow a-head against the current from the south-west, the lead being our only guide. The depth of water about the Horboon was from ten to twenty fathoms, increasing by degrees to ninety-five, with muddy ground. Fearing the barren and woody islands, we towed to the south-west till midnight of the 13th, when, reaching the depth of sixty fathoms, we brought-to. Shortly after, two large leathern boats came to our assistance, in consequence of a letter I had sent the day before, by means of a small bidarka, to announce our arrival, in one of which was captain Bander, deputy-commander of the Russian establishment here. The weather was so thick and dark, that he found us merely by the noise we made in furling our sails. His own stay with us was short, but he left his pilot on board, who brought the vessel into the harbour about two o'clock in the afternoon. On passing the fort, we were saluted

13th.

by eleven guns; and as soon as the anchor was down, Mr. Bander returned, accompanied by several Russians, who were eager to congratulate us on our happy arrival. It is not easy to express what I felt on this occasion. Being the first Russian that had hitherto performed so long and tedious a voyage, a degree of religious fervour mixed itself with the satisfaction and delight of my mind.

I now supposed my voyage to be at an end for the present year; but it turned out otherwise. Mr. Bander, soon after my arrival, put a paper into my hands, which confirmed the account I had heard at Caracacoa, that our settlement in Sitca Sound had been destroyed by the natives; and he begged my assistance in opposing the savages, and restoring things to their former state. He gave me farther to understand, that the commander-in-chief, Mr. Baranoff, had gone there himself in the spring with an equipment, consisting of four small ships, manned with a hundred and twenty Russians, and of three hundred bidarkas, containing about eight hundred Aleutians,* and that he was there still.

Convinced of the importance to the Russian trade of recovering this establishment, I complied with his request, and I resolved to prepare for sea immediately. Orders were therefore given to overhaul the rigging, and do whatever else was necessary to hasten our departure. Ten days would have been sufficient for every purpose, if the rainy weather had not stopped

---

* The natives belonging to the Russian Company are commonly called by this name.

1804.
July.

our unloading, and easterly winds had not opposed us. These winds blew so constantly, that a ship belonging to the United States of America, which I found in the harbour, called the Okeen, from the name of her captain, was detained by them upwards of six weeks; and our delay was but little less.

In the interval of this delay, we explored the bay of Chiniatskoy, and took occasional observations, by which we found the harbour of St. Paul to be in the latitude of 57° 46' 36" north. I also adjusted my chronometers; and it appeared, that No. 136, instead of losing 42" 2, as I had allowed from the Sandwich Islands, now lost 48" 4 a-day; and that No. 50, instead of 10", was losing 13". The variation of the compass was reckoned by my azimuths at 25° 52' east.

August 15th.

On the 15th of August, about five o'clock in the afternoon, we entered on our new voyage. We soon cleared the shore, having come out of the harbour by the north passage, which is much shorter than the one by which we entered it. From the idea of rendering a particular service to our country by the expedition we had undertaken, our spirits were buoyant, and, as if to encourage us in our purpose, the westerly winds enabled us to make a rapid course. Nothing of importance occurred during the run.

19th.

From the latitude of 56°, sea-leeks and large trunks of trees passed us continually; and at six in the morning of the 19th, land was seen to the north half east, but indistinctly, from the weather being hazy. At noon we observed, in latitude 57° 8' north, and longitude 136° 46' west. At this time Cape Edge-

HARBOUR OF St PAUL.
1805.

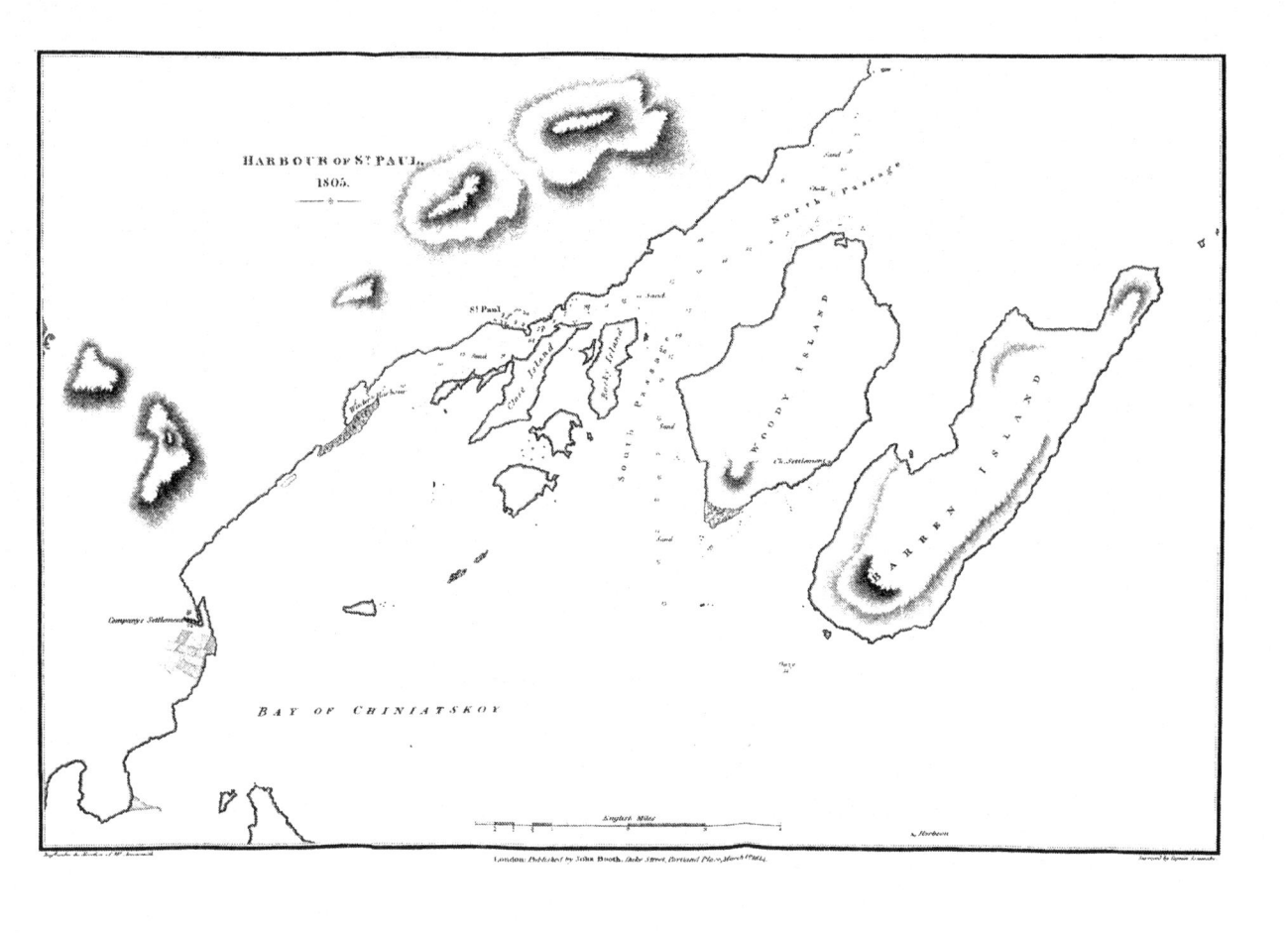

cumbe bore north 72° east, distant twenty-five miles. The wind was now become so light, that we did not get a-breast of Mount Edgecumbe till ten at night. What was still more disagreeable, we could not come up with a vessel, that was plying to the southward, which we afterwards found was the Okeen, that had sailed from Cadiack a few days before us.

1804.
August.

On the 20th we had light breezes, till nine o'clock in the morning, when the wind settled to the westward. We took advantage of the flood, and, on approaching the offings of Cross Bay, in the afternoon came to anchor in fifty-five fathoms, muddy ground. From our entrance into Sitca Sound, to the place where we now were, there was not to be seen on the shore the least vestige of habitation. Nothing presented itself to our view but impenetrable woods, reaching from the water-side to the very tops of the highest mountains. I never saw a country so wild and gloomy; it appeared more adapted for the residence of wild beasts, than of men.

20th.

With respect to the Sound itself, there is plenty of room to work to windward every where, except between the second point from Mount Edgecumbe and the islands opposite, called Middle Islands. In case of necessity, a vessel also may find there tolerable anchorage. The ship we had seen the day before was at anchor under the second point. On our dropping anchor, a small canoe with four natives made towards us. At first they seemed afraid; but, on my beckoning to them, they approached the vessel. I invited them on deck; but no one would venture, though I threw brass buttons and other trifles among them as an allurement. I thought I had at last

U

1804.
August.

succeeded in gaining their confidence, when two large leathern boats from Cross Bay making their appearance, they left us, and paddled towards the shore, giving us to understand, by signs, that the men in the boats were their enemies. These boats proved to be Russian, and belonged to the company's vessels, the Alexander and Catharine, which had arrived ten days before. They had come from Yacootat, or Behring's Bay, and were waiting for Mr. Baranoff, who was gone with a party of Aleutians, under a convoy of two small armed vessels, to hunt the sea otter. From the officer who accompanied the boats, I learned, that the inhabitants of Sitca had fortified themselves, and were resolved not to suffer the Russians to make a second settlement amongst them, without a trial of strength.

Towards sun-set, our countrymen having left us, the canoe, that had come alongside before, returned with other men in it, who were also afraid to venture on board, but invited me by signs to their settlement. The faces of these men were painted black and red; one in particular had a black circle extending from the forehead to the mouth, and a red chin, which gave the face altogether the complete appearance of a mask. The men were all armed with muskets, and asked me if I had any to sell, offering in exchange for one, two sea-otter skins. Though they behaved in a very friendly manner, yet, thinking it prudent to be on my guard, I ordered, that, during our stay, all the guns should be kept loaded, some with grape and others with round shot.

As contrary winds would not permit us to sail into Cross Bay, we were obliged to warp into it; but the depth was every where so great, that we could not reach the anchorage till the 22d, when we secured the ship, by mooring head and stern close to the shore.

On the 25th, the Okeen came into the bay. She had left her former situation, under the idea that we were carrying on a brisk trade with the natives for otter skins, whereas we had not seen a single article of that kind since our arrival.

In the afternoon of the 26th, a canoe, with three young men in it, came alongside of the American ship. Being informed that one of these youths was the son of our greatest enemy, I could not resist the desire I felt of having him in my power; and the moment the canoe left the Okeen, I dispatched a jolly-boat in pursuit of it; but the natives rowed so lustily, that they outstripped the boat; and when our party fired upon them, they intrepidly returned the fire, showing us thereby, with what sort of persons we should have to deal. During the day, I visited the company's ships, the Catharine and Alexander; and found them deficient in many necessary articles, with which I immediately supplied them; ordering, at the same time, two good guns to be added to each vessel.

From the day of our pursuit of the canoe, no natives made their appearance till the 31st at noon, when a large boat was observed under the shore, rowed by twelve naked men, whose faces and bodies were painted with different colours, and the hair of the head powdered with white feathers. As our boats were then fishing at a considerable distance from the ship, I was apprehensive that the intention of these savages was to attack

1804.
August.

them. I therefore ordered a few grape-shot to be fired: but the canoe soon passed a small inlet that was opposite to us, and took shelter amongst the islands, so that we could do it no harm.

In the mean time captain Okeen, in returning from the woods, was attacked. Hearing of the circumstance, I instantly sent an armed launch against the barbarians; but they escaped by conveying their canoe over a shoal into another bay, which it was impossible for the launch to enter. On the return of the launch, I sent it, accompanied by a large armed boat, in search of our fishermen; and they all returned together in safety at sun-set.

On passing the inlet I have mentioned above, the savages fired their small-arms; and so true were they to their aim, that they shot through my barge, which was then lowered. Their skill, as marksmen, was also apparent from the shattered state of captain Okeen's launch, as well as from the collar of his coat, through which a bullet had passed. On the captain's complaining of this treatment, I could not help observing to him, that as he had himself, like other of his countrymen, supplied these savages with fire-arms, he ought not to be surprised at any use they might make of them.

Sept. 8th.

In the morning of the 8th of September, captain Okeen set sail on his voyage homewards. As the hostile disposition of the natives, since our arrival at Cross Bay, would not suffer us to go far from the ships for exploring, we had chiefly been employed in fishing, and repairing our rigging. In the course of this day, however, I was employed in making observations, by which the latitude of the station where we were at anchor was fixed at 57° 8′ 24″ north, and the longitude at 135° 18′ 15″ west. At new moon the flood was observed to be at its height at ten minutes after one in the afternoon.

In he afternoon of the 19th, Mr. Baranoff arrived from his hunting expedition, in the ship Yarmak. I shall not attempt to describe the joy we felt at seeing him. Suffice it to say, that we had been more than a month in this unfavourable climate, anxiously expecting his return; and that we at last had begun to doubt of his being alive. He informed us, that during the whole of his excursion, the most distressing weather prevailed; that he had passed through Cross Sound, through Acoo, or Stephen's Passage, and through Hoosnoff, or Chatham's Strait; and that two days ago he had been separated in a gale of wind from his party, whom, however, he hourly expected.

Besides hunting the sea otter, in which he had been so successful as to obtain, in spite of obstacles, sixteen hundred skins, Mr. Baranoff had another object in view in the expedition he had just finished, which was that of punishing the savages who had assisted in destroying the settlement. In this attempt, his wishes were in some degree frustrated; for the Colushes* fled on his approach, and he was obliged therefore to content himself with demolishing their habitations.

The next day Mr. Baranoff paid me a visit on board the Neva, bringing with him a number of masks, very ingeniously

---

* A name given to the natives from Chatham's Strait to Charlotte Islands.

1804.
Sept.

cut in wood, and painted with different colours (See Plate I. Fig. *b*). He had found them in the habitations he had destroyed. These masks were formerly worn by the Colushes in battle, but are now used chiefly on festivals. They are placed on a neck-piece of wood (Plate I. Fig. *c*), that extends from the lower part of the neck to the eyes, with indentations, *o*, at the edge, to see through, and fastens behind. Some of them represent heads of beasts, others of birds, and others of imaginary beings. They are so thick, that a musket-ball, fired at a moderate distance, can hardly penetrate them. Mr. Baranoff brought with him also two other curiosities; one of which was a thin plate, made of virgin copper, found on the Copper River, to the north of Sitca (Plate I. Fig. *f*): it was three feet in length, and twenty-two inches in breadth at one end, and eleven inches at the other, and on one side various figures were painted. These plates are only possessed by the rich, who give for one of them from twenty to thirty sea-otter skins. They are carried by the servants before their master on different occasions of ceremony, and are beaten upon, so as to serve as a musical instrument. The value of the plate depends, it seems, in its being made of virgin copper; for the common copper ones do not bear a higher price than a single skin. The other curiosity was a rattle, (Plate I. Fig. *e*), which is used in dancing, and was very well finished, both as to sculpture and painting.

23d.

Hearing nothing of the hunters that had been separated in the gale, an armed vessel was on the 23d sent in search of them, and every thing in the mean time prepared for their reception, in a small bay opposite to us. At eight o'clock in the evening, sixty bidarkas belonging to this party, among whom were twenty

Plate I.

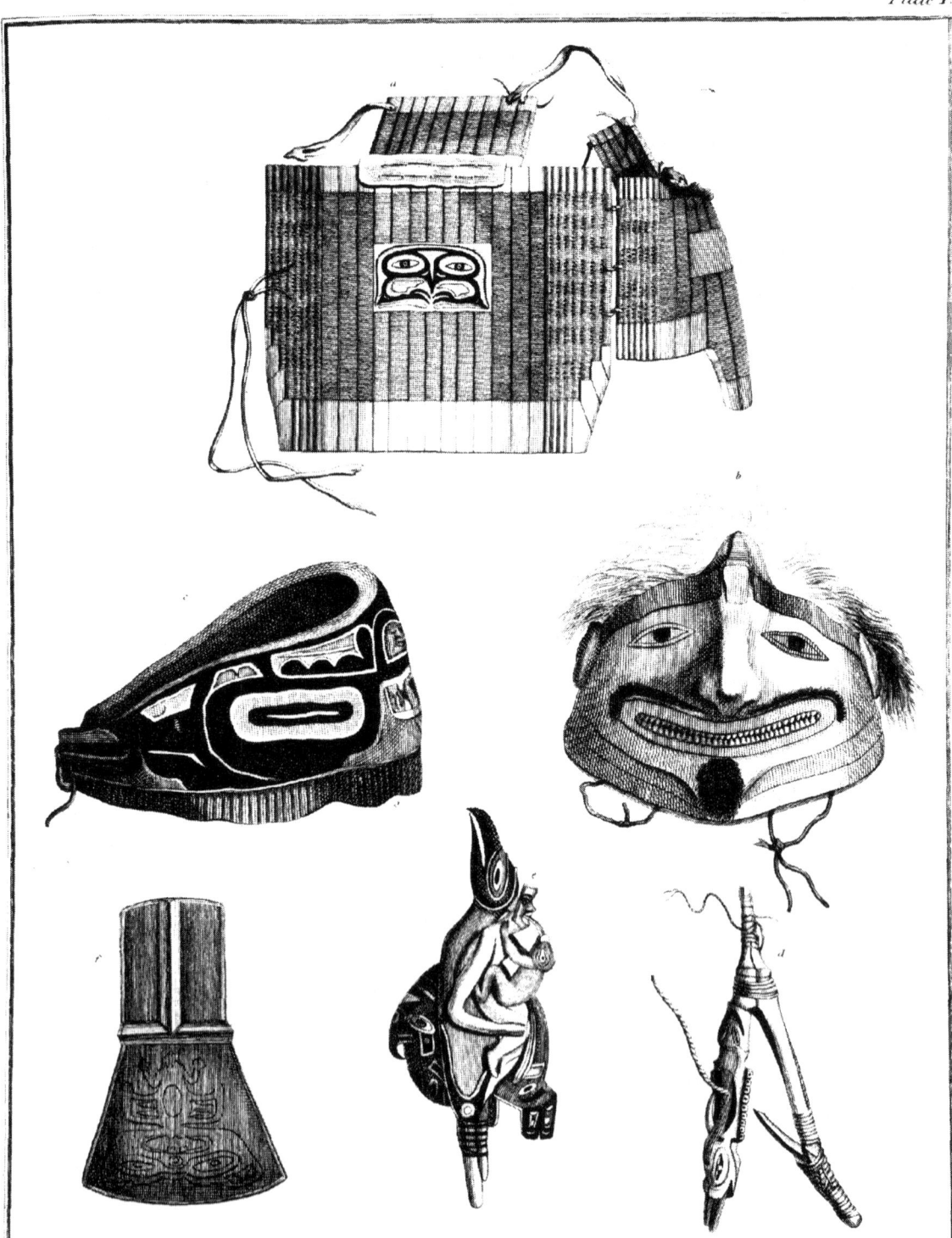

Russians, arrived, under the command of Mr. Kooskoff, who, on passing us, fired a salute of muskets; in answer to which, I ordered two rockets to be sent up. Expecting more of these bidarkas in the course of the night, we hung out a lantern to each top-gallant-mast head of our vessel.

1804.
Sept.

The next morning as soon as it was light, observing the shore, to the extent of three hundred yards, completely covered with the hunting-boats, we sent our launch, armed with four swivels, to cruize in the Sound, to prevent them from being attacked by the Sitcans; and shortly after I went with some of my officers on shore,—where the picture that presented itself to our view was new to us.

24th.

Of the numerous families of hunters,* several had already fixed their tents; others were busy in erecting them. Some were hanging up their clothes to dry, some kindling a fire, some cooking victuals; some again, overcome with fatigue, had stretched themselves on the ground, expecting, amidst this clash of sounds and hum of men, to take a little repose; whilst at a distance boats were seen arriving every moment, and, by adding to the numbers, increasing the interest of the scene. On coming out of the barge, we were met by at least five hundred of these our new countrymen, among whom were many toyons.

Having passed a few hours in contemplating this busy group, I was returning on board, when a report was spread by some

---

* They always keep together in families, and are under the direction of toyons or chiefs.

1804.
Sept.

hunters who had just arrived, that the natives were attacking a few boats they had left at a short distance behind. The Russians in the company's service were instantly afloat; and the moment I reached my ship I dispatched my barge and jollyboat, armed, under the command of lieutenant Arboosoff, to assist them; and in the course of half an hour, the entrance of the bay appeared choked with craft. Not knowing where the canoes were, that the natives were said to have attacked, we could only watch the motion of this little fleet; which, after quitting the bay, was quickly out of sight. Towards evening it returned, no enemy being to be found. Lieutenant Arboosoff, however, understood that the natives had taken a single bidarka, with two men in it, whose heads they immediately cut off.

25th.

In the morning of the 25th, tents were seen all along the bay; the whole of Mr. Baranoff's scattered party having arrived, except thirteen bidarkas. The manner in which the Aleutians form their tents is simple, though singular. A bidarka or boat is turned up sideways, and at the distance of four or five feet, two sticks, one opposite to the head and the other to the stern, are driven into the ground, on the tops of which a cross stick is fastened. The oars are then laid along from the boat to the cross stick, and covered with seal skins, which are always at hand for the purpose. Before every tent a fire is made, round which the persons belonging to the boat are continually employed in roasting or boiling, and especially in the morning.

As we shall have frequent occasion to make mention of the

hunting party, it will not be amiss to give the reader an idea of what sort of persons it was composed. It was formed of the inhabitants of different places; for instance, Alasca, Cadiack, Kenay, or Cook's River, and the Choohaches, or people of Prince William's Sound. When it first set off from Yacootat, or Behring's Bay, it consisted of four hundred bidaraks, and about nine hundred men; but there were now only three hundred and fifty bidarkas and eight hundred men, the rest of the men having been sent back to Yacootat from sickness, or having died on the voyage. The party is commanded at present by thirty-six toyons, who are subordinate to the Russians, in the service of the American Company, and receive from them their orders. They used to defend themselves with the same instruments which they employ in the hunt, such as spears and arrows; but muskets have lately been distributed amongst them by Mr. Baranoff.

During the 27th and preceding day, our ship was filled with these Aleutians. I treated them all with a degree of hospitality, and regaled their toyons with brandy in my cabin. Their imagination was so struck with every thing they saw on board, that they left the ship with the persuasion that I must be the richest man in the world.

In the afternoon we were invited by the Choohaches to see their dances on shore. These people were curiously dressed, and had their heads powdered, like the twelve men we saw on the 31st ultimo, with small feathers and down. They advanced to meet us, singing as they came. Every man had an oar in his hand, except the toyon, who was dressed in an old

1804. Sept.

cloak, made of woollen cloth, had a round hat on his head, and marched by the side of his troop. The instant we met them, they formed a ring, and began their dance; which consisted of writhing and twisting of the body into various forms, every one, as he chose, accompanying the distortions with singing, or beating on an old broken kettle. They at length worked themselves up to such a pitch of frenzy, that the scene to us became frightful, while to the native spectators this was the moment of rapture. On the termination of this curious amusement, I ordered some tobacco to be distributed among the performers, and returned to my ship but little gratified with what I had seen.

Towards evening, the vessel that had been sent to sea on the 23d, returned with the remnant of Mr. Baranoff's hunters; and our whole force being now collected together, we determined to attack our enemy, the Sitcans, without farther delay, unless they consented to our forming quietly a second settlement amongst them.

28th. Accordingly, on the 28th towards noon, we moved out of Cross Bay. The weather was so calm, that our ships were obliged to be towed till ten in the evening, when we anchored for the night, at a short distance from the old settlement of the Sitcans. The Neva could not have reached this station, but for the united assistance of upwards of a hundred bidarkas, which, though small in size, pulled with uncommon strength. Our equipment was not a little formidable, and seemed to have alarmed our enemies; for an extraordinary noise was heard amongst them on shore, proceeding, as we supposed, from the ceremony of *shamaning*,* which is practised by them on every important occasion.

The next day we landed and took possession of the settlement, which was situated on a hill of a tolerable height, and well adapted for a fortification. Mr. Baranoff would, no doubt, on his first arrival in the country, have preferred this spot to the unfortunate one, where, in establishing himself, about thirty of our countrymen two years ago lost their lives, as will be related hereafter, had it not been at that time in the possession of those whose friendship he was seeking to cultivate. To ascertain whether the enemy was near, we discharged, before we landed, several guns and muskets from the ships, in different directions, to places where we imagined the natives might be lying in ambush; and I sent lieutenant Arboosoff in a launch to reconnoitre the neighbouring shores. About noon, we had several field-pieces and two long six-pounders mounted on the hill, to which I gave the name of New Archangel. Shortly after, a large canoe of the enemy was observed lurking at a distance among the islands. Our launch immediately attacked it, and it blew up. With great difficulty six of its crew were saved, of whom four were very much wounded. It appeared afterwards, that this party was on its return from a place called Hoosnoff, with a supply of powder and flints. The chief was in the canoe, but had quitted it on perceiving our ships, and had returned by land to his settlement. I was sorry for this, as he was a person of consequence, and of a violent character; and by taking him we might possibly have finished our enterprise without further

---

* Operation of witchcraft, by men called shamans or wizards.

1804.
Sept.
bloodshed. Towards evening, an ambassador arrived from the Sitcans, with amicable overtures. He was told, that we had no objection to a treaty with his countrymen, provided they would send their chiefs to agree upon the conditions; and that, if they rejected this offer, their former treachery would be punished by us with the utmost rigour. With this answer he departed in the night.

The next morning the same ambassador returned, accompanied by another native, who, to prove the good intentions of their countrymen towards us, was sent as a hostage. They were in one canoe, and sung as they approached a sort of song of a melancholy strain. On landing, the hostage threw himself flat on his back in the shallow water, according to the custom of the country, and continued in this posture, till some of our people arrived, who were sent to lift him up, and conduct him, with his companion, into the fort; for so we called our fortified station on the top of the hill.

The ambassador received a present of a warm dress from Mr. Baranoff, in return for an otter skin he had brought with him for that gentleman. He was then sent back with the same answer as before, that we required, as a necessary preliminary to pacification, that the chiefs themselves should come to us. At noon we saw thirty men approaching, all having fire-arms. They stopped when at the distance of a musket-shot from the fort, and commenced their parley; which, however, was quickly terminated, as they would not agree to a proposal made by Mr. Baranoff, that we should be permitted to keep perpetual possession of the place at present occupied by us, and that two other respectable persons should be given as hostages. On the conclusion of this interview, the savages, who were sitting, rose up, and after singing out three several times *Oo, oo, oo!* meaning End, end, end! retired in military order. However, they were given to understand by our interpreters, that we should instantly move our ships close to their fort (for their settlement was fortified by a wooden fence, as represented in Plate II), and they would have no one to reproach but themselves for any consequences which might ensue.

1804.
Sept.

On the 1st of October we carried this menace into execution, by forming a line with four of our ships before the settlement. I then ordered a white flag to be hoisted on board the Neva, and presently we saw a similar one on the fort of the enemy. From this circumstance, I was not without hope that something would yet occur that might prevent bloodshed; but finding no advances on their part, I ordered the several ships to fire into the fort. A launch and a jolly-boat, armed with a four-pounder, under the command of lieutenant Arboosoff, were then sent to destroy the canoes on the beach, some of which were of sufficient burthen to carry sixty men each, and to set fire to a large barn, not far from the shore, which I suspected to contain stores. Lieutenant Arboosoff, finding he could do but little execution from the boats, landed, and taking with him the four-pounder, advanced towards the fort. Mr. Baranoff, who was then on board the Neva, seeing this, ordered some field-pieces to be landed, and, with about a hundred and fifty men, went himself on shore to the aid of the lieutenant. The savages kept perfectly quiet till dark, except that now and then a musket was fired off. This stillness was mistaken by Mr. Baranoff; and,

October 1st.

1804.
October.

encouraged by it, he ordered the fort to be stormed: a proceeding, however, that had nearly proved fatal to the expedition; for as soon as the enemy perceived our people close to their walls, they collected in a body, and fired upon them with an order and execution that surprised us. The Aleutians, who, with the aid of some of the Company's servants, were drawing the guns along, terrified at so unexpected a reception, took to their heels; while the commanders, left with a mere handful of men belonging to my ship, judged it prudent to retire and endeavour to save the guns. The natives, seeing this, rushed out in pursuit of them; but our sailors behaved so gallantly, that, though almost all wounded, they brought off the field-pieces in safety. In this affair, out of my own ship alone, a lieutenant, a master's mate, a surgeon's mate, a quartermaster, and ten sailors of the sixteen who accompanied them, were wounded, and two killed; and if I had not covered this unfortunate retreat with my cannon, not a man could probably have been saved. Of the two that were killed, one was immediately exhibited to our view on the spears of the barbarians. Mr. Baranoff, who proposed the attack, was himself also wounded in the arm.

This business, which terminated about six o'clock in the evening, disquieted us considerably; and though, from the stillness of our enemies during the night, we inferred, that they had suffered perhaps more than ourselves, it afforded us but slender consolation.

2d.

The next morning one of my wounded sailors died; and I received a note from Mr. Baranoff, who had retired the preceding evening to his fort on shore, informing me, that he was unable to come to me, on account of his arm; begging me, at the same time, to take upon myself the future management of the contest with the Sitcans, and to act in it as my judgment might dictate. In consequence of this request, I resorted to the plan I wished at first should have been adopted, that of annoying the enemy from the ships, and I instantly ordered a brisk discharge of guns on the fort. This proceeding had the desired effect; or, at least so far brought the Sitcans to their senses, that in the afternoon they sent to sue for peace, offering to place in our hands some of their best families as hostages, and to deliver up all the Cadiack people, who, at different times, had been taken prisoners by them. I received this overture amicably; but insisted at the same time, among other things, that none of their canoes should quit the place where they were stationed, till the conditions of it, on their part, were fulfilled.

Before it was dark, a youth was sent as a hostage, and the rest, it was said, would follow the next day. This youth proved to be of importance to us, as by his means we became acquainted with the number of toyons or chiefs that were in the settlement, as well as with the state of their provisions and ammunition, and how many muskets and guns they possessed. I was the more anxious about this last article, as our rigging had been much damaged by them. Though appearances were favourable, we kept a good look-out during the night, aware of the treacherous character of the enemy; but nothing material occurred.

On the 3d a white flag was hoisted by the natives; and, in the

1804.
October.

course of the day, other hostages were sent on board. I was, however, obliged occasionally to fire on the fort, as individuals were seen picking up our exhausted shot, that lay on the beach, which was contrary to the stipulations we had made.

4th.

The next day we received three more hostages, and a Cadiack man and two women. Understanding from these last, that there were still some ill-disposed toyons in the fort, we demanded hostages also on their part. In the afternoon Mr. Baranoff came on board; and, after consulting together, we resolved as the last and most essential preliminary to a treaty, to insist on a surrender of the fort. This demand was accordingly made towards evening, on purpose that the natives might have time, during the night, to reflect upon so important a point, and be able to give us their answer in the morning: and to show how much we were in earnest, I moved my ship still closer to the settlement. While these things were going on, our Aleutians had not been indolent; on the contrary, they had over-run the woods in all directions, plundering whatever they could find. In one place they discovered a considerable hoard of woollen cloth, and as much dried fish as would have loaded a hundred and fifty bidarkas.*

5th.

In the morning of the 5th, we received two hostages more; one of whom, a Cadiack girl, informed us, that the enemy had sent to the inhabitants of Hoosnoff, to solicit assistance. On hearing

---

* The inhabitants of Sitca Sound, always conceal in the woods such things as they do not immediately want, to prevent their being stolen, which would be the case if they kept them in their houses. The cloth mentioned above, had been furnished by ships of the United States, from which they derive large supplies of various other articles.

this, we dispatched our interpreter to demand the surrender of the fort immediately: he returned, however, with an evasive answer; and several other embassies were exchanged, which terminated in our consenting to wait till the next day, when the chief toyon promised to evacuate the fort with all his people.

1804.
October.

In the morning, having hoisted anew the white flag, we sent to inquire if the inhabitants were ready to quit the place; and received for answer, that they were only waiting for high-water. At noon, observing the flood to be at its height, and that no preparations were made on the part of the natives to perform their promise, our interpreter was ordered to hail them; and as they made no reply, I recommenced my fire, believing they were merely protracting the time till a reinforcement should arrive. I ordered also a float or raft to be made, on which our guns could be conveyed quite close under the fort. During the day we took two large canoes, one of which belonged to the old man, who, like another Charon (a name by which we called him), had in general brought the hostages to us. Shortly after, he came himself on board to demand his canoe, assuring me that just as he was quitting the fort, it had accidentally got loose and floated away. Knowing that he was telling me a falsehood, I refused his demand, and advised him to go back and persuade his countrymen to evacuate the fort as soon as possible, if they valued their safety. He consented to this; and added, that if they complied with our wishes, it would be made known to us in the night, by their singing out, *Oo, oo, oo!*

6th.

About eight o'clock in the evening our ears were saluted with this cry, which we immediately answered with an hurrah; after which followed, on the part of the savages, a song, expressing, that now only the Sitca people could reckon themselves free from danger.

When morning came, I observed a great number of crows hovering about the settlement. I sent on shore to ascertain the cause of this; and the messenger returned with the news that the natives had quitted the fort during the night, leaving in it, alive, only two old women and a little boy. It appears that, judging of us by themselves, they imagined that we were capable of the same perfidiousness and cruelty; and that if they had come out openly in their boats, as had been proposed, we should have fallen upon them in revenge for their past behaviour. They had therefore preferred running into the woods, leaving many things behind, which, from their haste, they had not been able to take away. By this unexpected flight we obtained a supply of provisions for our hunters, and upwards of twenty large canoes, many of which were quite new. Mr. Baranoff ordered the fort to be completely destroyed; to effect which, three hundred men were sent on shore, with a sufficient guard, under an officer from my ship.

It was on the 8th that the fate of Sitca Fort was decided. After every thing that could be of use was removed out of it, it was burned to the ground. Upon my entering it, before it was set on fire, what anguish did I feel, when I saw, like a second massacre of innocents, numbers of young children lying together murdered, lest their cries, if they had been borne away with their cruel parents, should have led to a discovery of the retreat to which they were flying! There were also several dogs,

Fathoms

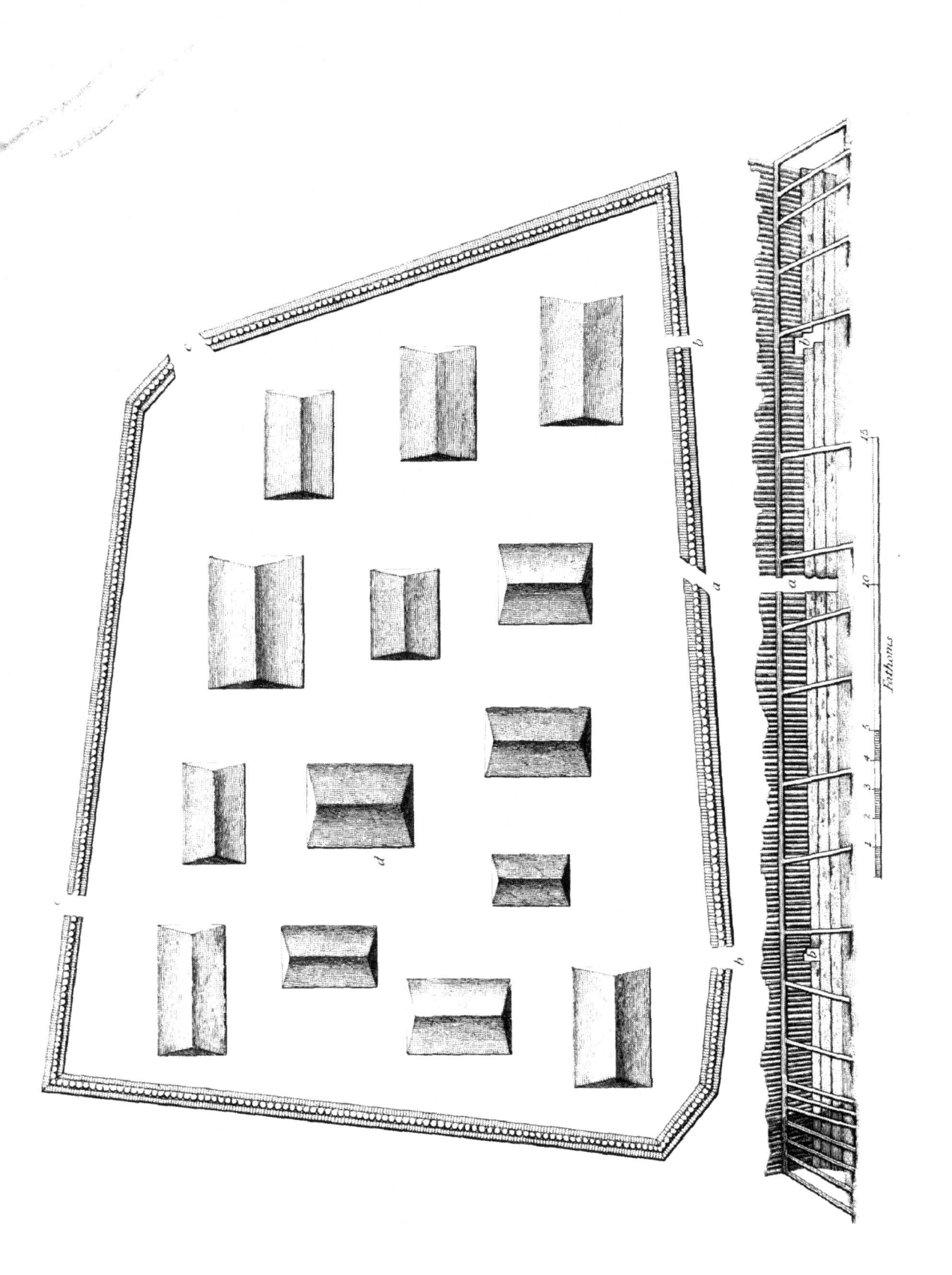

that, for the same reason, had experienced the same fate.—O man, man! of what cruelties is not thy nature, civilised or uncivilised, capable?—But I turn from this scene of horror to pursue my narrative.

1804.
October.

The fort was an irregular square, its longest side looking towards the sea. It was constructed of wood, so thick and strong, that the shot from my guns could not penetrate it at the short distance of a cable's length. As represented in Plate II., it had a door, *a*, and two holes, *b*, for cannon in the side facing the sea, and two large gates, *c*, in the sides towards the wood. Within were fourteen houses, or barabaras, *d*, as they are called by the natives. Judging from the quantity of dried fish, and other sorts of provision, and the numerous empty boxes and domestic implements which we found, it must have contained at least eight hundred male inhabitants.

We have reason to believe, from information we obtained, that the chief cause of their flight was the want of powder and ball; and that, if these had not failed them, they would have defended themselves to the last extremity. By this fortunate termination of the contest, we added two small cannon to our artillery, and we picked up about a hundred of our exhausted shot.

Upon returning the next day to the fort of New Archangel, we estimated our loss at six Russians, and a few Aleutians, who had been killed.

9th.

Had the plan which I suggested been followed, of molesting

1804.
October.

15th.

the enemy from the ships, cutting off their supply of fresh water, and hindering them from having communication with the sea, I am persuaded that our wishes would have been obtained without the sacrifice of a single man. But Mr. Baranoff was anxious to terminate the affair quickly; and that anxiety led him into the error, of placing too much reliance in the bravery of his people, who had never been engaged in a warfare of this kind before.

From the 10th to the 15th of the month, the weather was so bad, that we could hardly do any thing on board; we however persevered in carrying on the buildings on shore. With respect to the Sitcan troop who had fled, we were wholly ignorant what had become of them, though our fishermen and hunters were dispersed almost every where.

For some time we had been able to catch no fish but the halibut. Those of this species, however, which we caught were fine, some of them weighing eighteen stone, and were of an excellent flavour. This fish abounds here from the month of March to the month of November, when it retires from the coast till the winter is at an end. The natives catch it with a wooden hook, twelve inches long (Plate I. Fig. *d*).

Between the 15th and the 21st our sportsmen killed five sea lions; the largest of which weighed a hundred and fifty-seven stone, and the others from a hundred and thirty to ninety stone each. The flesh of this animal, in taste, a little resembles beef, and may be eaten in cases of necessity; the kidneys, the tongue, the lips, and the fins or feet, were extremely good.

On the 21st, one of our fishermen was shot from the woods; which proved, notwithstanding the peace which had been agreed upon, that the enmity of the natives was still unsubdued. But this was no matter of surprise to us: for what faith as to treaties, or what reliance as to humanity, was to be placed in men, who had coldly shed the blood of their own helpless and unoffending offspring?

1804.
October.
21st.

A few days after this unfortunate event, our old Charon came on board the Neva, not on the part of his former friends of Sitca, but from the people of Hoosnoff, who had sent him with assurances of their friendship towards us. He brought, as presents, two sea-otter skins, and received several articles of equal value in return, with a friendly declaration on our part, that we should be happy to live on terms of amity with all our neighbours, and with the good people of Hoosnoff especially. This venerable ambassador, on receiving so favourable an answer, immediately, like the wily snake, unfolded himself; and, in a speech of some length, requested, in behalf of those who had sent him, that they might be permitted to make war against and subjugate the Sitcans, who did not deserve to be considered as an independent people. They were indeed, he said, held in such contempt by his countrymen—for he was himself a native of Hoosnoff, but had married a woman of Sitca—that the very name was used by them as a term of reproach: and he gave as an instance of this, that if a Hoosnoff child committed a fault, he was told, by way of reprimand, that he was as great a blockhead as a Sitcan.

25th.

Though not wholly ignorant of the character of savages, I

1804.
Nov.

Having, as far as was in my power, succeeded in the object for which I left Cadiack, I took leave of Mr. Baranoff to return to that island, where I hoped to find the repose that was necessary both for myself and my people.

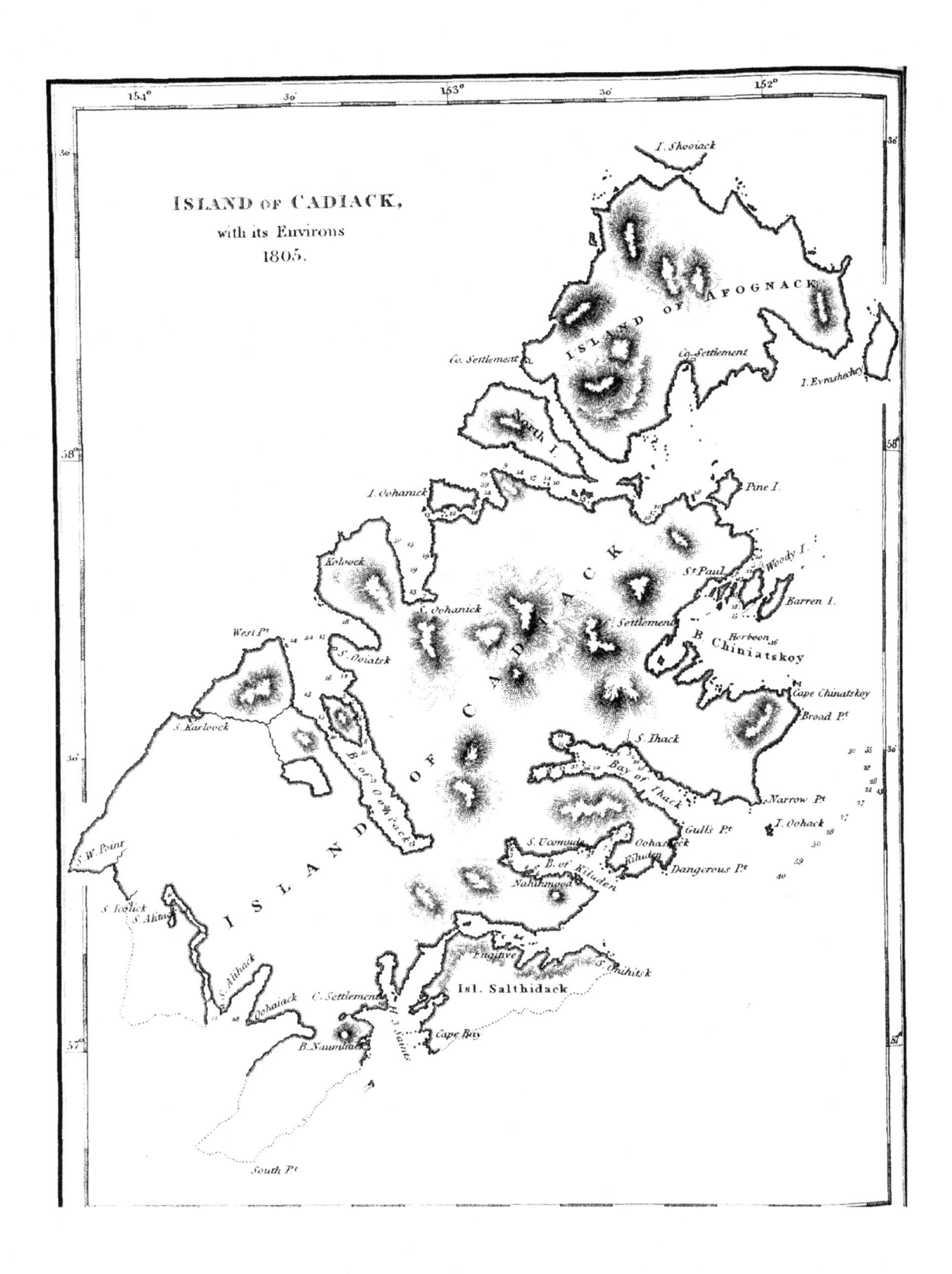

ISLAND OF CADIACK,
with its Environs
1805.

CHAPTER IX.

RETURN TO THE ISLAND OF CADIACK, TO PASS THE WINTER.

Particulars of our Run from Sitca to Cadiack. Moor the Ship for the Winter. Winter Amusements. State of the Weather. Set out to explore the eastern Part of Cadiack. Settlement of Ihack. Conversation with the Chief. New volcanic Island. Visited by an old Shaman, or Wizard. Bay of Ihack. Bay of Kiluden, and Settlement of Oohasheck. Land at a Settlement that has only Women and Children. Curiosities at Dranker's Bay. Harbour of Three-Saints. Fugitive Settlement. Account of Mr. Shelechoff. Huts appropriated for Women. Curiosities at Cape Bay. Tea and Supper in a Barabara. Stupidity of the Aleutians. Singular Custom on the Death of Relatives. Tame Eagle. Mountain tumbled into the Sea by an Earthquake. Straits of Sulthidack. Female Surgeon. Return to the Harbour of St. Paul. Explore the western Part of Cadiack. Account of Cook's River. Intelligence respecting the Russian Settlement of Nooscha.

We set sail on the 10th of November, with light breezes, and at eight o'clock in the evening passed Cape Edgecumbe. In coming out of the Sound we were becalmed three times. The wind, however, at length enabled us to gain the open sea, and then blew so fresh from the east, varying occasionally to south-east, till the 13th, that our run, during that period, was at the rate of eight miles an hour.

On the 14th, in the morning, Evrashechey Island and Cape

1804. Nov.

Chiniatskoy were in sight. About noon, the wind became contrary, and blew with such violence, that we were obliged to wear the ship every two hours, till evening, when it became more moderate, and allowed us to steer to the north-east. In the night it shifted to east-south-east, when I brought the ship's head to the southward. As soon as it was light we saw the island of Oohack; and, as the weather cleared up, we were able to approach the harbour of St. Paul. In consequence of the buoys having been taken away, we got a-ground in the Passage; but we sustained no damage, and were soon at anchor in the very station where we had been moored on arriving from Europe. The next day, having unrigged the vessel, and secured her for the winter, we disembarked, and took up our quarters on shore.

15th.

16th.

The reader may easily conceive how happy we now were; and will no doubt agree with us, that, after having been so long at sea, and especially after the late disagreeable adventures, even a barren land was preferable to the best vessel in the world. The settlement of St. Paul, however, small in extent, and with few civilised inhabitants, it may well be supposed, could afford us little occupation or amusement, during the five months of winter which we should have to stay in it. Something of this kind it was my duty to discover, the better to render my people orderly, contented, and healthy. Shooting and fishing were obvious resources. During the festival of Christmas, I employed them in constructing two immense ice hills, so large and of so gradual an ascent, that they could take with them a sledge to the top, and, placing themselves in it, slide to the bottom. This, though a common amusement in Russia, was new to the people of Cadiack, and especially to the Aleutians, who came from all parts to enjoy the sight, and, under the guidance of my sailors, to partake of the sport. I also took care to supply my crew with ship-muskets, powder and shot, that they might procure something like game for themselves. This was of great use, and by degrees rendered them expert marksmen. Sometimes they caught fish for the supply of their table; but when the weather was too cold for that pursuit, the shooting of crows was an inexhaustible employment. The crows here are small, and being stewed with vinegar were found no unpalatable food. I must own, that I set the example to the rest, by having sometimes a crow fricasseed for my own table; and though not very delicate, it was a considerable relief to the perpetual uniformity of salt meat, and proved as healthful as any provision we could be supplied with. I cannot dismiss my account of our residence here, without recording my obligations to Mr. Bander, who, in the absence of Mr. Baranoff, commanded the settlement. Being an old soldier, and a pleasant companion, he made many a day pass in cheerful and lively conversation, when cold or bad weather would not allow us to stroll far from home.

During the month of December, though the winds blew from the north, the weather was tolerably mild. The thermometer was not lower than thirty-eight degrees till the 24th, when it sunk to twenty-six. The ground was then covered with snow, and remained so several months. The winter, however, was not supposed to set in till the beginning of January. During its continuance, a few days excepted in February, the air was dry and clear, and the winds blew fresh from the points between the west and south-west. The severest frost was on the 22d of

1805.
Jan.

January, when the thermometer fell to zero. The last days of February, and the beginning of March, were also so cold, that the mercury often stood between thirteen and fourteen. During this period, I purposely measured the thickness of the ice in the ponds near the settlement, and found it to be eighteen inches.

March 9th.

On the 9th of March commenced the return of spring, and with it our repairs on board, and other preparations for resuming our voyage. While these things were doing, I applied myself to astronomical observations, by which the longitude of the harbour of St. Paul proved to be 152° 8′ 30″ west. I also entered upon a plan I had formed, to explore the eastern part of the island of Cadiack; and I took with me for the purpose, the ship's master, and one of the fore-mast men, and left the harbour

22d.

on the 22d of March in three bidarkas. On reaching the rock Horboon, the weather changed; and the clouds beginning to gather to the southward, I thought it prudent to pass the night ashore, on the side of the island where we then were, accommodating ourselves, by means of our boats, in the best manner we were able.

23d.

The next morning, the weather being beautiful, I set out again on the business of exploring, and about noon was a-breast of the island of Oohack. In passing between this island and the island of Cadiack, we were completely drenched by the surf, occasioned, as I supposed, by the south wind acting against the current. We however reached the settlement of Ihack without any other inconvenience, and stopped at a comfortable house belonging to the Company.

From Cape Chiniatskoy to Broad Point, the shore is so steep, that it was impossible to land any where, but on the north side of that point. It consists of dark stone like slate, and is overgrown, in places, with a rough sort of grass and low poplar. I saw no pine-trees, except about Cape Chiniatskoy, and there the number was few. The only means I had of measuring the distance between the harbour of St. Paul and the bay of Ihack, was the rate of going of the bidarkas; and by that I estimated it at forty-five miles.

1805.
March.

The next morning, after exploring the bay, I went on board a small vessel belonging to our American Company, which, on its way from Kamchatca had anchored there, from not having been able to reach the harbour of St. Paul. In the afternoon I visited the settlement of Ihack, which consisted only of eleven houses, or barabaras; the poverty and filth of which were extreme. As it was low water, all the people residing there, were busily employed along the beach in search of shell-fish, which constitute their chief food during this season of the year; the children only, who were too young, being left at home. From a very good meridian altitude I found the latitude of the settlement to be 57° 29′ 58″ north.

24th.

After dinner, the chief of Ihack with his wife came to pay me a visit. On entering my room they crossed themselves several times, and then sat down on the floor, and begged snuff. In the course of conversation their poverty was mentioned, when I endeavoured to convince them that their extreme indolence was the chief cause of it; and I suggested various ways, by which they might improve their situation, and render life more com-

1805.
March.

fortable. I advised them to build better habitations; to lay in regularly a sufficient stock of winter provisions, which they almost always neglect; to attend more to the article of cleanliness; and lastly, to cultivate different culinary plants near their houses, by which they would be relieved from the trouble of collecting wild roots and herbs, which were neither so palatable nor so nutritious. In speaking of food, they gave me to understand, that the flesh of the whale was deemed the best; though, during the fishing season, the whalers were reckoned unclean, and nobody would eat out of the same dish with them, or even come near them.

Of these whalers a story prevails, that when the fishing season is over, they conceal their instruments in the mountains, till wanted again; and that they steal, whenever they can, the bodies of such fishermen as die, and were known to have distinguished themselves in their calling, which they preserve in caves. These bodies are said by some to be stolen, from the idea that the possession of them conduces to render the fishing season prosperous; and by others, that a juice or fat is extracted from them, into which if an arrow be dipped, the whale, when wounded by it, dies the sooner.

During my conversation with the chief of Ihack, I learned a circumstance very unfavourable, I am sorry to say, to one of my countrymen. The first Russian vessel that had been seen on the south side of Cadiack, was in the year 1768; and the captain of this vessel, he said, treated the islanders so ill, that they took a dislike to all strangers; and when another vessel from Russia touched there, the following year, they acted hostilely towards it, and forced it to retire without any of the crew having communication with the shore.

In the evening of the 26th, while I was alone, writing the memorandums of my journal, a Russian introduced himself, who had resided on the island of Oonalashca, when a new island started up in its vicinity. I had heard of this phænomenon, and was therefore desirous to learn what he knew respecting it. He said that, about the middle of April, 1797, a small island was seen where no island had been seen before. That the first intimation of its appearance had been brought by some Aleutians to Captain's Harbour, who, returning from fishing, observed a great smoke issuing out of the sea: that this was the smoke of the volcano, which was then gradually rising above the surface of the sea, and which in May 1798, burst forth with a blaze, that was distinctly seen from a settlement called Macooshino, on the island of Oonalashca, at the distance of no less than forty miles to the north-west. This new island is tolerably high, and about twenty miles in circumference. It has been remarked, that it has not increased in size since the year 1799; and that no alteration has taken place in its appearance, except that some of the highest points have been thrown down by violent eruptions.

On the 28th, I had a still more curious visitor, in an old man of the name of Minack. He was about eighty years of age, and the most celebrated shaman, or wizard, in the island. Wishing, probably, to astonish me by his magic powers, he told me, that he had immediate intercourse with the devil, and was thereby able to foretell events to his countrymen. Observing, however, a smile of disbelief on my countenance, he became extremely angry, and abruptly left the room.

The bay of Ihack is about twelve miles long, and has several good anchorages, and two very fine but small harbours at its extremity. In entering it, a vessel should keep near the south shore, as the opposite one is rather unsafe. The inner shores of the bay are mountainous, with only a few inhabited spots here and there. There are alder, birch, and poplar trees in abundance; the last of which is strong enough for props and beams to houses, though not durable. Many small rivers run into the bay; which, during summer, are well stocked with fish. The quantity of ducks is also so great, that many hundreds of them may be killed in a day. They are of different species; and in the morning before sun-rise they make a prodigious noise. On our first arrival we killed an immense number; we likewise shot four black birds, that were nearly as large as the domestic hen, with red beaks and red feet.

29th. The next day the weather was fine and calm; and at seven in the morning I went to the bay of Kiluden with its chief, who had come on purpose to convey me thither. On the way we landed at the settlement of Oohasheck, and found its inhabitants in great distress, on account of the death of the chief's son, who had been buried the night before. I saw the mother, her sister, and another female relation, weeping over the grave of the deceased; but, on my offering a pinch of snuff to each, their sorrow seemed to abate, and their countenance to brighten.—The coast here, to the extent of about eight miles, is steep, and, when the east or south-east winds blow, must be dangerous for such frail boats as the bidarkas.

On approaching the Bay of Killuden we saw a number of small poles erected on one of the high clefts of the mountain, which were meant as a signal, some inhabitant having fallen from thence into the sea. Such precautions are very necessary in a country where fear acts more powerfully than common sense.

In the afternoon we arrived at the chief's house. He pointed out to me two islands in the vicinity, which, he said, had formerly been inhabited by fourteen different families, and fortified, though at present no vestige of habitation remained.

Except a few hours, which were employed in shooting, the whole of the 30th was taken up in examining the bay, which very much resembles that of Ihack. There are two places in it where ships may anchor with safety. We could not well determine the depth of water, the weather being so rough that, from our little bidarkas, we could with difficulty use the lead. In passing it we landed at a settlement, in which we only found women and children, the men belonging to it having been absent with Mr. Baranoff since the preceding spring. From not having laid in provisions in sufficient quantity for the winter, these poor wretches were literally half-starved. Wishing to afford them what aid was in my power, I distributed among them the stock of dried fish I had in the boats, and left this abode of wretchedness with no very pleasurable sensations. It was indeed a heart-rending scene to see these emaciated beings crawling out of their huts to thank me for the trifling relief I

1805.
March.
had afforded them.—I had this day an observation near the head of the bay, in latitude 57° 17′ 43″ north.

Though the weather was the next morning very disagreeable, I went to Drunkard's Bay, where I witnessed the same meagre traits of poverty. Of the inhabitants I purchased several curiosities, consisting of images, dressed in different forms. The best were cut out of bone (Plate III. Fig. *a, b*). They are used here as dolls. The women, indeed, who have no children, keep them, I was told, to represent the wished-for infant offspring, and amuse themselves with them, as if they were real infants. If we may judge by these figures, the inhabitants of Cadiack must have lost much of their skill in carving, their old productions of this kind being greatly superior.

April 1st.
On the 1st of April we had to encounter both rain and snow; but we were not to be diverted from our course, and we proceeded courageously for the harbour of Three Saints, where we arrived in the afternoon. In our way we visited a village called the Fugitive, which was in a thriving condition. The inhabitants appeared much healthier than those of Ihack or Killuden, and lived better. On our arrival, the chief's wife brought us a bason of berries, mixed with rancid whale oil, begging us to refresh ourselves. This delicate mess, produced at a time when the berries are not in season, is regarded by the islanders as no small proof of opulence. I gave this treat, however, to my Aleutians; and, after distributing tobacco and other trifles among the family, took my leave.

The next morning, as soon as my arrival at the harbour of

Three-Saints was known in the neighbourhood, several of the toyons came together to see me. After the usual compliments, and a treat of snuff* on my part, the conversation began on the common topic, of poverty; when I endeavoured, with some earnestness, to persuade them to throw off the sloth and idleness so visible amongst them, and exert themselves: and I stated, as I had done in a previous instance, the many comforts they would derive from it, of which they were at present perfectly destitute. The toyons listened attentively to my advice, and assured me they should be happy to follow it, but that there were many circumstances to prevent them; and I must confess I blushed when I heard, that the principal of these was the high price fixed by the Russian company on every necessary article, and especially its iron instruments, which rendered it impossible for the islanders to purchase them. While this is the case, what improvement can be expected in these people? or how can it be recommended to them with effect, to attend to the cultivation of the ground, which it was a part of my instructions to do?

This led to the general conduct of the Russians, and particularly to their first settlement in the island, of which the oldest of the toyons gave me the following account.—When Mr. Shelechoff arrived at the harbour of Three-Saints, the first step he took was to demand hostages of the natives, as a security for their good conduct. Wishing, however, to have nothing to do with them, they refused to comply with the demand; and, apprehensive of hostile proceedings in consequence, they assembled from

---

* Snuff is the best treat that can be offered to these people, who will often go twenty miles out of their way to get merely a pinch or two of it.

1805.
April.

all the neighbourhood around, and agreed to fortify themselves on a high rock, situated on the east side of the island of Salthidack. But the first hostile measure proceeded from themselves. So far from resorting to violence, Mr. Shelechoff conducted himself amicably towards them, till he had been suddenly attacked in the night; when, supposing his peaceable disposition to have been misconstrued into timidity, he ordered an assault to be made on the rock, and the place, which had been deemed impregnable by the islanders, was quickly taken. After this, many skirmishes took place between the Russians and the natives, in which the latter were worsted, and were obliged at last to resign the island to the strangers. Upon my inquiring, what number of persons had assembled on the rock, the toyon informed me, that it scarcely amounted to four hundred, including women and children: Mr. Shelechoff, however, to enhance the importance of this conquest, has estimated it at four thousand.

5th.
On the 5th we visited the bay of Naumliack. On our approaching the beach, some of the inhabitants who came to meet us, entered the water, and carried me on shore, in the bidarka, on their shoulders. I stopped at the toyon's hut for an hour or two. In examining the different apartments, it was with difficulty I succeeded in getting into the rooms called joopans, from the smallness of the entrance, which obliged me to squeeze myself through on my hands and knees. But of these rooms I shall have occasion to speak hereafter.

This settlement pleased me more than any I had yet seen on the island. There was an air of order in it, and a supply of every thing necessary for a well-inhabited place. Having satisfied my curiosity, I returned to the harbour of Three-Saints towards evening.

1805. April.

The whole of the next day was spent in Cape Bay, on the island of Salthidack. In examining the barabara of the toyon, at which we stopped, I was obliged again to bend my body to enter the joopans; my curiosity, however, did not go unrequited. In one of them I saw a man and woman, with their hair cut short, and their faces blackened with soot; which I understood, by my interpreter, were emblems of deep mourning. Before the Russians came among these people, this mode of expressing sorrow for the dead used to be observed for the space of a whole year; but at present it continues for a month only, and sometimes not so long.

6th.

Amongst other things, the baskets called ishcats, in which the Aleutians keep all their valuables, caught my attention here. They are made of the thin roots of the pine-tree. Those of the men contained arrows, small pieces of wood, of different kinds and for different uses, a small crooked knife, a tooth, a piece of stone, and an implement resembling a small adz. Those of the women were filled with rags, strings made of the entrails of animals, beads, and other trifles, which a beggar in Europe would have thrown away.

Towards evening the weather becoming cold, we made a fire in the middle of our barabara, which was soon surrounded by the inhabitants, young and old. They were very much amused at seeing us drink tea; but, I have no doubt, were still more grati-

1805.
April.

fied when I ordered some dried fish to be distributed amongst them, which was a rarity at this season of the year. The master and mistress of the house were invited to partake of our beverage, and they seemed to plume themselves upon the circumstance, as if distinguished by it from the rest of the party. During our tea repast, the family were at their supper, which was served up in the following manner. The cook having filled a wooden bowl with boiled fish, presented it to the master of the house, who, after eating as much as he could, gave the rest to his wife. The other dishes were served up in similar order, beginning with the oldest of the family, who, when he had eaten his fill, gave the dish to the next in age, and he again to the next; and thus it passed in rotation till it came to the youngest, whose patience, as the family was numerous, must have been a little exhausted. Perceiving, at length, that our companions were becoming drowsy, I advised them to go to rest, which they did, wishing us several times a good night, and expressing how satisfied they were with our kindness.

7th.

The next morning when I arose at day-light, and was proceeding to take a walk, I found all the men sitting on the roofs of their houses. This is their favourite recreation after sleeping; though they are also fond of sitting on the beach, and looking for hours together at the sea, when they have nothing else to do. This practice resembles more a herd of beasts, than an association of reasonable beings, endowed with the gift of speech. Indeed these savages, when assembled together, appear to have no delight in the oral intercourse that generally distinguishes the human race; for they never converse: on the contrary, a stupid silence reigns amongst them. I had many opportunities of noticing individuals of every age and degree; and I am persuaded, that the simplicity of their character exceeds that of any other people, and that a long time must elapse before it will undergo any very perceptible change. It is true, that on my entering their houses, some sort of ceremony was always observed by them; but by degrees even this so completely disappeared, that an Aleutian would undress himself to a state of nudity, without at all regarding my presence; though at the same moment he considered me as the greatest personage on the island.

At six o'clock in the morning, I dispatched my ship's master to examine a bay in the neighbourhood, and about eleven returned myself to the harbour of Three-Saints; where I had observations, and found its latitude to be 57° 5′ 59″ north, and its longitude 153° 14′ 30″ west. This harbour is a fine and safe anchorage, being secure from all winds, and having a depth of water from four and a half to ten fathoms, with ground of mud and black sand. It is easy of access, and bears, from the south point of the island of Salthidack, west-north-west. Its shores were formerly tolerably high, but since the earthquake of 1788, they have sunk so much, that the equinoctial floods cover them almost to the very mountains. It has at present only one small company's settlement, but was a few years ago in a more flourishing state.

Having finished all I had purposed to do in this part of the island, we left it on the 8th, to return to the harbour of St. Paul. Though the weather was fine in the morning, the wind freshened so much in the course of the day, that we

1805.
April.

thought it prudent to stop at the Fugitive settlement, and pass the night there.

As I observed before, this settlement is superior to many, though, like all that we saw, extremely filthy. The habitations, except that of the toyon, were miserable places. In one of the small buildings, or kennels, as they may very properly be called, was a woman who had retired into it in consequence of the death of her son. She had been there several days, and would have remained for the space of twenty, had I not entreated the toyon to permit her to quit it, representing that the weather was too bad for continuing long in so disagreeable a place. However ridiculous this custom may appear to an enlightened mind, it is so strictly observed by the inhabitants of this island, that they can scarcely be induced to abridge the period of its duration, though death itself should be the consequence of their pertinacity.

9th.

The next day I removed to another settlement not far distant, where I was again obliged by the weather to pass the night. In the evening, I was amused by a tame eagle, which flew into the barabara, and at sun-set placed itself by the fire-side, as orderly as if it had been one of the family. After warming itself, and deliberately adjusting its feathers, it fell asleep. This bird, they say, is so sagacious, that it will recognise at sea the bidarkas belonging to its master, and on seeing them return from fishing, will follow them home. The people of Cadiack keep tame eagles for the sake of the feathers, which they use for arrows.

10th.

In the morning of the 10th we stopped at the bay of Shashgat, in the neighbourhood of Ihack, to examine a lofty precipice, which, the inhabitants say, once formed a part of the conic mountain that, in the earthquake which happened here in the year 1788, was tumbled into the sea. What had been a fine sandy beach was so completely filled up, that it now presents nothing to the eye but a long rocky shoal. While in the village, I had an opportunity of witnessing a curious method of bleeding. A young woman performed this office of the surgeon. She first transpierced the vein of the arm with a stout needle, fixed in a wooden handle, and then cut the skin that was upon the needle with a copper instrument, which was far from being sharp. As she did not succeed in drawing blood the first time, she repeated the operation, when the blood gushed out in a stream. Though to me this was no very agreeable sight, the patient sat with the most perfect composure, which surprised me, when I understood that he had never been bled in this manner before.

Between the harbour of Three-Saints and the Bay of Killuden we passed the Strait of Salthidack, which is about eight miles broad at the extremities, but draws so close towards the middle, that in the narrowest part of it the space does not exceed a quarter of a mile. In this contracted part two floods meet, one entering from the north and the other from the south. The shores are low here, and thinly covered with trees. Though the weather would not permit us to sound this strait properly, I am persuaded there is sufficient depth of water every where for small vessels.

We passed the night of the 10th at Ihack, and proceeded the next morning for Oohack, which has four very good bara-

1805.
April.

baras. The toyon of this settlement interested me much. He had lately buried his father, and was erecting a monument over his grave. We remained on this island but a short time, as the weather gave no promise of change for the better, and I wished to reach the harbour of St. Paul before night. Though the distance was not great, we did not arrive there till nine o'clock in the evening, and were perfectly drenched by the rain, and the sea, which rolled so high, especially about Cape Chiniatskoy, that we should have been in danger, in any species of canoe but bidarkas, which are as able to contend with rough weather as boats that have decks.

On my arrival at St. Paul's, I found all my people in good health, and the rigging nearly repaired. The Easter holidays had commenced; and as soon as they were over (for I was unwilling to interrupt my people in their pleasures), I resolved on fitting out for sea. The large cargo, however, that we were preparing for Canton and Sitca, was not the business of a day; and it detained us yet for some time. Meanwhile I sent my ship's master to survey the western part of Cadiack, a task which he executed to my satisfaction. He not only reached the settlement of Carlook, but explored also the islands of Afognack and Evrashechey, and took many very accurate observations both of latitude and longitude on his way.

May.
19th.

The year had now advanced to the middle of May, and the weather was so warm, that the lower part of the mountains were clothed with verdure. On the 19th, however, a sharp frost took place, and the ground was covered half an inch deep with snow, which remained at least twelve hours. So sudden a change, which is common here, might have produced in Europe much mischief; but in this part of the world, there is so little cultivation, that no injury could ensue. The natives, on the contrary, consider such changes as the forerunners of good luck: and in this instance it so happened; for the next day, a dead whale, thirty-five feet in length, was brought into the bay; and though, to our sense of smelling, it stunk shockingly, it was quickly cut up and divided amongst the delighted inhabitants.

We had hardly finished the stowage of our cargo, when furs were brought us from the Bay of Kenay, or Cook's River. There were also some curious dresses of the natives, several of which I purchased from curiosity.

The person who came from the Bay of Kenay with this cargo of furs, informed me, that the natives were of a quiet disposition, but had so great a dislike to our priests, that they threatened to take away the life of the first that should dare to come amongst them. This dislike commenced in the year 1796, in consequence of the imprudent zeal of one of our missionary monks, who, having prevailed on many of them to embrace Christianity, had too rigidly insisted on their throwing aside, all at once, their native prejudices and customs, and, by authority of his holy office, compelled some of them to marry in conformity to the rites of the Greek church. Provoked at last by the daring encroachments of this fanatic stranger, they put him to death, and vowed at the same time perpetual hatred to the whole Russian priesthood.

1805.
May.

From the same person I obtained some intelligence respecting our settlement at Nooshca. He told me, that one of our countrymen had been killed on the Copper River, whither he had been sent to establish a communication with the inhabitants, who had always been an implacable foe to the Company: and that another Russian, a Mr. Bogenoff, who had ascended the river as far as a hundred and fifty miles, for the same purpose, would have experienced a similar fate, but for the contrivance and kindness of a female native with whom he fortunately became acquainted, and whom, out of gratitude for having saved his life, he afterwards married. He added, that the river abounded in virgin copper, but the inhabitants kept the spots where large pieces of it were to be found a profound secret.

Having mentioned the Bay of Kenay, I shall conclude this division of my narrative with a short account of it.

This bay has fourteen settlements, and about three thousand inhabitants, who have a language of their own. Their canoes are sheathed with the bark of trees. The families, however, who live near the sea, use only the common bidarkas. Though the people profess the Greek religion, and are baptized, polygamy and witchcraft are as much in vogue among them as among the other inhabitants of the coast. They live better than the Aleutians; because, besides the article of fish, there are wild animals which they hunt, and especially wild sheep, the flesh of which is excellent. The other wild animals are the black and common bear, rein-deer, martins, foxes of different sorts, river-otters, rabbits, ermines, beavers, and squirrels.

The inhabitants of Kenay bury their dead in wooden boxes, and pile stones over their graves, to hinder the wild beasts from scratching them out of the ground. They express their mourning by singeing their hair, besmearing their faces with black paint, and lacerating their bodies in different places. In other respects their manners differ but little from those of the people of Cadiack.

CHAPTER X.

DESCRIPTION OF THE ISLAND OF CADIACK.

Climate of the Island. Plants. Wild Beasts. Birds. Number of Inhabitants. Customs. Dress. Food. Marriages. Burials. Manner of catching Fish, wild Animals, and Birds. Instruments used for the Purpose. Shamans. Games. Building of Bidarkas. Building of Barabaras. Filthiness of the Inhabitants. Nature of the Government.

1805. May.

CADIACK is one of the largest islands belonging to the Russian empire in the fourth quarter of the globe. It is very mountainous, and surrounded by deep bays, into which a number of small rivers fall. On the shores of these, many settlements might be formed; but the country elsewhere is in general too elevated, and is besides, for the greater part of the year, covered with snow. The materials of which the island is composed, are chiefly slate and common gray stone. The climate, from the account given of it by the inhabitants, and from what I experienced myself, is by no means agreeable; the air is seldom clear, and even in summer there are few days which may be called warm: the weather, indeed, depends entirely upon the winds; so long as they continue to blow from the north, the west, or the south quarter, it is fine; when from other points of the compass, fogs, damps, and rain, are sure to prevail. The winters very much resemble what we experience in Russia in a bad autumn; the one,

HARBOUR of S.T PAUL, in the ISLAND of CADIACK.

however, which we passed on the island proved to be an exception.

Poplar, alder, and birch grow on the island, though in no great quantity, and pine* is only to be found in the vicinity of the harbour of St. Paul, and farther to the northward of it. Till the arrival of the Russians, only wild plants and roots were to be seen; but at present cabbages, turnips, potatoes, and other culinary productions, are cultivated here and there, but not generally throughout the island, as they require great labour and patience, which are traits not belonging to the disposition of the natives. The dark and rainy weather is besides unfavourable to horticulture, as well as to tillage in general; though barley was sowed last year by the Company, and in many places succeeded; and hopes are thence entertained of similar success as to other grain.

The native animals here are but few; they consist of bears, foxes of different kinds, ermines, dogs, and mice. Since the time of Mr. Shelechoff's establishment on the island, cattle, goats, pigs, and cats, have been introduced. I had also the pleasure of adding, during my stay, a Russian ram and an English ewe, which, before I left Cadiack, had already brought forth young; and the breed of this useful domesticated animal will no doubt be multiplied. The feathered tribe, on the contrary, is very numerous; it is composed of eagles, partridges, plovers, crows, magpies, cranes, sea-parrots, fen-ducks, and many other water-fowl.

---

* For want of fir, we made a new bowsprit of one of these pine trees, which answered admirably.

1805.
May.

Several species of the ducks fly away in the spring, and are replaced by geese and swans, which remain, in some places, the whole summer. There are three kinds of small birds, one of which, of a dark gray colour, regularly sings its song preparatory to bad weather. Cadiack abounds also in fish; which are halibut, cod, flounders, loaches, perch, herrings, and different kinds of salmon: the last come into the rivers, from the month of May to that of October, in such abundance, that hundreds may be caught in a short time with the hands only. The rivers, indeed, are sometimes so completely filled with them, that the wild beasts, and especially bears, will eat only the head, which they seem to consider as the most delicate part. The bears go into the river and catch these fish with their paws in a very dextrous manner. As they bite off the head, they throw the rest of the body on shore. The coast abounds in whales, porpoises, sea-lions, sea-dogs, and sea-otters. Sea-bears* also were formerly tolerably numerous, but are now very seldom seen. In the spring, sea-crabs are caught in plenty: I saw them enter the bay of St. Paul in pairs, two and two together, united by their claws.

The population of this island, when compared with its size, is

---

* At present, sea-bears are caught by the American Company on the islands of St. George and St. Paul. Though they are not so plentiful there now as heretofore, yet with good management they will always abound. Formerly each person in the employ of the Company used to kill two thousand of these animals in a year. It is to be lamented, that there is no good harbour on these islands, as ships which lie in the open sea must get under sail on the appearance of foul weather. I was told that the two islands were very different, that of St. George being high, and that of St. Paul low. There is no fresh water in either. The people belonging to the Company who reside in them, drink the water which is collected in ponds from melted snow. They live entirely on the flesh of the sea-bears, and eggs of sea-birds.

very small. As will be seen by the annexed account, which is the result of the minutest research, it amounts only to four thousand souls. It is also in a decreasing state; but as the Company have lately introduced several new regulations in favour of the inhabitants, I have no doubt it will soon be otherwise.

In the district of the harbour of Three-
    Saints, are - - - - 83 barabaras
In that of Ihack - - - 57
In that of Carlook - - - 34
In that of Alitack - - - 25
On the Wood Island - - - 3

        Which give a total of 202 barabaras.

Now, if we multiply this number by eighteen, the average estimate of persons (men, women, and children) in a barabara, the number of natives will be - 3636
And, if we add the Kaurs or Aleutians* in the Company's service, which are - - - - 364

        The amount of the population will be 4000

The oldest inhabitants of the island say, that when the Russians arrived amongst them the population was double what it is now. Supposing this, it must even then have been short of ten thousand souls: yet Mr. Shelechoff, in the account of his

---

* These Aleutians are fed and clothed by the Company.

1805.
May.

voyage, says, that he subjected to the crown of Russia about fifty thousand men on the island of Cadiack.

The islanders are of a middle stature, and of a copper complexion. They have large round faces and broad shoulders; their eyes, eye-brows, and hair, are jet black. The last is strong and straight. The men cut it short, or wear it long and loose: the women wear theirs flat upon the forehead, with the points cut extremely even, but twist it in a club behind. The dress of both sexes consists of parkas and camleykas, both of which nearly resemble in form a carter's frock. The first are made of the furs of animals, or the skins of sea birds; and the other of the intestines of seals, sea-lions, and sea-bears, or of the whale's bladder. Formerly, the rich clothed and decorated themselves with the skins of sea-otters, river-otters, and foxes; but they are now obliged to sell these furs to the Company for tobacco and other luxuries; which, introduced at first by Europeans, are become necessaries of life. The men wear girdles round their bodies, with a square piece or apron reaching to the mid-thigh. The women wear only a sash round the waist, about two inches broad, made of the skin of the seal. Both sexes wear caps, made of the skin of sea birds, or hats, of the fine roots of trees, platted: on the upper part of these hats some whimsical figures are generally painted. They have nothing on their feet, except when they go to a distance from home, in very cold weather; they then put on occasionally a sort of boot, made of the skin of the seal, or of some other skin equally strong.

The people of Cadiack are very fond of ornaments. Both

sexes pierce the ears all round, and embellish them with beads. The women also wear beads on the neck, arms, and feet. Formerly they wore strings of beads suspended from apertures in the lower lip, or else placed in these apertures small bones, resembling a row of artificial teeth, and had besides a bone passed through the gristle of the nose; while the men had a stone or bone, four inches long, in a cut made in the lower lip (Plate III. Fig. *d*): but these embellishments are now seldom seen. The fair sex were also fond of tatooing the chin, breasts, and back; but this again is much out of fashion.

Amber amongst these savages is held in as high estimation as diamonds are in Europe. It is worn instead of ear-rings. I made a present of a small piece to a toyon's son, and I thought he would have lost his senses from joy. On grasping the precious article, he exclaimed, " Now Sava," which was his Christian name, " is truly rich! He was known before by his alertness and courage, but now he will also be famous by possessing amber." I was afterwards told, that this youth travelled over the island to exhibit this bauble as a curiosity.

The food of the inhabitants consists of fish of different kinds, shell-fish, and amphibious animals. The fat of the whale, however, is the prime delicacy. It is eaten raw, as are also the heads of salmon. The other viands are boiled in earthen pots, or roasted on sticks, simply fixed in the ground before the fire. In a time of scarcity, which seldom fails to occur in winter, and is almost unavoidable during the spring, the islanders live entirely on shell-fish; they therefore form a settlement near some large bank, as the best situation for the means of subsistence.

1805.
May.

On the arrival of the Russians, the islanders believed alike in good and in evil spirits; but made their offerings to the last only, conceiving the first to be incapable of doing injury. At present many of them profess to be Christians of the Greek church, though all their religion consists in being baptized, in having but one wife, and in crossing themselves on entering a Russian house. They know nothing of the principles of the Greek faith; and profess the religion from mere interest, that they may receive a cross, or some other present. I knew several who, for the sake of getting a shirt or a handkerchief, had been baptized three times.

The real history of the first peopling of this island is not known, though every old man has his story to tell about it. Toyon Kolpack, who is held in great esteem for his cleverness, and whose story obtains most credit, told me, that the true origin of the people was this:—To the northward of the peninsula of Alaska lived a toyon, whose daughter cohabited with a male of the canine species, by whom she had five children, three males and two females. The toyon being displeased with this degenerate conduct of his daughter, took an opportunity, in the absence of her lover, of banishing her to an island in the neighbourhood. The lover, coming home, and finding none of his family, grieved for a long time: at last, discovering the place of their exile, he swam towards it, and was drowned on the way. The whelps in the mean time were grown up, and the mother had acquainted them with the cause of their banishment; which exasperated them so much against their grandfather, that when he came to see them they tore him to pieces. The mother, on this melancholy event, resolved to return to her native place, and gave free leave to her offspring to go wherever they chose. In consequence of this permission, some went northward; while others, passing the peninsula of Alaska, took a southerly course, and arrived at the island of Cadiack, where they increased and multiplied, and were the founders of the present population.

On my asking the toyon, by what means they reached the island, he very gravely affirmed, that it was formerly separated from Alaska by a river only; and that the present channel was made by a large otter, in the bay of Kenay, who one day took it into his head to push himself through between it and the peninsula.

Another islander told me a very different tale of the origin of the first peopling of the island. The raven, it seems, is considered by many of the islanders as a divinity; and a raven, he said, brought the light from heaven, while a bladder descended at the same time, in which a man and a woman were enclosed. At first this pair of human beings enlarged their dungeon by blowing, and afterward by stretching their hands and feet; and it was thus mountains were constructed. The man, by scattering the hair of his head on the mountains, created trees and forests, in which wild beasts sprung up and increased; while the woman, by making water, produced seas, and by spitting into ditches and holes, formed rivers and lakes. The woman, pulling out one of her teeth, gave it to the man, who made a knife of it; and, cutting trees with the knife, threw the chips into the river, which were changed into fish of different kinds. At last this human pair had children; and while their first-born,

1805.
May.

a son, was playing with a stone, the stone all of a sudden was converted into an island. On this island, which was the island of Cadiack, a man and a she-dog were then placed; and it was set afloat on the ocean, and arrived at its present situation. The man and the she-dog multiplied, and the present generation are their descendants.

These fables, which have a degree of analogy, plainly show, how slow is the progress of civilisation; or, at least, how little effect has been produced on these people by an intercourse of more than twenty years with the Russians.

Formerly, polygamy was in use on the island. The toyons had then as many as eight wives, and private persons a smaller number, according to their situation and property. The shamans had persuaded their ignorant countrymen, that they ought to cohabit with as many women as the supernatural being, their patron, would allow them. Those who marry according to the rites of the Greek church, have now but one wife.

The manner of courtship of the country is this:—A young man, on hearing that in such a place is a girl that he thinks will suit him, goes thither, carrying with him the most valuable things he is possessed of, and proposes himself for a husband. If the parents of the girl are satisfied with him, he makes them presents till they say—Enough. If they are not pleased with him, he returns home with all he brought. The husband always lives with the parents of the wife, and is obliged to serve them, though occasionally he may visit his own relations. When they are not married by the Greek church, there is no rite observed; having agreed to be man and wife, the young couple go to bed together without ceremony. The next morning, however, the husband rises before day, to procure wood, which is very scarce in many parts of the island; and is obliged to prepare a hot bath, for the purification both of himself and his partner.

There are no feastings at the time of marriage; but if the son-in-law should happen to kill a beast or fish of value, the father-in-law makes a parade of sending pieces of it to his friends. This ostentation, however, is only practised in a season of plenty: at other times there are no givings; every one keeps what he gets to himself.

Of all the customs of these islanders, the most disgusting is that of men, called schoopans, living with men, and supplying the place of women. These are brought up from their infancy with females, and taught all the feminine arts. They even assume the manners and dress of the sex so nearly, that a stranger would naturally take them for what they are not.* This odious practice was formerly so prevalent, that the residence of one of these monsters in a house was considered as fortunate; it is however daily losing ground.

The Cadiack people seem more attached to their dead than

---

* As a proof how easily this mistake may be made; it once happened, that a toyon brought one of these unnatural beings to church to be married to him, and the ceremony was nearly finished, when an interpreter, who came in by chance, put a stop to the proceedings, by making known to the priest, that the couple he was joining in wedlock were both males.

1805.
May

to their living relatives, and often weep when their names happen to be mentioned. They dress the dead in their best apparel, and then lay them in state, commonly in the place where they sickened and died. While the grave is digging, the relations and friends howl bitterly. When it is ready, the body is wrapped up in furs and seal-skins, and placed in it. Over the grave large stones are piled, and blocks of wood. The melancholy business of interment being ended, the distant relations and friends return home; but the parents of the deceased remain on the spot, wailing till sun-set. Formerly, on the demise of a great man, a slave or *calga*, as it is called here, used to be killed, that he might be buried with his master; but this is no longer allowed. At present the only difference is, that broken beads and granules of amber are strewed over the bodies of the wealthy; and even this is but seldom practised. With the hunters that die, their arrows, spears, and harpoons, are generally buried; and the frame of a bidarka is placed over them. I saw instances of high poles being erected over the graves of persons of consequence.

They express their mourning by cutting the hair short, and daubing the face with soot. A wife, on the death of her husband, retires for a certain period to another settlement; and a husband does the same on the death of his wife. When a child dies, its mother must seclude herself, for a period of from ten to twenty days, in a hovel built apart; of which, in my account of the Fugitive settlement, I have cited an instance that came under my observation.

A curious custom prevails here on occasions of lying-in. To be delivered, the woman retires into a small low hovel, built of reeds and covered with grass, where she must remain after the birth of the child twenty days, whatever may be the season of the year, summer or winter. During this period she is considered so unclean, that nobody will touch her, and food is given to her on sticks. When the twenty days are expired, she washes herself and child, first in cold water and in the open air, and then in a warm bath. During the first washing, a small perforation is often made in the gristle of the infant's nose, and a thin twig, like a small wire, drawn through it; an incision is also made under the lower lip, or small holes are bored in it.

This custom extends also to women during their periodical courses, when they are not allowed to remain in their barabaras, but must retire to similar hovels; nor are they permitted to come out, till they have observed the customary ablutions. Those females to whom this occurs for the first time, are even obliged to retire for ten days; during which, from being considered as unclean, they are fed as in the instance of child-birth. I had the curiosity to measure one of these hovels; the length of which was three feet two inches, the breadth two feet seven inches, and the height two feet four inches.

Of the different diseases to which these people are subject, the most common are, venereal, colds, consumption, itch, and ulcers. The two last are so unavoidable, that there is hardly a person to be found on the island without one or the other. They have three methods of cure; shamaning, cutting away the part affected, and bleeding. I was told, that slight venereal taints are removed by means of some decoction; but that when the disease

1805.
May.

touches the nose, each nostril is pierced through, and sometimes the gristle itself.

The mode of education here is similar to that of other savage countries. The people are able to bear cold, from having been habituated to it, in various ways, from their cradle. It often happens that a mother plunges her noisy child into water, even in winter, and keeps it there till it leaves off crying. To teach them to bear hunger, they have no occasion for lessons, necessity being a sufficient master; for they have often nothing to eat for several days together. The men are taught early to construct bidarkas, and to manage them at sea; to make arrows, and to shoot with them: and the women are exercised from their infancy in needle-works, in making nets, lines, and other things adapted to their sex. The men are all, without exception, brought up to fishing, and killing wild animals and birds. The whale-fishing, however, belongs almost exclusively to particular families, and is handed down in succession to those children who prove to be the most expert at it. But this art is not brought to such perfection in the island of Cadiack, as in Greenland, and many other places. A Cadiack whaler, in a single bidarka, attacks only small whales; and for this purpose he is provided with a harpoon, the spear of which is made of slate-stone, and so fixed into the handle, as to detach itself when the whale is struck. When wounded by it, the whale runs to sea and dies, and is perhaps never seen again, unless the currents and winds should throw it on the coast. Thus no whaler is sure of his prey. The spears of the whale harpoons are marked by the whalers, so that every one knows his own.

The mode of hunting the sea-otter is different, and the prey so sure, that scarcely one animal out of a hundred can save itself from its pursuers. The method is this. A number of Aleutians, more or less, go out together in separate bidarkas. As soon as any one of them perceives an otter, he throws his arrow at it, if he can, and, whether he can or cannot, pulls to the place where it plunges. He here stations his boat, and then lifts up his oar. The rest of the hunters, on observing the signal, form a circle round it. The moment the animal appears above water, the hunter that is nearest throws his arrow, and then hastens to the spot where the animal replunges, and makes it known, as in the preceding instance, by raising his oar. A second circle is then formed; and in this manner the chase continues, till the poor beast is perfectly exhausted by the blood flowing from its wounds. I was told by very expert hunters, that these animals were sometimes easily caught; whereas, at other times, twenty bidarkas would be employed half a day in taking a single otter: and that this animal has been known to tear the arrow from its body in order to escape. The first plunge of an otter exceeds a quarter of an hour; the second is of shorter duration, the third still shorter; and thus the intervals gradually diminish, till at last it can plunge no more.

1805.
May.

When these hunters attack a female otter, swimming with her young one, a picture of maternal affection presents itself, that would induce a feeling mind to desist from its cruel purpose: but a Cadiack man, hardened to his trade, has no frailties of this kind, and can pass nothing without darting his arrow at it. When she finds herself pursued, the poor mother takes her cub in her arms, if I may so speak, and plunges with it, to save it.

1805.
May.

As the cub, however, cannot long remain under water, she soon, instigated by affection, rises again, and is easily struck by the weapons of the hunters. Sometimes the hunters come upon her by surprise, and separate her from her young one, in which case her loss is inevitable, for the cub is sure to be taken; and when she hears its cries, she swims, fearless of danger, to the very bidarka from which they proceed. It is said, that if a female otter has two cubs with her when she is attacked, she will destroy one herself, or leave it to its fate, that she may be the better able to protect the other.

The Cadiack people, exercised from their childhood to this sort of hunting, are very expert at it. In fine weather, they know the course of the otter under water, after it has plunged, by the bubbles that appear on the surface; and in rough weather they are equally acquainted with it, as the otter always swims against the wind.

The killing a sea-otter is matter of great triumph to these people. It is expressed by a shout, proceeding at once from all the party concerned in the hunt; then follows the inquiry to whom the prize belongs. The highest claim is his who first wounded the animal; if several wounded it at the same time, the right side has the preference over the left, and the nearer the wound is to the head, the more weight has it in the scale of decision. When two or more arrows are struck into the same part of the animal, and the lines of the arrows are broken,* the

---

* The line of the sea-otter arrows is made of the sinews of the whale; one end is fastened to the spear of the instrument, and the other to the handle.

Plate III.

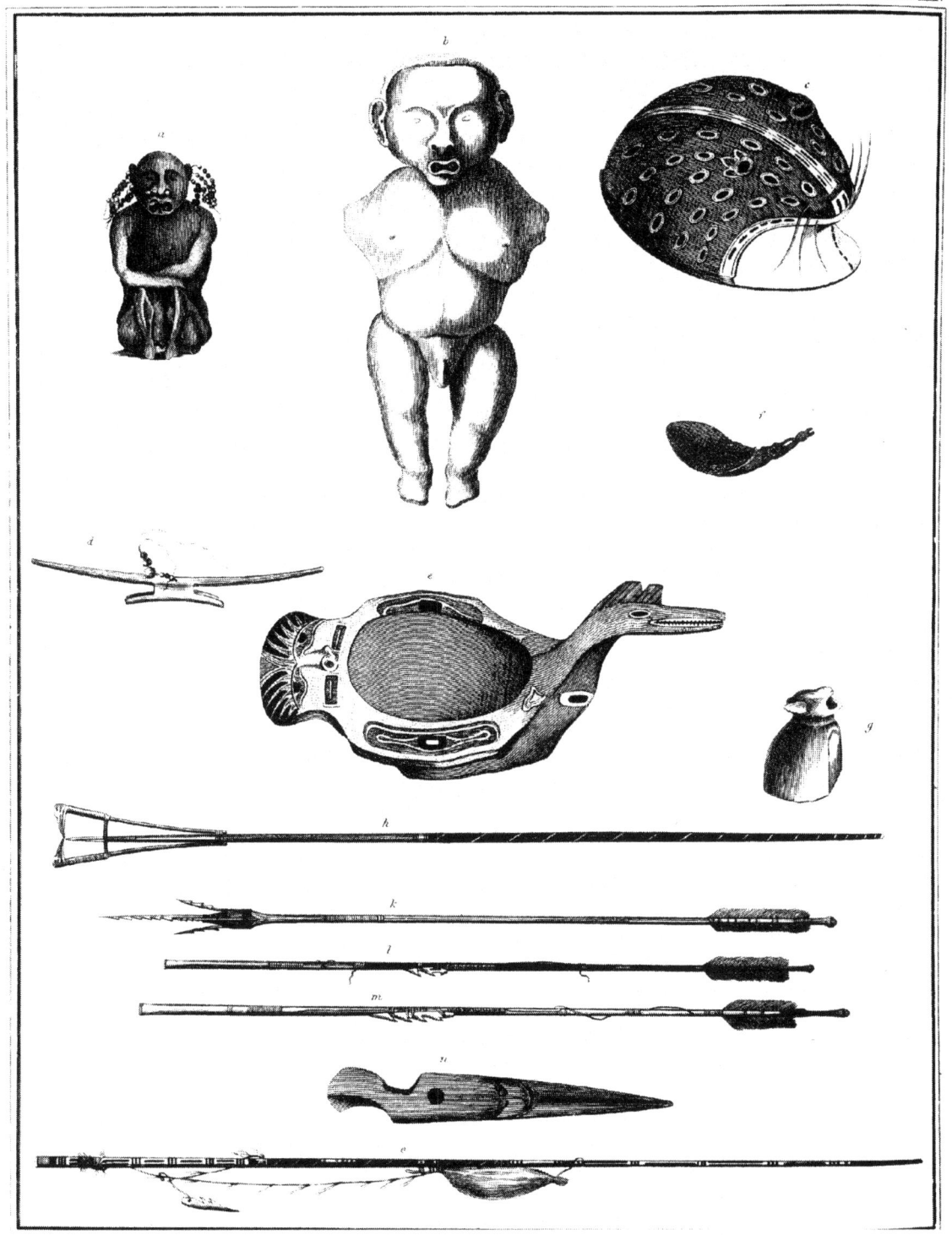

longest piece of line determines the preference. From this complication of rules, disputes often arise; and in such cases, some Russian is called in to determine the point.

Next to the otter, the most valuable animal, in the estimation of the Cadiack men, is the species of seal or sea-dog, called by the Russians Nerpa. It is caught with nets, made of the same material as the line of the sea-otter arrow; or killed when asleep: or, which is the easiest manner of taking it, enticed towards the shore. A fisherman, concealing the lower part of his body among the rocks, puts on his head a wooden cap, or rather casque, resembling the head of a seal (Plate III. Fig. c.), and makes a noise like that animal. The unsuspicious seal, imagining he is about to meet a partner of his own species, hastens to the spot, and is instantly killed.

The catching of birds called ooreel or sea-raven, from the skin of which handsome warm gowns or parkas are made, is also a business of importance. It is done by a net, the lower part of which is stretched on a pole fourteen feet in length, while a string is passed through loop-holes in the upper part, and fastened to the extremities of the pole. These birds always keep on high and steep rocks and precipices. The sportsman, getting as near as he can to the birds, throws the net over them; and when by fluttering they are sufficiently entangled, he draws the net to a bag by means of the string, and sometimes takes a whole flight at once. The length of the net is about eighty feet, the breadth fourteen only.

Fish in the rivers are caught, either with the hands only,

1805.
May.
or by bags tied to a long pole. Sometimes they are taken by being struck with a spear about five feet long, made for the purpose (Plate III. Fig. *h, k*). At sea it is done by hooks made of bone, which are fastened, instead of a line, to a sea-leek, that grows sometimes to the length of nearly two hundred feet, and is the eighth of an inch thick. This production of the sea answers better for fishing, than a line made of the sinews of the whale; which, by stretching too much in the water, becomes impaired in strength.

The Cadiack people use long spears, harpoons, and arrows, for killing the large sea animals, such as whales, seals, sea-otters, and others. Formerly, in their wars with one another, bows and arrows were in use; but at present this weapon is seldom to be seen. The whale harpoon is about ten feet long; the spear or point is of slate stone, and of the form of a knife, sharp on both sides, and is set loose into the handle. The seal harpoon is but little shorter, and has a barbed spear made of bone. A bladder is fixed to the middle of the handle, to prevent the harpoon from sinking, or the seal from plunging beyond a certain depth after being wounded by it (Plate III. Fig. *o*). There is also a particular sort of arrow used against the seal (Plate III. Fig. *m*), nearly similar to that used against the sea-otter (Plate III. Fig. *l*), the length of which is about four feet. The arrows are thrown from a narrow and pointed board, twenty inches long, which is held by the thumb and three fingers (Plate III. Fig. *n*.) They are thrown straight from the shoulder with astonishing velocity.

Their working tools are very few. They consist of a small

iron adz, which was formerly made of stone; a crooked knife, which has taken place of a shell; a stone for polishing, and a tooth, fixed in a wooden handle. With the assistance of these simple instruments, the Cadiack men make various articles, and finish them neatly. In the art of carving, however, which had been carried by them to tolerable perfection, they have so greatly declined, that there is now scarcely an individual who can execute any thing decently in that way.

With respect to the needle-work of the women, it is no where surpassed but in Oonalashka. I have a great many specimens of their skill, that would do credit to our best seamstresses. Every thing is sewed with thread made of the sinews of the whale, or other sea animals, some of which is as fine as the thread of silk. The most beautiful twists and braids are made of it. Before the Russians came, the needles were of bone: the instruments for boring the eye in them, are still found in almost every family. The hair of the rein-deer and of goats, are used here for ornamenting the dresses of the women; as also is the European shaloon, out of which they draw the threads, and form them into tufts, each according to her fancy.

On the island of Cadiack, as through the whole of what we saw of the north-west coast of America, shamaning is held in great veneration. The professors of it are brought up to their business from their infancy. They persuade the people, they have a correspondence with the devil, and can by his means foretell what will come to pass. They pretend that some children are doomed to be shamans; and that their destiny is made known by a dream. Though every shaman has in his practice some

1805.
May.

particular mummery, the foundation of the pretended art is the same in all. The ceremony generally observed on these occasions, is this:—The skin of a seal or other animal being spread on the ground, in the middle of a barabara or elsewhere, and a vessel of water placed near it, the shaman enters, and, placing himself on the skin, takes off his ordinary dress, and puts on a camleyka, turning the fore part behind. He then disguises himself by a wig of human hair, to which two feathers are attached, one on each side, to resemble horns. Opposite to him stands the person who wishes to consult him about his affairs. The question to be solved being stated, the shaman begins to sing, the company joining in the song by degrees, till it comes to a chorus, or rather a yell. During this incantation, the shaman makes the most frightful grimaces and twistings of the body, till at last he appears perfectly exhausted and falls to the ground. He falls, however, only to rise again; and he repeats this foolery several times before he gives the answer, which, in his trance, he pretends to have received from the evil spirit.

The shamans are consulted also as physicians in dangerous cases, and are rewarded very handsomely if the patient recovers, but receive nothing if he dies. The mode of cure consists, in like manner, in incantations.

Next in rank to the shamans are the kaseks, or sages, whose office is to teach children the different dances, and superintend the public amusements and shows, of which they have the supreme control. The islanders generally call our priests by this name.

The people of Cadiack, whelmed in ignorance, can do nothing without some superstition mixing in the business. If merely a piece of twist or line is made, it is under the auspices of some lucky root, herb, or stone, which owes its power to its scarcity. A person who possesses none of these happy influences, these gifts of fortune, is considered as the poorest of his species. Even the small sea nut, which abounds on the beach in the warmer climates, is esteemed in this way here, because seldom found. It is from this superstitious feeling that, at the commencement of spring, the whale-fishermen go into the interior of the island to search on the mountains for eagle-feathers, bear's hair, and different stones and roots. The abominable custom, which I mentioned before as prevailing amongst the whalers, of stealing the dead bodies from the graves and secreting them in caverns, has the same origin. This is carried so far, that a father at his death bequeaths this cavern to the son whom he appoints to succeed him in the whale-fishery, and the son endeavours to augment the precious collection; so that a whaler may be found possessing upwards of twenty of such corses.

In my narrative I have represented the whalers as unclean, in the eyes of their countrymen, during the fishing season. Nevertheless, they have great respect paid them, and are regarded as the purveyors of their country.

These islanders pass their time in hunting, festivals, and abstinence. The first takes place in the summer; the second begins in the month of December, and continues as long as any provisions remain; and then follows the period of famine, which

1805.
May.

lasts till the re-appearance of fish in the rivers. During the last-mentioned period, many have nothing but shell-fish to subsist on, and some die for want. Their festivals consist chiefly of dancing, which differs but little from that of other savage nations, except that masks of the most hideous figures are worn. I was present at some of these festivals, but found nothing pleasant or amusing in them.

The Cadiack men are so fond of gaming, that they often lose every thing they possess at play. They have a very favourite game called *kroogeki*. Four or more men play at it; that is, two against two, or three against three. Two skins are spread on the ground, at the distance of about twelve feet from each other. On each skin is placed a round flat mark made of bone, about four inches and a half in circumference, with a black circle and centre marked on it. Every player has five wooden pieces, like what are called men in the game of draughts or back-gammon, and distinguished in the same manner by colour. The players kneel, and stretching themselves forward lean on the left hand, throwing the draughts with the right, one after another, adversary against adversary, aiming at the round mark. If a man hits the mark, his antagonist endeavours to dislodge the draught, by placing his own there. When all the draughts are expended on both sides, it is examined how they lie, and they are counted accordingly: for every draught touching the mark, one; for that which lodges on it, two; for that which cuts the black circle, three, &c. In this manner the game continues till the number of a hundred and twelve, which is the point of the game, is gained. The numbers are counted by small sticks made for the purpose.

There is another favourite game called *stopka*, which is a small figure cut out of bone (Plate III. Fig. g). It is thrown up into the air, and if it falls on its bottom, two are counted; if on its back, three; and if on its belly, one only. This game consists in gaining twenty, which are also marked with short sticks.

The Cadiack men deserve great credit for the invention of the bidarka, which is lightly constructed of wood, fastened together with whalebone, and covered over with seal-skins, the seams of which are so well sewed that not a drop of water can get through. At present there are three sorts in use: the first carries three persons, the second two, and the third only one (See Plate, View of St. Paul's Harbour). Before the arrival of the Russians, the two last only, called the single and the double bidarkas, had been built. The islanders had also large leathern boats, of sufficient burthen to carry seventy persons, which were used in their wars and long voyages; but these boats are kept now only by the Russians. The bidarkas paddle very fast, and are safer at sea in bad weather than European boats; especially when provided with good hatchway cloths, which are always drawn over holes, answering to hatchways, and extend round the waists of the people sitting in them. It is common to send one of these craft as far as the island of Oonalashka, or to Sitca Sound. For such voyages, however, the rowers must be furnished with new camleykas, which they always fasten tight round the neck and arms, as a guard against the waves of the sea, which often roll over them. When there are several of these vessels in company, and a storm overtakes them, they fasten together in parties of three or four, and thus ride it out, like so

1805.
May.

many ducks tossed up and down by the waves, without the smallest danger. At first I disliked these leathern canoes, on account of their bending elasticity in the water, arising from their being slenderly built; but when accustomed to them, I thought it rather pleasant than otherwise.

The following table gives the dimensions of each of the three kinds of bidarka.

For three Men.	Feet.	Inches.	For two Men.	Feet.	Inches.	For one man.	Feet.	Inches.
The length . .	26	7	. . . . . .	19	7	. . . . . .	14	6
The breadth . .	2	8	. . . . . .	2	7	. . . . . .	2	4
The depth . .	1	3	. . . . . .	1	1	. . . . . .	1	
From stern to the first hatchway .	4	6	Between the hatchways	4	11	Between the stem and the hatchway .	7	8½
From the first hatchway to the main ditto	4	1	From the fore hatchway to the stem .	7	4			
From the stem to the fore hatchway .	7	11	From the stern to the main hatchway .	4		Diameter of the hatchway . . .	1	6½

It is astonishing that a people, capable of inventing the bidarka, should pay so little attention to the building of their barabaras, which are wretchedly constructed. A barabara here consists of a large room, with a door about three feet square, and an opening in the roof to let out the smoke. In the middle of the room a large hole is dug for a fire place. The sides of this dwelling are divided by boards into different store-rooms. In short, a barabara answers the purpose of a court-yard, a kitchen, and, when requisite, a theatre. In this room the natives dance, build their bidarkas, clean and dry their fish, and perform every other domestic office. It is never cleaned, except that now and then some fresh grass is thrown over the floor, to give it a sort of decent appearance. Adjoining to this filthy hall are small rooms, called by the natives joopans, each of which has a particular entrance, or rather hole, through which a man can with difficulty thrust himself. It has also an opening in the roof covered with bladder, or dried intestines sewed together, which are a very good substitute for glass, and admit the light freely. These joopans serve for drawing-room, bed-room, and sometimes even for graves. The one I entered at Naumliack measured thirteen feet ten inches, by fourteen feet seven inches. Except at the entrance, blocks of wood were placed all round the room, at the distance of three feet and a quarter from the walls, in which narrow space seal skins and straw were laid, for the convenience of sitting and sleeping. These blocks were ornamented with teeth of the sea-otter, which greatly resembled human teeth, but were larger. While they served as a partition for the room, they were used also as bolsters to sleep on. It was surprising to me, how these people could lie, breadthwise, in so narrow a space as that between the wall and the blocks; but I found, upon inquiry, that they lie mostly on their back, with the knees cocked up nearly to the chin. These rooms are convenient in winter, as, from their size and construction, they will keep tolerably warm from the respiration only of those who live in them. They are, however, in very cold weather, warmed with heated stones; and in this manner are sometimes converted into hot baths. The construction of a barabara is a very simple one. A large square space is dug about two feet deep in the ground. In the corners of this space, pillars, about four feet long are fixed, upon which a high roof is erected, thickly covered with grass. The sides of this building are boards plastered over with mud, which gives it an appearance not very unlike a dunghill.

It may justly be said, that the inhabitants of Cadiack, if we except the women during their monthly periods and their lyings-in, have not the least sense of cleanliness. They will not go a step out of the way for the most necessary purposes of nature; and vessels are placed at their very doors for the reception of the urinous fluid, which are resorted to alike by both sexes. Urine indeed is used by them for preparing the skins of birds; but they also wash themselves, as well as their clothes, with it: and even in the hot bath, of which the men and women are alike fond, because they love to perspire, it is with this fluid they sometimes make their ablutions.

The island of Cadiack, with the rest of the Russian settlements along the north-west coast of America, are superintended by a kind of governor-general, or commander-in-chief, who has agents under him, appointed, like himself, by the Company at Petersburg. The smaller settlements have each a Russian overseer. These overseers are chosen by the governor, and are selected for the office in consequence of their long services and orderly conduct. They have the power of punishing, to a certain extent, those whom they superintend; but are themselves amenable to the governor, if they abuse their power by acts of injustice.* The seat of government is the Harbour of St. Paul, which has a barrack, different store-houses, several respectable wooden habitations, and a church, the only one to be found on the coast. To these store-houses, all the valuable peltry from the various settlements are brought, to be conveyed, as opportunities offer, to Ochotsh, from whence a part goes to Russia, and the rest for sale to Kiakta, which is the mart of the Russian commerce with China.

---

* Mr. Langsdorff has drawn a most frightful picture of the barbarity of these overseers, and others above them in authority; and affirms, that he had ocular demonstration of its truth. " I have seen," he says, " the Russian *promusclinicks*, or fur-hunters, sport with the lives of the natives, and put these defenceless creatures to a horrible death, from the mere caprice of their own arbitrary will." To facts which a person asserts came under his own observation, I am not so rude as to give a direct denial; but I must be permitted to remark, that no such cruelties presented themselves to my sense of seeing, nor did I hear of any such, though I was more than a twelvemonth on the coast, and made many inquiries respecting the treatment of the natives. In my opinion, the greatest cause of complaint on the part of the poor Aleutians, is the severe labour that is required of them, and the hardships they have to endure in the long voyages they are obliged to perform in their small canoes in the business of hunting.

There is another representation by Mr. Langsdorff, as to these overseers, in which I cannot agree with him. He says, " they are Siberian malefactors, or adventurers." The truth is this:—Some years ago, about twenty exiles were sent to Cadiack; but they were employed as common labourers only, not as overseers of districts.

That mistakes of this nature should be made by Mr. Langsdorff, is not to be wondered at, when we find him thus speaking of himself:—To examine a country accurately, three things are requisite, not one of which I at this time enjoyed; leisure, serenity of mind, and convenience." To this might be added, that he was but a short time in the country of which he speaks, and was ignorant of the language both of the natives and of the Russians.

CHAPTER XI.

SECOND PASSAGE FROM CADIACK TO SITCA.

Feelings of the Russian Inhabitants on our leaving Cadiack. Arrive at New Archangel. Improved State of this Settlement. Account of the Destruction of the old Settlement. Explore the Coast round Mount Edgecumbe. Sitcan Embassy, and Ceremonies attending it. Excursion to the Top of Mount Edgecumbe. Arrival, at New Archangel, of another would-be Ambassador. Hot Baths. Plan of the ensuing Course of our Voyage.

1805.
June.
14th.

On the 14th of June, at eleven o'clock in the morning, we sailed out of St. Paul's harbour. Mr. Bander took leave of us in the offing beyond the woody island, and about five in the afternoon we were able to steer a direct course for Sitca. On quitting the harbour, we took, as in the former instance, the north passage, which is the best for coming out, though impracticable for sailing in, because, with the easterly and northerly winds, a thick fog generally prevails. On passing the fort, we were saluted by the cannon; and the inhabitants flocked to the shore to take a last farewell, wishing us a safe and good voyage to our native land. There were many amongst them, I am sure, whose hearts ached to be of our party; longing once more to behold their mother-country, from which poverty alone, perhaps, kept them banished.

20th.

At three o'clock in the afternoon of the 20th, Mount Fair-

Weather was observed to the north 6° east; and soon after many other elevations appeared, amongst which was Mount Edgecumbe, bearing by the true compass south 60° east, distant about forty miles. We flattered ourselves with being able to reach the anchorage in a few hours; but the weather becoming calm, obliged us to keep at a distance from the shore; which, from being covered with snow, could not be distinctly seen in the night, though we might be close to it. This precaution was also necessary on account of the easterly currents, which had pushed us forward, during the last five days, 2° 47', and still flowed in the same direction.

The next morning we approached Mount Edgecumbe, which, with other elevations of Sitca Sound, presented a landscape similar to the one we had seen on our first arrival at Cadiack. The tops of the mountains being covered with snow, proved that the winter had not yet left these environs; though in many places of the same latitude, summer already reigned in its full splendour. At noon we found ourselves, by observation, in the latitude of 57° 30"; from which it appears, that Cape Edgecumbe, which bore from us then north 69° east, must be placed at 57° north. We had now a southerly breeze, but it was so light that we could not reach the entrance of the harbour till late in the evening; when, meeting with a strong counter current, we were obliged, once more, to retire for the night to a station beyond the Middle Islands.

On the 22d we succeeded in entering the harbour of New Archangel, which, however, we should not have done, on account of light breezes from the north-west, had not Mr. Baranoff sent

1805.
June.

to our assistance three large leathern boats, which towed us in about noon. As the ebb tide would not permit us to enter the passage by which we had sailed out the preceding autumn, I found myself obliged to go to the leeward of it, and I took my station to the east of the fort of New Archangel. As soon as we let go our anchor, Mr. Baranoff came on board, whom I was happy to find perfectly recovered of the wound he had received in the contest with the Sitcans. Towards evening the ship was moored east and west, with about fifteen fathoms of cable each way; the fort of New Archangel bearing west-north-west, and point Coloshenskoy north-east by east.

23d. The next morning I went on shore, and was surprised to see how much the new settlement was improved. By the active superintendence of Mr. Baranoff, eight very fine buildings were finished, and ground enough in a state of cultivation for fifteen kitchen-gardens. His live stock also made no despicable appearance. It consisted of four cows, two calves, three bulls, three goats, a ewe and a ram, with many swine and fowls: an acquisition altogether of great value in this part of the world.

The weather continued fine for many days after our arrival;
29th. and on the 29th I went, with Mr. Baranoff and some of my officers, to the place where formerly stood our old fort of Archangel. There were still some buildings left, which had either escaped the ravages of the flames, or which probably the savages had not thought it worth while to destroy to the foundation. We took our dinner on these ruins; and, having paid a last respect to the manes of our countrymen, who lost their lives in defending this place, we returned home.

HARBOUR of NEW ARCHANGEL, in SITCA or NORFOLK SOUND.

As I have several times in my narrative referred to this unfortunate event, I shall state here a few particulars of it. The settlement had been built but two years; and it was with the perfect concurrence of the natives, with whom Mr. Baranoff, who superintended it, was on good terms. Having occasion to go to Cadiack, he left the care of it to a Russian overseer, between whom and the principal toyons there was a still greater cordiality; for they often passed a day together, he at one or other of their houses, and they at his. With so fair a face of friendship, no enmity could be suspected, and the fort was occasionally left in a sort of unprotected state; the Russians and Aleutians being engaged in hunting the sea-otter, or in the still more necessary business of procuring a supply of provision for winter. It was an opportunity of this nature which the Sitcans embraced for the execution of their nefarious plan; and so secret were they in its management, that, while some stole through the woods, others passed in canoes by different creeks, to the place of rendezvous. They were about six hundred in number, and were all provided with fire-arms. Though the attack was wholly unexpected, the few Russians in the fort courageously defended it. But vain was defence against such numbers: it was quickly taken by storm. The assault commenced at noon, and in a few hours the place was leveled to the ground. Among the assailants were three seamen belonging to the United States, who, having deserted from their ship, had entered into the service of the Russians, and then took part against them. These double traitors were among the most active in the plot. They contrived combustible wads, which they lighted, and threw upon the buildings where they knew the gunpowder was kept, which took fire and were blown up. Every person who was found in the fort was

1805.
June.

put to death. Not content with this, the Sitcans dispersed in search both of Russians and Aleutians, and had many opportunities of exercising their barbarity. Two Russians, in particular, were put to the most excruciating torture. The place was so rich in merchandise, that two thousand sea-otter skins, and other articles of value, were saved by the Sitcans from the conflagration.

July 2d.

On the 2d of July, I dispatched my ship's master to explore the coast round Mount Edgecumbe, and find out the channel beyond it, that, as I was told by the natives, led to Cross Bay. At the same time Mr. Baranoff sent an interpreter to the Sitcans, with whom he had had no personal communication during the whole winter, to acquaint them with our arrival from Cadiack, and that we had brought back several of their hostages.* It appeared as if they still retained inimical feelings; since, during the long period of our absence, not a toyon could be induced to come to the fort. They had passed the winter in a scattered state, but were now united again, and had built themselves another fort, opposite to the settlement of Hoosnoff, in Chatham's Strait, similar to the one we had destroyed. It is well situated in a small shallow bay, and is defended on the water side by a large rock. Other tribes residing about Sitca, had also, it was understood, been busily employed in fortifying their settlements; so that, it is to be feared, our countrymen here will in a short time be surrounded by very formidable and dangerous neighbours.

---

* I had taken all the hostages with me to Cadiack last autumn, of which I now brought back three, a Sitca youth, and two men belonging to another tribe.

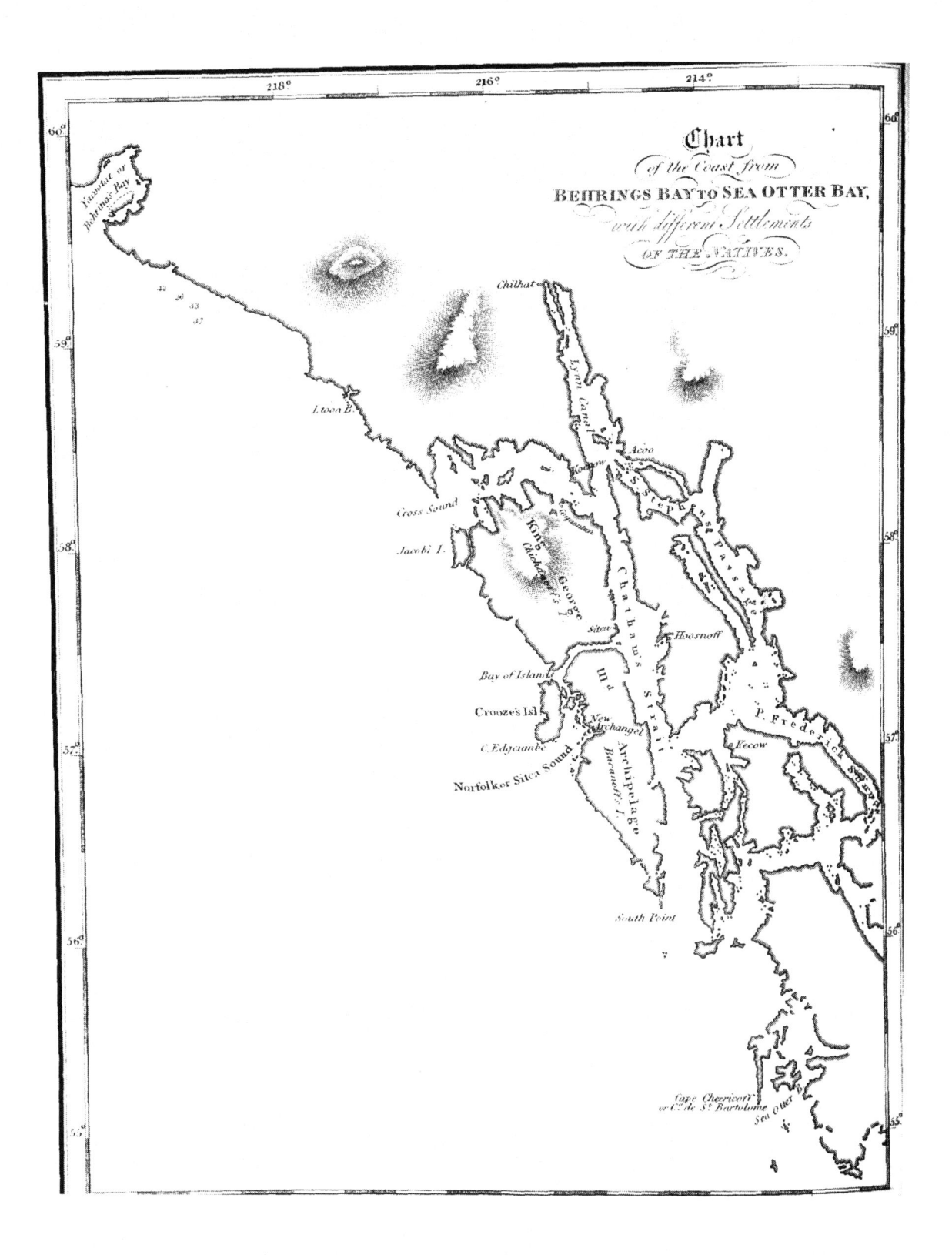

Chart of the Coast from BEHRINGS BAY TO SEA OTTER BAY, with different Settlements OF THE NATIVES.

On the 7th my ship's master returned from his expedition. He had found the channel, and surveyed the whole island on which Mount Edgecumbe stands. To this island I gave the name of Crooze, in honour of our late admiral, to whom I am chiefly indebted for my naval preferment: as he kindly took me under his protection from my youth, and gave me every opportunity of instruction, I cannot help ascribing to him, also, whatever qualities I may possess for undertaking this long and difficult voyage.—In the course of this day we changed our old mizen-mast for a new one made of pine.

In the morning of the 11th our interpreter returned from the Sitca settlement, bringing for answer, that the toyons wished for further assurance of good intention on our part, before they would venture to come to the fort. Accordingly, to conquer their reluctance, the same person was sent back with presents, and a message of invitation couched in the civilest terms.

On the 16th he returned, accompanied by a Sitcan ambassador and his suite, to settle the terms of a formal pacification; and we prepared to receive them with the respect due to their dignity. Although the people here may be said to live in a state of perfect barbarism, they are fond of parade, and scrupulous observers of ceremony. The party, who were in five boats, made their appearance about four o'clock in the afternoon, rowing up all together in front of the fort. When at a short distance, they began to sing, and our Aleutians sallied forth to meet them, while the Choohaches, who were appointed to conduct them to the fort, instantly prepared for the office, by powdering their hair with the down of the eagle, and dressing themselves in their best ap-

1805.
July.

parel. It was difficult to refrain from laughter at the odd appearance of these gentlemen-ushers. Many of them had nothing on but a thread-bare waistcoat, and others paraded naked, with the exception of an old hat or a pair of tattered breeches; yet, with these rags, they were as vain as the most finical beau in Europe. The embassy stopped when close to the beach, and commenced dancing in the boats. The toyon himself jumped and capered in the most whimsical manner, fanning himself at the same time with large feathers. The song, which they sung as an accompaniment to the dancing, was execrable. This farce over, another of a similar kind commenced on the beach, on the part of the gentlemen-ushers; which, though it lasted only a quarter of an hour, completely tired our patience.

Our visitors were now brought on shore in their boats by our Aleutians, and I supposed the introductory ceremony to be ended; but I was mistaken; the embassy still remained in their boats, though ashore, admiring the contortions and singing of the Choohaches, which were renewed.

At length, the ambassador, being lifted out of the boat, was placed on a carpet, and conveyed to the place appointed both for him and his followers, who were carried in the same manner, but on a less costly vehicle. When settled in their apartments, Mr. Baranoff gave orders that they should be treated with hospitality; but, as it was late, postponed seeing them to the next day.

In the morning, previously to the interview, the ambassador paid me a visit, accompanied by the whole of his suite, in one of Mr. Baranoff's boats. On leaving the shore, they sung and danced. One, who stood at the head of the boat, was employed in plucking out the feathers of a bird's skin, and blowing them in the air. When near the ship, they danced again, and when on board resumed this favourite exercise, and kept it up for at least half an hour. I then invited the ambassador and his wife, and a Cadiack toyon who was of the party, into the cabin, while the rest were entertained on deck. Having regaled them with tea and brandy, I desired the three hostages to be brought to me; one of whom was the ambassador's son. The old man, seeing his boy taller and stouter than when he had parted from him, expressed a degree of gratitude for my kind treatment of him: but there was no kindness shown by the father to the son, or by the son to the father, in this meeting; which gave me no favourable opinion of the esteem in which either parental or filial affection is held by these people. The destruction of our old settlement by his countrymen being mentioned, the ambassador assured me, that he had had no participation in their guilt: on the contrary, he had endeavoured to restrain their violence, and, when he found that he could not succeed, had retired to Chilchat, a settlement in Lynn Canal, that he might not be present at so nefarious a proceeding. As I knew he had always been well-disposed towards the Russians, I gave credit to what he said.

My visitors having been upwards of two hours on board, at last proposed to depart. As soon as they were on the deck, they again began to dance, and returned on shore with the same ceremony, in this respect, as they had observed when they quitted it. These people are so fond of dancing, that I never

1805.
July.

saw three of them together without their feet being in motion. Before the departure of the ambassador, I allowed him to fire off one of our twelve-pounders, which he did with a firmness I little expected, exhibiting no surprise either at the report of the cannon or its motion.

In the afternoon I went on shore, and was present at the interview between Mr. Baranoff and the Sitcans. Mr. Baranoff presented the ambassador with a handsome red cloak trimmed with ermine, and each of his companions with a common blue one. Pewter medals were then distributed amongst them, as tokens of peace and amity with their country. To give importance to this pacification, an entertainment had been prepared in Mr. Baranoff's house, to which the whole embassy were invited; and so much honour did they do to the feast, that in the evening they were carried to their apartments in a state of perfect inebriety.*

The dress of the Sitcan party, on this occasion, consisted merely of a square piece of European cloth thrown over the shoulders; while the face of each was painted of different colours, and their hair powdered, first with soot and then with down. This mode of ornamenting the head is considered as magnificent here, and is only practised on particular occasions. The appearance of the ambassador's wife was the most singular. Her face was besmeared with black paint, and her hair completely covered with soot only. She had a cut through her lower lip,

---

* Mr. Langsdorff represents the Colushes as not liking brandy or other spirituous liquors.

into which a round piece of wood, two inches and a half long and an inch thick, was inserted; so that the lip, projecting horizontally from the countenance, greatly resembled a spoon. When it was necessary for her to drink, she was obliged to act with the greatest care, for fear of injuring this charming feature. She had a child with her, that was carried in a basket. Though it could not be more than three months old, it had the nose and lower lip pierced and hung with strings of beads.

The next morning the Sitcan embassy left us to return home. They set off as they came, singing. On taking leave, Mr. Baranoff, as a last sign of friendship, presented the ambassador with the Russian arms made of copper, fixed to the top of a long pole, and ornamented with eagle's feathers and ribbands. This present was apparently received with the utmost respect, as well as delight. The ambassador also was permitted to exchange his eldest son, the hostage, for a younger one, whom he promised to send.

Among the Aleutians who were present at yesterday's entertainment, were two from Cadiack, who, I was informed, had been last autumn on the top of Mount Edgecumbe. I had often wished to visit this place, but had been prevented from carrying my wishes into execution by not knowing the road, two-thirds of which lies through almost impenetrable woods. I therefore instantly engaged these people as guides; and taking lieutenant Powalishin with me, we set off on the 21st, at seven in the morning. About noon we landed in a small bay, opposite Cape Island; and, resolving to pass the night there, we pitched our tents on the beach, and made a large fire. With

1805. July.

my lieutenant I took a survey of the environs, and found that the whole shore was formed of lava. We passed a clift about thirty feet high, which extended in length to more than the eighth part of a mile, and was composed of the same volcanic matter mixed with clay. Its summits were crowned with tall pines. On returning to the tents, one of the sailors gave me some wild pease and strawberries he had gathered, which, though not ripe, were pleasant enough to the taste.

22d. The next morning a thick fog reigned on the mountains. I determined, however, to commence my journey, trusting that the weather would clear up as the day advanced. Relying upon what our guide said, that we should be able to return to our tents by night, we only provided ourselves with a little bread. The road was bad, and, as we proceeded, became worse and worse. The obstruction from ditches, and fallen trees of an immense size, and the prickly bushes through which we were continually obliged to force our way, so completely tired us, that in two hours we found it necessary to rest. We now discovered our mistake in taking so scanty a supply of provision. In addition to this misfortune, the fog, instead of clearing, increased, and our guides wandered out of the road. Regardless of these difficulties, I was determined to go on; and, while we rested, I sent back one of the Cadiack men for provision and warm jackets. Towards noon we were so exhausted, that we could not walk a step further; and we had no choice but to stop for the night on a small eminence near a brook of clear water. The weather in the mean time, as if taking compassion upon us, began to brighten; but it was only to show us, that for the attainment of the object of our enterprise, much time would be necessary.

Though in so weary a state, we set to work as well as we could, and towards evening had succeeded in constructing two huts, or rather bowers, of the branches of the cedar tree. Having made a blazing fire before each, we passed the time till midnight, bewailing our situation; having craving appetites, and nothing to eat; exposed to cold and mist, and no suitable clothing to defend us. The night proved so keen, that the thermometer fell to 40°. It was to very little purpose that I attempted to sleep; and I rose so early as two o'clock, and found my companions in difficulty, turning from side to side, in the torment of half sleep, which is worse than wakefulness. They had covered themselves with the bark of trees, to screen them at once both from cold, and from the heat of the fire, close to which they had crept. At day-light, the fog still prevailing, I fired my gun; and, to my great joy, the report was answered by a cry from the Cadiack man, and some of my people from the boats, who had accompanied him, bringing an ample supply of every thing we wanted. A favourable change soon after taking place in the weather, our joy was complete; and having made a hearty meal, we proceeded on our way. The road was steep, but less disagreeable than that in which we had travelled yesterday. At noon we cleared the woods, and, after reposing a while, ascended the top of the mountain by a path lying between deep cavities filled with snow. In some places it was narrow, and strewed with small volcanic fragments: the ascent, however, was regular and easy, so that we finished our task between one and two o'clock. The first object that struck us on reaching the summit, was a bason, about two miles in circumference, and forty fathoms deep; the surface covered with snow. From the information of our guides, I expected to have

1805.
July.

found it full of water; instead of which it was perfectly dry. I have no doubt, when our guides visited it, that the heavy rains of autumn had filled the bason, and given it the appearance of a lake. I have no doubt also, that at the bottom of this bason are cavities, through which the water flows, when the bason contains any, and thus forms the rivulets and ditches which so much incommoded us in our ascent. Having made the tour of the summit, I wrote our names on a piece of paper, and enclosed it in a bottle, which was buried under a heap of stones, as a memorial of our having visited this spot.

The views from this summit were the most beautiful in nature. Innumerable islands and straits, extending to the very entrance of Cross Sound, with the continent stretching itself far and wide towards the north, lay under our feet; while the mountains, on the other side of Sitca Sound, appeared as if reposing on clouds that hung motionless at their base. To add to the enchantment, the sun, after a shower of a few minutes, shone forth in all its lustre.

On this spot we spent three delightful hours, contemplating the great works of the Creator, as displayed in the scene; and towards evening returned to our new-built huts, where we passed the night in more comfort than before; the weather being warmer, and ourselves provided with food and clothing.

24th. Early the next morning we set off for our tents, where we arrived after a walk of about five hours.

The perpendicular height of Mount Edgecumbe I estimated at about eight thousand feet. The side towards the sea is steep, and was covered with snow; that towards the bay, smooth and of gradual ascent, and overgrown with woods to within a mile and half of the top. This upper space exhibits a few patches of verdure, but is in general covered with stones of different colours. To judge from the appearance of the top of this volcanic mountain, it may be concluded that it was formerly much higher, but, the eruptions having ceased, that time has crumbled to pieces the highest points, and filled up the abyss out of which the materials forming the exterior mountain were vomited. Many years must have elapsed since this volcano was in action, as several sorts of the ejected lava are turning to earth. The hardest lava is of a dark colour: it was originally a gray stone, but is now glass, having been vitrified by the volcanic heat. I have a piece in my collection, half of which is glass, and the other half, the gray stone in its natural state: this vitrified lava, when struck against steel, produces a spark. The gray lava is also firm and hard: the shore where we landed was composed of nothing else. The other sorts, for instance, the red, resembling brick, and the white, were light and brittle.

On the 25th, at two in the afternoon, we returned to the ship. We came just in time to see a party of Aleutians preparing for the hunt of the sea-otter. Three hundred bidarkas were ready to take them on board. The hunters were dressed in their best apparel; but their faces were so besmeared with paint of different colours, that they looked more like monsters than men. Having taken leave of Mr. Baranoff, they all set off together.

On the 28th, two small armed vessels were dispatched to join the party, with whom they were to remain, as a guard, till the

1805.
July.

hunting season was over. In the afternoon a Sitcan toyon, whose name was Kotlean, arrived at the fort. This man had always been a declared enemy to the Russian company, and was the principal agent in the destruction of their former settlement. He was accompanied by eleven of his countrymen. Previous to his landing, he sent a present to Mr. Baranoff, of a coverlet made of the skin of the silver-gray fox, with a request, that he might be received with the same honours as had been paid to his predecessor; to which Mr. Baranoff returned for answer, that as all his Aleutians were absent, no ceremony could be observed. He however sent some men to draw his boat on shore, and take him out of it on their shoulders. On the arrival of this self-important personage, I went with Mr. Baranoff to see him. In the course of the interview the governor spoke to him freely of the unprovoked injuries his family had done the Russians: upon which the toyon, with apparent sincerity, acknowledged himself to blame, and promised to be in future a faithful friend. Mr. Baranoff then gave him a blue cloak trimmed with ermine, and some tobacco. I also distributed this favourite plant amongst the party, and was presented in return with otter skins, roots called gingam, and cakes made of the rind of the larch-tree. On our taking leave, Kotlean expressed great mortification at the absence of the Aleutians, as he and his companions, he said, excelled all their countrymen in dancing. To display his skill in this accomplishment, I have no doubt, was one motive of this visit. A still stronger motive was ambition: the preceding toyon had boasted of our treatment of him; and this man could not rest till he had made an attempt to be received with the same honours.

This second party were painted and powdered in the same manner as the first, but were better clothed. Kotlean himself was dressed in a cuaca, or loose gown, resembling a little a smock-frock, but of blue cloth, over which was a great-coat of English baize. He had a black fox-skin cap on his head, the tail of the animal hanging over from the top of it. He was of a middling stature, and of an agreeable countenance, with a scanty beard, and a pair of whiskers. He is reckoned an excellent marksman, and has an armoury of no less than twenty of the best muskets. Notwithstanding the cold reception he met with, he staid at the fort till the 2d of August, dancing with his company nearly the whole of every day.

On the 7th of August I repaired with some of my sick people to the hot baths, where we remained till the 15th. The weather was beautiful; and we should have passed our time agreeably, but for the gnats and a small species of flies, with which the woods swarmed, and especially with the last, the head, body, and wings of which are black, and the legs white. They alight imperceptibly, and occasion a swelling where they bite. There is a still smaller sort of these flies, which always attack the part immediately under the eyes, and produce a blue swelling.

The hot baths proved serviceable to our invalids. The spring that supplies them, flows from a hill about three hundred yards from the shore, into a large bason dug purposely in the ground: the heat of the water at its head is a hundred and fifty-one degrees, and in the bason, on an average, about a hundred. It is chiefly impregnated with sulphur, but has a mixture of salt and magnesia. The Sitcan people often resort to these baths, and

1805.
August.

are benefited by them, especially such as are afflicted with scurvy and ulcers. The baths are situated on the east side of Sitca Sound, beyond what are called the South Islands, and are about twelve miles from the harbour of New Archangel.

16th.

On my return to the fort on the 16th, I found our old ambassador there. He had come to announce to us his elevation to the dignity of chief toyon of the Sitcan nation, in the place of Kotlean. This new dignity had so elated him with pride, that he made no use of his legs for walking, but was invariably carried on the shoulders of his attendants, even on the most trifling occasions. He had no objection however to dance, or distort himself, with any of his people. It would seem as if some superstition mixed itself with his fondness for this amusement; for the place in which he was most in the habit of enjoying it, while with us, was near a monument erected over the grave of a favourite brother. This was the only monument which had not been destroyed by us: it was preserved out of respect to the deceased, who had always been a friend to our countrymen. Mr. Baranoff considered the visit of this toyon as a great compliment; and, knowing him, like his deceased brother, to be attached to the Russians, he presented him with a Russian coat of arms made of brass, and gave him the privilege of wearing it on his breast. About noon this great personage was borne in state from the fort.

17th.

The Company's brig Elizabeth arrived in the harbour the following day, from the island of Oonalashca, and two ships from the United States, one of which, commanded by captain Wolff, came in for repairs. Whilst off Cape Horn she had struck, in the night, against another vessel in company with her; both at the time were under storm stay-sails, in consequence of a heavy gale of wind, and both were greatly damaged. The other ship that arrived was commanded by captain Trescot; whose object was to dispose of such articles as he had left of his cargo, and then to proceed to Canton.

The settlement of New Archangel will always be a place of resort for ships trading on the coast; as the Russian company are ready to purchase flour, brandy, woollen cloth, and every necessary, at a profit of at least fifty per cent to the trader; which is more than he would obtain at Canton, besides the chance of his being obliged to sell there at a loss.

On the 17th and 18th I took forty-five lunar distances; and, upon comparing them with thirty others, which I had taken on the 2d and 3d, I found the longitude of New Archangel, calculating by the mean rate of these distances, to be 135° 7′ 49″ west; from which it follows, that Cape Edgecumbe must be 135° 33′.

Though the weather for several days had been very bad, we had been so busily employed, that on the 22d the vessel was ready to sail with the first fair wind.

In the further prosecution of my voyage, I resolved not to go near the Sandwich Islands, but, on reaching the latitude of 45° 30′ and the longitude of 145°, to steer west, as far as 165° and 42° north. Thence I intended to proceed to 36° 30′, and to keep in that parallel till I arrived at 180° west, and then to take a direct course for the Ladrone or Marian Islands. By this plan, I should have

1805.
August.
an opportunity of examining the places where captain Portlock met with a seal in 1786, and where we ourselves saw an otter. Besides, as this course would lead the ship as far as the tropics, through a tract of sea never yet explored by any navigator, I might not unreasonably expect to make new discoveries. The idea of passing as far as 180° to the westward in the latitude of 36° 30' north, was suggested by the instructions of count Roomantzoff, which say, that formerly a large and rich island, inhabited by white people, was found in the latitude of 37° 30', and at the distance of about three hundred and forty Dutch miles from Japan, or between the longitude of 160° and 180°.

24th.
The weather was fine on the 24th, the thermometer stood at 72°; and, but for a fresh breeze of wind that prevailed, the mercury, I have no doubt, would have risen to eighty.

Since my arrival at Sitca, I had never neglected my chronometers, and I now finished the task of regulating them. No. 136 was losing 54" 3, No. 50, 5" 3, and No. 1841, 1' 11" per day.

Having made acquaintance with the commander of the brig Elizabeth, lieutenant Sookin, I embraced the opportunity of inquiring again about the new island that had appeared in the neighbourhood of Oonalashca. From what this gentleman told me, it is not so high as I had been led to believe. It has three summits, from which smoke is seen to issue. It is about five miles in circumference, and twenty-five distant from the island of Oonalashca. This account is more entitled to credit than what I received at Cadiack, as Mr. Sookin had passed near the island, and taken a drawing of it.

B&L

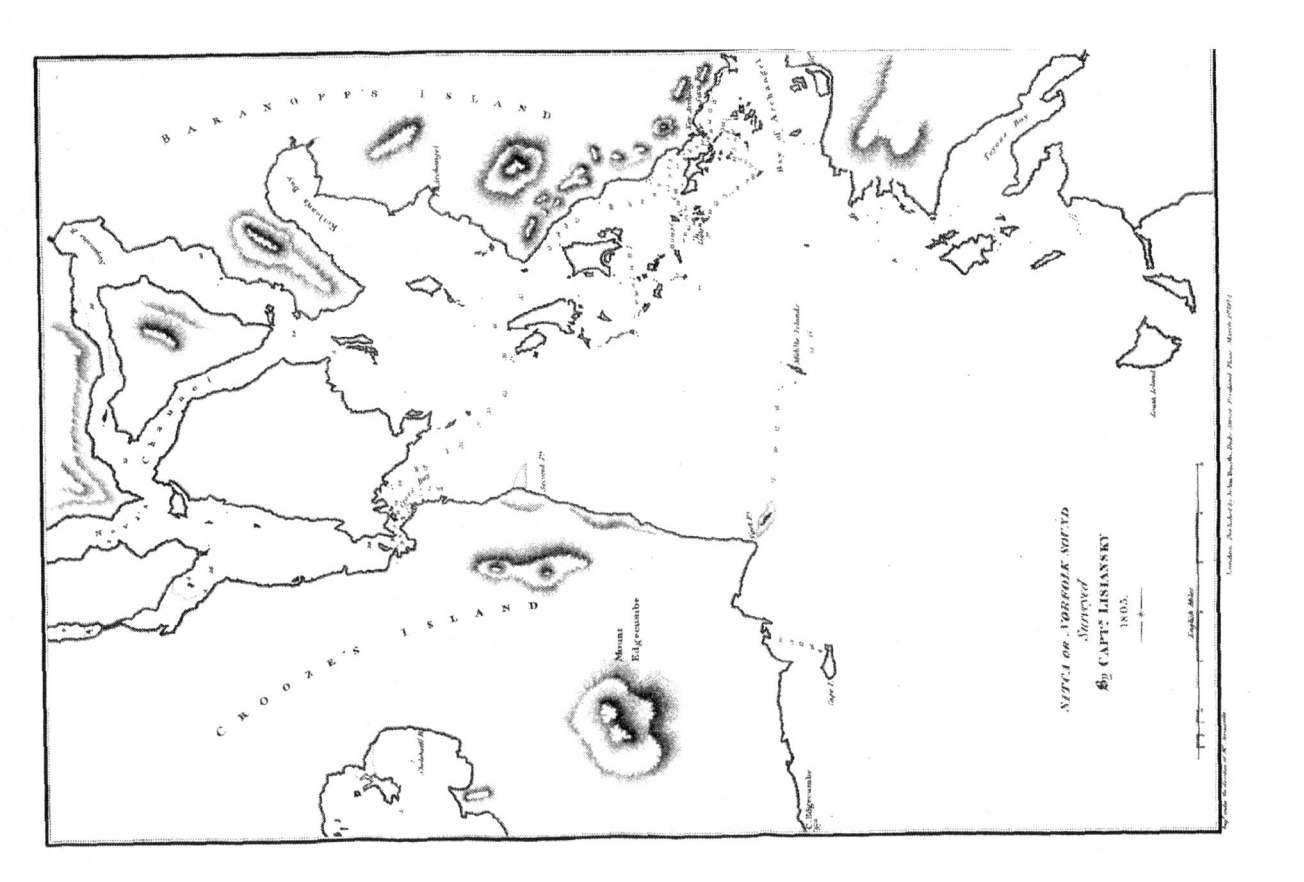

NITCA OR NORFOLK SOUND
Surveyed
by CAPT^n LISIANSKY
1805.

CHAPTER XII.

DESCRIPTION OF THE SITCA ISLANDS.

Reason of this Group of Islands being so denominated. Advantageous Situation of the new Russian Settlement. Productions of these Islands. Climate. People. Dress. Character. Food. Houses. Canoes. Custom of burning the dead. Arts. Tribes or Casts. Religion. Power of the Toyons. Custom respecting Females of cutting the Lip when they arrive at Womanhood.

THOUGH this part of the coast of America has been known to us since the period of captain Cheericoff's voyage, in the year 1741, we still were not sure whether it formed part of the continent or belonged to an island, till captain Vancouver's expedition, when Chatham's Strait was discovered, and other points of consequence ascertained, as may be seen in the narrative of that navigator. By our survey it appears, that amongst the group of islands, which in my chart I have denominated the Sitca Islands, from the inhabitants, who call themselves Sitca-hans, or Sitca people, are four principal ones, viz. Jacobi, Crooze, Baranoff, and Chichagoff. As the passage which separates the island of Jacobi from that of Chichagoff was not explored by us, I can only state, that a vessel belonging to the Company is said to have once passed through it, and to have found there a sufficient depth of water. The channel, to which I gave the name of Neva, and that called Pagoobnoy, or Pernicious, are both deep.

1805.
August.

1805.
August.

The first joins Sitca Sound, and the second Chatham's Strait. The Pernicious derives its name from a party of Aleutians having been poisoned there some years ago, by eating muscles.

Our first settlement here was formed in the year 1800 by Mr. Baranoff, with the consent of the natives, who afterwards, as I have already stated, treacherously destroyed it.

Our present settlement is more advantageously situated than the former one. It is surrounded by woods, that never felt the stroke of the axe, and is well supplied with fresh water. In my opinion it will soon become the chief establishment of the Russians. Besides other advantages, it is in the neighbourhood of the best places for hunting the sea-otter, of which eight thousand might be procured annually, if the ships of the United States did not interfere with the trade: at present, the yearly amount does not exceed three thousand. The woods will also yield a handsome revenue, when the Russian commerce with China shall be established.

The Sitca Islands are all, indeed, plentifully supplied with wood, consisting chiefly of pine, larch, and cedar, called by the Russians the smelling-tree. There are also fir, alder, and a few others to be found, but in no great quantity. The apple-tree deserves notice. Its leaves resemble those of the European apple-tree, but it bears a small fruit like the white cherry, and has the taste of a sourish apple. The islands abound in wild berries. Exclusive of the sorts found on the island of Cadiack, there are blackberries, strawberries, black currants, a particular kind of raspberry, and what is commonly called the red berry, which grows on large bushes, and has a very pleasant taste.

1805.
August.

The rivers, during the summer, are full of excellent fish. Herrings swarm in the Sound every spring; fine cod-fish also may be caught, and hallibut of great weight, with the hook and line only. There are few land animals; but a great quantity of almost every species of amphibious ones, such as the sea- and river-otter, the sea-lion, the sea-bear, and the common seal. The birds, too, are not so numerous as on the island of Cadiack: the few that we saw were nearly of the same species as in that island; one however excepted, which was a magpie of a blueish colour, with a tuft or crown on its head.

The climate of these islands is such as, in my opinion, would favour the cultivation of barley, oats, and all sorts of European fruit and vegetables. The summer is warm, and extends to the end of August; the winter differs from our autumn in this only, that there are frequent falls of snow. The population here is estimated at eight hundred males; the females amount probably to a greater number: of the males, about a hundred reside in the isle of Jacobi, and the rest on that of Chichagoff, in Chatham's Strait. They are of a middling stature, have a youthful appearance, and are active and clever. Their hair is lank, strong, and of a jet black; the face round, the lips thick, and the complexion dark, or copper-colour: some of them, and especially the women, if they did not daub themselves with different paints, which injure the skin, would be much fairer. Painting the face, and powdering the hair with eagle's down, are considered as the necessary appendages of beauty. The men cover their body with

1805.
August.

square pieces of woollen cloth, or buck-skin: some dress themselves in a kind of short pantaloon, and a garment resembling a shirt, but not so large. Their war habit is a buck-skin, doubled and fastened round the neck, or a woollen cuaca, to the upper part of which, in front, iron plates are attached, to defend the breast from a musket-ball. Formerly a sort of coat of arms was worn, made of thin pieces of wood nicely wrought together with the sinews of sea animals, as represented in Plate I. Fig. *a*. The cuacas are not made by the natives, but are furnished by traders from the United States in exchange for sea-otter skins. In the cold season they occasionally wear fur dresses; though woollen cloth is mostly in use. The rich wrap themselves up sometimes in white blankets, manufactured in the country, from the wool of the wild sheep, which is as soft and fine as the Spanish merino. These blankets are embroidered with square figures, and fringed with black and yellow tassels. Some of them are so curiously worked on one side with the fur of the sea-otter, that they appear as if lined with it, and are very handsome.

Though the Sitca people are brave, they are extremely cruel to their prisoners, whom they torture to death, or consign to hard labour for life. Their cruelty is chiefly exercised against Europeans. If a European is so unfortunate as to fall into their hands, he will, in general, receive no mercy. On these occasions, men, women, and children, fall upon the poor wretch at once. Some make gashes in his flesh, others pinch or burn him, others cut off an arm or a leg, and others again scalp the head. This last cruelty is also practised upon an enemy, when killed and left on the field of battle. It is performed by the shamans, who first cut the skin round the head, and then pull away the scalp by the hair. The head is then cut off and thrown away, or stuck up any where as a mark. They have fire-arms, as I have already stated, and small cannon, which they obtain from the traders of the United States. Their former instruments of war, such as spears and arrows, are almost wholly out of use.

The common food of these islanders consists, during the summer, of different sorts of berries, fresh fish, and the flesh of amphibious animals. During the winter they live on dried salmon, train oil, and the spawn of fish, especially that of herrings, of which they always lay in a good stock. On the first appearance of these fish in the spring, the people assemble on the coast, and are active in catching them. For taking the spawn, they use the branches of the pine-tree, to which it easily adheres, and on which it is afterwards dried. It is then put into baskets, or holes purposely dug in the ground, till wanted. To this list we may add a particular sort of sea weed, and cakes made of the rind of the larch-tree, which are about a foot square and an inch thick. They roast their meat on sticks, after the Cadiack manner; or boil it in iron, tin, and copper kettles, which they purchase of the Russian settlers, or of chance traders. The rich have European stone-ware, such as dishes, plates, basons, &c.: the poor, wooden basons only, of their own manufacturing, and large spoons, made either of wood, or of the horns of the wild sheep (Plate III. Fig. e and f).

The barabaras of the Sitcan people are of a square form, and spacious. The sides are of planks; and the roof resembles that of a Russian house, except that it has an opening all along the top, of the breadth of about two feet, to let out the smoke.

1805.
August.

They have no windows; and the doors are so small, that a person must stoop very low to enter. In the middle of the building is a large square hole, in which fire is made. In the houses of the wealthy, this fire-place is fenced round with boards; and the space between the fire-place and the walls partitioned by curtains for the different families of relations, who live together in the same house. Broad shelves are likewise fixed to the sides of the room, for domestic purposes.

The canoes of these people are made of a light wood, called *chaha*, which grows to the southward. A canoe is formed out of a single trunk, and is, in some instances, large enough to carry sixty men. I saw several that were forty-five feet long; but the common ones do not exceed thirty feet. When paddled, they go fast in smooth water. The largest are used for war, or for transporting whole families from place to place. The smallest serve for fishing, or other purposes that require but few hands. They are ingeniously constructed.

The manners and customs of the Sitca people, in general, so nearly resemble those of the island of Cadiack, that a description would be a repetition. The Sitcans appear, however, to be fonder of amusements; for they sing and dance continually. There is also a great difference in their treatment of the dead. The bodies here are burned, and the ashes, together with the bones that remain unconsumed, deposited in wooden boxes, which are placed on pillars, that have different figures painted and carved on them, according to the wealth of the deceased.

On taking possession of our new settlement, we destroyed a

hundred at least of these, and I examined many of the boxes. On the death of a toyon, or other distinguished person, one of his slaves is deprived of life, and burned with him. The same inhuman ceremony is observed when a person of consequence builds a new house; with this difference, that on this occasion the unfortunate victim is simply buried, without being burned. The bodies of those who lose their lives in war are also burned, except the head, which is preserved in a separate wooden box from that in which the ashes and bones are placed. This mode of destroying dead bodies originated, I was informed, in the ridiculous idea, that a piece of the flesh gave to the person who possessed it, the power of doing what mischief he pleased. The body of a shaman is interred only; from another absurd notion, that, being full of the evil spirit, it is not possible to consume it by fire.

But few arts are to be found amongst these people. They have, however, some skill both in sculpture and painting. On seeing their masks, their different domestic utensils, which are painted, and carved with various figures, and their boxes, the tops of which are curiously inlaid with a shell resembling human teeth, one might suppose these productions the work of a people greatly advanced in civilisation. The custom of painting the face every day, contributes, I have no doubt, to their skill in painting other things. Black, light green, and dark red, are the colours generally preferred. The use of the needle is said to be but little understood by the women. I have seen, however, some of their dresses that were neatly sewed, and extremely well made.

1805.
August.

The Sitca people are not so expert in hunting as the Aleutians. Their principal mode is that of shooting the sea animals as they lie asleep. As they cannot destroy many in this way, the sea-otter abounds in their neighbourhood. The Aleutians, on the contrary, from their skill, are sure to commit dreadful depredations wherever they go. As an example of this, along the coast, from the Bay of Kenay to Cross Sound, where the sea-otter was formerly very common, there is hardly a trace of this valuable animal to be found.

What I have said of the Sitcans, applies alike to all the inhabitants residing between Jacootat, or Behring's Bay, to the fifty-seventh degree of north latitude, who call themselves Colloshes or Collushes. These people live in different settlements, independent of one another; though they speak the same language, and are almost all related. They amount to about ten thousand, and are divided into tribes; the principal of which assume to themselves titles of distinction, from the names of the animals they prefer; as, the tribe of the bear, of the eagle, the crow, the porpoise, and the wolf. The tribe of the wolf are called Coquontans, and have many privileges over the other tribes. They are considered as the best warriors, and are said to be scarcely sensible to pain,* and to have no fear of death.

---

* We had an instance of the indifference to pain of this tribe, in a Coquontan lad, of the age of nine or ten years, who was one of our hostages. He was so addicted to theft, that nothing was safe from him. Having tried remonstrances in vain, we at length threatened him with the whip, when, deriding our threats, he bared his bosom to show the many lacerations that had been made in his flesh to harden his feeling: and when under the whip, he continued his derision, without once exhibiting the slightest appearance of suffering.

If in war a person of this tribe is taken prisoner, he is always treated well, and in general is set at liberty. These tribes so greatly intermix, that families of each are found in the same settlement. These families, however, always live apart; and, to distinguish the cast to which they belong, they place on the top of their houses, carved in wood or painted, the bird or beast that represents it. The different tribes seldom go to war with one another, and are always ready to make common cause, in case of an attack from any strange tribe.

The Colloshes believe there is a creator of all things in heaven, who, when angry, sends down diseases amongst them. They also believe in a wicked spirit, or devil, whom they suppose to be cruel, and to inflict them with evils through his shamans.

The right of succession is from uncle to nephew, the dignity of chief toyon excepted, which passes to him who is the most powerful, or has the greatest number of relations. Though the toyons have power over their subjects, it is a very limited power, unless when an individual of extraordinary abilities starts up, who is sure to rule despotically, and, as elsewhere, to do much mischief. These toyons are numerous: even in small settlements there are often four or five.

A strange custom prevails in this country respecting the female sex. When the event takes place that implies womanhood, they are obliged to submit to have the lower lip cut, and to have a piece of wood, scooped out like a spoon, fixed in the incision. As the young woman grows up the incision is gradually enlarged, by larger pieces of wood being put into it, so that the lip at last projects at least four inches, and extends from side to side to six inches. Though this disfiguring of the face rendered, to our eyes, the handsomest woman frightful, it is considered here as a mark of the highest dignity, and held in such esteem, that the women of consequence strive to bring their lips to as large a size as possible. The piece of wood is so inconveniently placed, that the wearer can neither eat nor drink without extreme difficulty, and she is obliged to be constantly on the watch, lest it should fall out, which would cover her with confusion.

CHAPTER XIII.

PASSAGE FROM SITCA SOUND TO CANTON.

State of the Weather on leaving Sitca. Number of Sick from Fatigue. Precautions for future Health. Ill Effect from the Use of Bread. Curious Shells. Clouds mistaken for Land. New Disappointments as to the Discovery of Land. Danger of the Ship from grounding on a coral Bank. Discover a new Island. Particulars relating to it. Discover a new Bank. Limit the Crew in their Allowance of Bread. Advice respecting the westerly Winds in the Southern Ocean. Make the Islands of Saypan and Tinian. Encounter a Hurricane. Putrid State of the Ship's Cargo. Loss sustained by it. Enter the Chinese Seas. Arrive at Macao, and meet Captain Krusenstern. Pirates. Macao described. Proceed to Whampoa to dispose of the Neva's Cargo. Chinese Customs relative to Commerce. Repair of the Neva. The Nadejda and Neva detained by Order of the Chinese Government. Services rendered by Mr. Drummond in this Business. The Ships released.

We sailed out of the harbour of New Archangel, on the 1st of September. At four o'clock in the afternoon we had a light northerly breeze, which however died away, and a thick fog coming on in the night, we dropped anchor when we had passed the Middle Islands, in forty fathoms of water. At six the next morning we again weighed, having a similar breeze from the north; but this also being shortly succeeded by a dead calm, we were obliged to employ all the boats in towing a-head till midnight, when, getting a fresh wind from the north-west, we proceeded in a south-westerly course. I had before taken leave of Mr. Baranoff; but, during the detention of the vessel, he kindly

1805.
Sept.
1st.

1805.
Sept.

5th.

made me another visit. I shall enter into no laboured panegyric of this gentleman, greatly as I admire his character:—but I must observe, in justice to his talents and patriotism, that the Russian company could not have selected a person better qualified for the superintendence of their affairs.

In the morning of the 5th, the wind shifted to the south-west, but soon returned to its former point. At noon we reached the latitude of 52° 33′ north, and the longitude of 139° west. When we quitted the port of New Archangel, we had ten men on the sick list, whereas there were now only two who could not perform duty. So great a number of invalids was occasioned, I have no doubt, by the badness of the weather, and the hard labour my crew had been obliged to perform during the last week, and especially while working the vessel out of the sound, which occupied more than twenty-four hours, during which no one on board had taken the slightest rest.

As my people were now habituated to different climates, I was persuaded their health would be good to the end of the voyage; yet, resolving to be on the right side, I laid in, while at New Archangel, a large stock of sorrel, two casks of which were prepared in the manner of sour crout, as well as an ample supply both of the juice of the hurtle-berry, and of the berry itself, which being put into small casks, and the casks filled with water, will keep a long time. There had hitherto been no appearance of scurvy on board, and with these antiscorbutics I had little fear of the disease. Considering, however, the length of the run to Canton, I put the distribution of the provisions for my crew, under a sort of preventive regulation; and I ordered for their dinner, five days in the week, soup made of salt beef and sorrel, with a requisite allowance of vinegar and mustard, and on the other two days portable and pea-soup mixed; and with their breakfast, on Sunday and Monday, a pint of beer made of essence of malt or of spruce, on Wednesday tea, and on Thursday the hurtleberry or its juice.

While at Cadiack, I added to my ship's company two men of that island, and four boys, the offspring of Aleutian mothers by Russian fathers: the first I wanted for managing the bidarka, and the boys I meant to bring up as sailors. For a day or two past the two Cadiack men had complained of a pain in their bowels. Believing this to proceed from the use of bread, to which they were not accustomed, I requested that in future a smaller portion of it might be given them. I understand, that the Russians themselves suffer greatly from this complaint, when, after having lived long upon fish, they return suddenly to bread, though accustomed to the use of it from their infancy.

On reaching the latitude of 48° 17' north, and the longitude of 139° 29' west, which was on the 8th, we saw a great number of sea-bears, and I immediately ordered the cleverest of my people aloft to look out: nothing however was seen, though the weather was fine, and they were on the watch till night.

The sea-bears made their appearance again the next day, though not in so great a number. Judging that we could not be far from their place of concealment, for this species of seal is said never to venture out to sea to any distance, I resolved to discover it if possible; but, towards noon, the wind shifting to

1805. Sept.

the westward, blew so hard, that I was obliged to relinquish my enterprise, and bear southerly.

14th.

On the 14th, when we were in 44° 24' north, and 147° 32' west, we found the whole surface of the sea covered with small triangular shells, not unlike a muscle, but less strong, that were stuck together in bunches, and looked like flowers swimming on the water. Our Cadiack men told me, that these shells were the chief food of the sea-otters, and that they grew on the branches of inundated trees. Be this as it may, I am firmly persuaded, that during the whole period of time from the 8th instant we were not far from some unknown land.

16th.

On the 16th we had a light breeze from the north-west, and fine weather. At sun-rise a number of small birds were seen flying about the ship. They were white, with patches of black on the back and wings. We had seen several of them the day before, but at a very great distance. At seven in the morning, a man from the fore-top-gallant-mast-head, called out that he saw land to the southward. I immediately sent my ship's master aloft to examine, and he also thought there was land a-head; but a fog coming on, prevented him from ascertaining it. For my part, knowing that we were near the place where captain Portlock caught a sea-calf, I could not help flattering myself that I should make some discovery, and I therefore shaped my course south-south-west till sun-set, when, as the day disappeared, my hopes vanished with it. In reality, we had been in pursuit of clouds only, which, from their singular appearance at the horizon, had been mistaken for land. The latitude, by observation at noon, was 44° 12' north, and the longitude 151° 4' west.

In the evening of the 27th we reached the proposed longitude of 165°; and the next day, as no sign of land appeared, where we had most reason to expect it, from having seen an otter in our former passage, I took a more southerly course, deeming it useless to proceed further westward.

In the morning of the 2d of October, the north-west wind, which had prevailed for forty-eight hours, died away, and the weather, which had hitherto been pleasant and refreshing, became rather sultry. At four in the afternoon we had lunar observations, by which the longitude was found to be 166° 6' west. The ship being now in the latitude of 36° 30', I steered westerly again, and purposed to continue in that course till we reached the longitude of 180°.

On the 4th at noon, we observed in latitude 36° 25' north, and longitude 167° 45' west: shortly after a gale of wind sprung up from the west, and obliged us to bear southward. Knowing from experience, that the westerly winds, when they once set in, continue for a long time, I gave up the idea of reaching the longitude of 180° west, and steered for the Ladrone, or Marianne Islands; in doing which, I took a different track from that of former navigators. In my preceding track, so far from discovering any thing like land, I can safely affirm, that between the latitudes of 42° and 36° 25', and the longitudes of 165° and 168°, we did not see a bird or animal of any kind, though the weather was fine the whole time.

We had now light airs and calms, which, from the prospect of their continuance, almost disheartened us. From the 6th to

1805.
October.

the 9th, the ship had scarcely moved from her station; and the heat was so powerful, that the boats, as well as our mizen-mast and bowsprit, were terribly cracked by it. I was obliged to caulk the first, and secure the last with wooldings.

8th.

On the 8th, we saw a curious sort of fish. It was thick, and about six inches in length; the singularity consisted in the fins, which were nearly as long as the body. In the course of this day we also saw some tropic birds, and a great number of flying-fish; which we considered as proofs of our having quitted the dismal climate where westerly winds and foggy weather are so annoying.

15th.

The light airs continued till the 15th, when they were succeeded by a moderate breeze, but still from the westward. At ten I took some lunar distances, and found the longitude at noon to be 173° 23′ west, and the latitude 26° 43′ north.

Though we had been for some time past visited by various birds and fish, we had never witnessed so great a number as on this day. The ship was surrounded by porpoises, benitas, pilot-fish, tropic birds, frigates, and ganets. One of the ganets alighted on our jib-boom, and was so tame that a sailor by climbing up had nearly caught it. From seeing so immense a quantity of birds and fish, my attention was roused, especially as Mr. de la Perouse had also observed near this place many signs which he thought would lead to a discovery of land. I accordingly desired my people to be on the watch, and remained on deck myself the whole of the day. We however perceived nothing; but at ten o'clock in the evening our courage was put to a most severe trial. I had given to the lieutenant of the watch my orders for the night, and was retiring to my cabin, when the vessel received a violent shock. I instantly put the helm a-lee and tacked, but it was to no purpose; before the ship came round to the wind, she grounded. All hands were summoned upon deck and set to work; and upon sounding, we found that we had touched on a coral bank. I now ordered the guns and the heaviest articles that had been stowed on the booms, to be thrown overboard; but with such precaution, that they might be recovered, should circumstances admit. The ship being thus lightened, we succeeded by day-light in getting her into deep water; when we perceived, at the distance of about a mile, a small low island to the west-north-west, and to south by west some high rocks that were beaten upon by a most tremendous surf, though the sea around was as smooth as glass. Notwithstanding our perilous situation, this sight greatly pleased us, and the crew all exerted themselves with alacrity. We were hardly however afloat, waiting for the ship's master, who had gone in a boat to sound, when a sudden squall came on, and drove us again on a more dangerous bank than the former one. The sea heaved greatly, and the ship struck continually against the ground with violence. This obliged me to throw overboard cables, anchors, and every heavy article however necessary. I had even determined to cut away the masts, should we be so unfortunate as not to get into deep water before night. This, however, with excessive labour, was effected. Though the ship was still in a critical situation, it was absolutely necessary to give rest to my people; and providentially a perfect calm reigned during the time, or we must all have perished.

1805.
October.
17th.

At day-light, the weather being fine, we again warped forwards; and shortly after I dispatched half of my crew in search of the different articles we had thrown into the sea; and to my great satisfaction, by five in the afternoon, every thing was recovered. While engaged in the search, they found a piece of the false keel of the vessel, which had been broken off by her striking; and as she struck repeatedly, but little of this keel could be left: yet, for the last twenty-four hours, the water in her hold had not exceeded twelve inches.

At seven in the evening, having reached a depth of eight fathoms, we cast anchor. When the depth of water, which, during the period of our difficulty, had been from three to six fathoms, is considered, it might be supposed, that we could have warped off much sooner; but it must be remembered, that the coral bottom, by continually cutting our cables, stopped the progress of our work: and that we had another obstruction, in the excessive heat of the weather. As I felt myself indisposed from fatigue, I did not, as had been my intention, go on shore this evening, but sent some of my officers, who, after an absence of two hours, returned, bringing with them four large seals, which they had killed on the beach with handspikes.

18th. On the 18th, the wind continuing perfectly calm, and the weather fine, we again warped with all possible expedition further northward. Desirous of examining the place, which, by its situation, appeared to be of great importance to navigation, I went on shore in the morning with several of my officers, leaving orders on board for the ship to go out to sea, should a fair wind spring up; and, after clearing every danger, to wait for us. The surf was so great, that we could with difficulty land at a small bay, where we found numerous birds of different kinds, and seals of an enormous size. On landing, we were much annoyed by the birds, many of which made their attack flying, while others ran after us, pecking at our legs: it was with difficulty we could keep them off, even with our canes. The seals lay on their backs along the beach, motionless. Some measured in length more than seven feet: they scarcely stirred at our approach, or even deigned to open their eyes. Though, at another time, the sight of these animals would have been extremely gratifying; yet, as we had objects in view of more importance, we passed on without molesting them. The heat of the day was excessive, and, almost at every step, we sunk up to our knees in holes, that were concealed by overgrown creeping plants, and contained the nests, as we supposed, of various birds; for we often heard their cries under our feet from being trampled upon. Towards evening, having examined every thing worthy of notice, we fixed a high pole in the ground, and buried near it a bottle, containing a description of our discovery of this island. We then returned on board, with no very pleasurable feelings, as we had the conviction from our search, that, should we be so unfortunate as to be unable to get clear of this island, we had nothing to do but resign ourselves quietly to the death that awaited us, since not a drop of fresh water was to be found. It is true, there was plenty of fish, birds, turtles, and seals, which would amply have satisfied our hunger; but with what were we to have quenched our thirst?—If our excursion to the new island was not pleasant, it was at least lucrative as to shells, coral, petrified

1805.
October.

sponges, and other curiosities, of which we brought away a great quantity.

This island promises nothing to the adventurous voyager but certain danger in the first instance, and almost unavoidable destruction in the event. It stands in the middle of a very perilous coral bank, and, exclusive of a small eminence on the eastern part, lies almost on a level with the sea. Its soil consists of coral sand, that is overgrown with creeping plants and grass, in the manner I have described. Amongst the birds we saw, the most worthy of notice was a species of wild pigeon; at least it resembled that bird, both in size and in colour: when flying in the night, it made a loud and disagreeable noise.

As there is no water, so neither are any trees to be seen on this island. We found, however, several large trunks of trees on the beach, which, no doubt, had been thrown up by the sea. The largest of these trunks, at the root end, measured twenty-one feet in circumference. They were like the red-wood tree, that grows on the banks of the river Columbia in America. I am at a loss what conclusion to draw from the appearance of these trunks of trees in so remote a place. If they could not have been drifted by the sea from America, on account of the great distance, it follows that they must have come from some nearer place. On the Sandwich Islands trees of this kind do not grow; and Japan, like America, is very remote. It is not therefore improbable, that, on the same line on which lie the Sandwich Islands, Necker Island, and the island now found, there are lands more to the north-west, which will owe their discovery to some future navigator: perhaps likewise on the same line lies the island, said by some writers to have been formerly discovered by the Spaniards in the latitude of 35° 30′ north, and the longitude of 170° east.

I also found on the beach a small callabash, which had a round hole cut on one side of it. This could not have been drifted from a great distance, as it was fresh and in good preservation. I cannot help regarding it as a great misfortune that the ship grounded, as I should otherwise certainly not have quitted the environs of this island till I had explored them thoroughly; but in her present damaged state, though the hope of discovery was dear to my heart, I dared not attempt it.

I shall insert here a plan of the island, that by comparing it with the description I have given of our situation, the reader may judge how great was our peril, and how miraculous our escape. When I reflect, that the ship might have grounded in many a worse place on this bank, and that the smallest breeze, especially from the north-east, would have been sufficient to dash her to pieces, I cannot help feeling grateful to Providence, persuaded that, without his aid, like Mr. de la Perouse and his companions, not one of us would ever again have beheld his native land: for even if we had escaped from a watery grave, it would only have been, as the island affords neither water nor wood, to have suffered a worse death by famine. To my ship's company I owe, on this trying occasion, a tribute of thanks, as well as a tribute of commendation: both officers and men were so incessantly employed, that they had hardly more than six hours' rest during the whole time we remained at the island; and

1805.
October.

so far were they from murmuring at this, that a cheerfulness, an alacrity, and a courage, were displayed by them, that have seldom been surpassed. To the south-east point of the bank where the vessel grounded, I gave the name of Neva; while the island itself, in compliance with the unanimous wishes of my ship's company, received the appellation of Lisiansky.

19th.

On the 19th a light breeze from the north-west happily for us sprung up, and allowed us to set sail about nine o'clock in the morning. At noon we observed in 26° 10′ north latitude. We were now at the distance only of about ten miles, yet could see the island but indistinctly, even from the mast-head. I here brought to, to hoist in our boats, and, sounding with a hundred fathom line, could find no ground, though but half an hour before, the depth was only twenty-five fathoms. From our last place of anchorage to the distance of a mile, we had nine and ten fathoms; when it increased to fifteen, twenty, and so on, gradually, till we were out of soundings. The bottom every where was full of corals, which in shallow water were seen nearly as large as common-sized trees.

20th.

The northerly wind, which had favoured us during the whole of yesterday, shifted the next morning to the north-east. During the night we had steered eastward, and we now shaped our course to the south-west. At noon, our latitude was 25° 23′ north, and the longitude 172° 58′ west. Having brought the ship to some order, and, as to myself, regained in some degree my strength, I applied to the calculation of the various observations I had taken since the 17th. By three meridian altitudes, the middle point of the island of Lisiansky appeared to be in

LISIANSKY'S ISLE
1805.

View of Lisiansky Island

Neva's Shoal

English Miles

Under the direction of Mr Arrowsmith

Surveyed by Captain Lisiansky

London: Published by John Booth, Duke Street, Portland Place, March 1st 1814.

the latitude of 26° 2' 48" north, and by fourteen lunar distances, including the observations of the 15th, in the longitude of 173° 35' 45" west.*

In the afternoon we saw at a distance two large flights of black birds; I therefore gave directions to carry only top-sails on the cap during the night. This precaution was also necessary on account of my people, who were greatly in want of rest. From this day, I resolved so to steer, as to reach the longitude of 180° west, when in the latitude of 17° north, in order to pass in the middle track of the two points given to captain Wake's Bank by Mr. Arrowsmith in his two Charts.

In the morning of the 23d we had a westerly wind, with rain. On the weather clearing up at noon, we found ourselves in the latitude of 22° 15' north, and the longitude of 175° 32' west. At the close of our observations, from the wind shifting to the southward, we steered westward; but had scarcely pursued that course one hour, when breakers were observed from the foretop, right a-head. I could myself see from the forecastle a great rippling before the ship, and I tacked instantly. Lieutenant Powalishin and the ship's master went aloft, and confirmed the report, that a little beyond the rippling were high breakers. At this time the clouds began to move with rapidity, and the wind was in a very unsettled state; expecting, therefore, bad wea-

---

* By the assistance of thirty-four other lunar distances, which I had afterwards opportunities of taking, I was enabled to calculate the situation of the middle of the island more accurately, and I found its true longitude to be 173° 42' 30". I have accordingly so placed it in my chart.

1805.
October.
ther, I thought it adviseable to retire to a distance from this station, and wait for a favourable opportunity, to take a survey of its environs. At three the weather became squally, and the fog was so thick, that we were obliged to sail sixteen miles to the southward, where we brought-to for the night.

From the account of the officers who were aloft, and from what I perceived myself from the deck, the new-discovered bank stretched north and south, about two miles. The surf, that was observed in one place only, was occasioned, it is natural to suppose, by a large rock, situated, by our reckoning, in the latitude of 22° 15' north, and the longitude of 175° 37' west. To this rock I gave the name of Krusenstern.

24th. On the 24th we were still unable to approach the bank, from the weather continuing thick and unsettled; and seeing no prospect of a change, I proceeded on my voyage. At eight in the morning a land bird was seen fluttering in the air, blown off, no doubt, by the squalls of yesterday, from some unknown land in the neighbourhood. At noon, by observation, we were in latitude 21° 56' north, and longitude 175° 21' west. Towards evening I again brought-to for the night; and I was determined regularly to pursue this plan till we should arrive in a track of the sea better known to us. By this precaution, nothing worthy of observation would escape us; and we should be as much on our guard as was practicable against unforeseen accidents, with which we were by no means in a condition to cope.

31st. Though the light and variable breezes continued nearly a whole week, we reached, on the 31st, the latitude of 18° 34', and the longitude of 178° 56'. I now deemed it prudent to diminish the daily allowance of biscuits by a quarter of a pound per man, fearing, as we had only a sufficient stock left for thirty days, that this indispensable article might fail us before we arrived at Canton; and I am happy to state, that the ship's company not only received this regulation without the least sign of dissatisfaction, but declared themselves willing to submit to any deprivations that should be found necessary.

1805.
October.

On the 2d of November, having a pretty fresh breeze from the northward, I ordered all sails to be set, and at noon arrived into the latitude of 16° 31' north, and the longitude of 180° 32' west. We had this day to congratulate ourselves upon having finished half of our circumnavigation, reckoning from the meridian of Greenwich, without the loss of a single man by illness. My people bore the hot climate as well as if they had been inured to it from their infancy; it seemed indeed to agree with them better than the cold climates. The practice, to which they had been habituated from early life, of using hot baths in their own country, was probably of advantage to them in this respect.

Nov. 2d.

In the afternoon the wind shifted to the north-east. It appears that the trade-winds, here, do not extend so far beyond the line, as in the Atlantic Ocean, or Indian Seas. Since the 25th ult. the weather had been calm, except now and then a light breeze, which sprang up always from the north, and shifted first to east, then to the south, and at last to the west, where it generally died away. We found the north-west swell very prevalent, which must have been occasioned by the winds from that quarter,

1805.
Nov.

which are very common in the high latitudes of this immense sea. We often had to encounter them in our way to America, while, on our return from thence, they prevailed still more constantly, for we had an easterly wind only twice during the whole time. It is to be lamented, that the sea between the Sandwich Islands and Japan is so little known, as it would be adviseable for ships bound to Camchatka to make the whole of their longitude when in 14° or 15° north latitude, and then steer directly north; as, by so doing, they would in a great measure avoid the inconvenience of the westerly winds, which might detain them in their course. It was for this reason, that, on my run to Cadiack, I resolved so to steer from the Sandwich Islands, as to reach the longitude of 165° west, in a low latitude, when I took a direct course for the place of our destination, where we arrived in about three weeks, notwithstanding the prevalence of winds from the west.

4th.
Having reached on the 4th the latitude of 13° 30' north, we considered the most dangerous part of our voyage from Sitca Sound to be surmounted. We had sailed through a sea as yet unexplored, and had probably passed near many a sunken rock, which, had we deviated ever so little from the course in which we fortunately steered, might have been our destruction, and especially higher towards the north. It struck me as singular, that from the time of our quitting the new-found island, no fish, except a grampus which once showed itself, had appeared till yesterday, when we saw some flying-fish. Birds, however, were seen every day.

From the latitude of 15°, we had so brisk a trade-wind from

the north-east, that on the 14th we were in 14° 29′ north, and 209° 14′ west. We could depend on the correctness of our longitude, as the result of our lunar observations had for the last four days scarcely differed from the chronometers. The flying-fish were less numerous here, than we had found them further to the north; but they were of a larger size. One which leaped upon deck measured fifteen inches and a half in length, and seven inches round; the length of the fore wings was eight inches, and that of the lower ones three inches.

On the 15th we had fresh breezes and fine weather. At noon we found ourselves in the latitude of 14° 48′ north, and in the longitude of 213° 4′ west. And at five o'clock in the evening we saw the islands of Saypan and Tinian; the former to the north-west by west, and the latter to the westward. As the sun was near the horizon, and I expected, from every appearance of the sky, that we should have a bad night, I steered north-west till half after six o'clock, and then plied to windward under an easy sail till day-light.

The weather, which had been squally and troublesome in the night, improved towards morning. At seven o'clock, observing the south-east point of Tinian Island, I made towards it, and entered between the islands of Aguian and Tinian about ten. At eleven we had passed both of these islands, and we then steered west by north. Nothing could be more safe and pleasant than this passage. I think there must be sufficient depth of water to the very shores of Tinian, for we saw no signs to the contrary, and the sea broke only on the north side of it, where it is craggy. The south-east point of this island is very

1805.
Nov.

steep; but the shore there on both sides rises gently, and is covered with trees. It is to be regretted that this island has not a good harbour, as it would in that case be of great service to ships navigating these seas. On the west side of the island we saw the anchorage of lord Anson, which appeared to be only safe from the easterly winds. By fifty-two lunar distances taken from the 11th instant, the longitude of the south-east end of the island of Tinian was estimated to be 213° 40′ 20″ west, and its latitude, by observation to-day, 14° 56′ 52″ north. The latitude of the island of Aguian was 14° 50′ 32″. I this day altered the rate of my chronometers. No. 136 was now losing 48″ 5; No. 50, 6″ 7; and Pennington's, 1′ 1″ 7, in twenty-four hours. At two o'clock we were out of sight of the Ladrones. The island of Saypan appeared to me to be the highest of the group. It may be seen in clear weather at the distance of thirty-five miles, which is ten farther than the island of Tinian can be seen. The first has the appearance of a sugar-loaf; the other is flat at the top. On taking a direct course for Canton, I could not restrain my joy at the idea that we were about to visit once more a civilised people, and should probably, in a short time, join the companions of the early part of our voyage, from whom we had been so long separated. From Sitca to the Ladrone Islands we had currents from the north-east and south-west. The last, which was the strongest, carried us a hundred and forty miles to the southward, and two hundred to the westward. Its force was very great near the tropic, but on our approaching the Marianne Islands it shifted to the west.

20th.
On our losing sight of land, the wind freshened; and at last, on the 20th, blew so hard that I was obliged to bear storm

stay-sails only. This, however, was but the prelude of what was to come.

1805.
Nov.

In the morning of the 22d the mercury in the barometer fell below all the divisions, and disappeared from the scale; and the storm, that had continued already for upwards of twenty-four hours, increased to a perfect hurricane, or typhoon, as it is called in these seas, which tore to pieces our mizen, the only sail we had set, and laid the ship so much on her side, that her hatchways were partly under water. About noon we saw our jolly-boat, which was hung over the ship's stern, washed away, and soon after our gangways and many other things shared the same fate. Meanwhile the water rushed into the hold through the seams of the lee-side, from which all the oakum was forced by the pressure of the sea, so rapidly, that it gained on all our pumps; and we should unavoidably have gone to the bottom, if this terrible storm had not abated, which it fortunately did towards evening; for the crew, who were all the time standing up to their knees in water, were so exhausted that they could pump no longer. Thus did Providence, seemingly for a second time, when we were in a perilous situation, interpose to rescue us from destruction. As the tempest diminished, the leak in the vessel diminished also, because, no longer kept down on her side by violence, she naturally righted herself.

22d.

During the night we had still a heavy gale to contend with; but with the dawn of the morning, the weather improved so much, that we were able to overhaul our rigging, some of which was greatly strained and chafed, and the whole rendered as

23d.

1805.
Nov.

white as if it had never been tarred. Having finished this task, our attention was next called to cleaning the ship, and drying such things as had become wet during the storm. Though every article was removed from below, and every place in the vessel fumigated with vitriol, so obnoxious a smell came from between decks, that I had no doubt of the furs in the hold being in a state of putrefaction.

24th.

Accordingly, as soon as my people arose from sleep on the 24th, I ordered the hold to be examined, and to my great mortification, my conjecture was verified. On taking off the main hatchway, a thick blue vapour, of so offensive a smell, issued out, that for some time nobody could stand near it.

A most unpleasant business now lay before us; for it was necessary that every fur should be examined, and that without delay. As soon therefore as the first noisome evaporation was over, we began to unload the larboard side; and in the mean time, to render the air as pure as possible, chafing-dishes with burning coals were hung in different parts of the ship, and a fumigator with vitriol was suspended over the place where the men were to work. The uppermost furs were in good condition; but the farther we went down the worse they were found; and when we came to the lower packages, they were so completely putrified, that we were obliged, from their rottenness, to hoist them up in bags and nets made of old ropes for the purpose. To render these putrescent labours less injurious, I divided the crew into three parties, who relieved each other alternately; for it was impossible for the same persons to continue long in the hold without feeling the most acute pain both in the head and eyes; and, as a further precaution, I prepared for them a beverage of water acidulated with vitriol, which I have no doubt had a good effect, for none of them suffered eventually in their health. About noon the wind shifted to the northward; but as our larboard side was nearly unloaded, I was obliged to lie-to on the same tack till sun-set, when I steered west-northwest. The smell from the hold was so strong in the fore part of the ship, that at night I was obliged to remove the crew from their births into the ward-room, while the officers took their rest in the cabin.

The next day at sun-rise my people resumed their task. From the burning coals and the fumigation having been kept up in the hold during the whole night, the air, however, was now so much purified, that they could work below for an hour at a time; whereas the day before, especially when the lowermost packages were hoisted up, they were unable to stay there longer than a few minutes. Towards evening the wind blew so strong from the north-east, that we were obliged to desist from our labours.

It was extremely fortunate that the wind moderated in the morning, as we should otherwise have been obliged to bear either for the island of Luconia, or the Philippines; because, being unloaded, the ship was wholly unable to withstand a gale. At noon, on taking an observation, I found myself in the latitude of 18° 48' north, and in the longitude of 231° 39' west. Towards night we finished unstowing the larboard side of the hold; when we found that, out of the cargo which it contained, we were obliged to throw overboard thirty thousand

1805.
Nov.

sea-bear skins, besides a great quantity of other valuable furs; a loss which I estimated altogether at forty thousand Spanish dollars.

27th. On the 27th we were annoyed again by the weather, which not only interrupted our work, but obliged us to close all the hatchways. In this unpleasant situation, however, I kept up my spirits with the hope, that the cargo of the starboard side would be found in better condition, and require less overhauling.

28th. The next day we had still fresh breezes from the north-east, and squally weather. At seven in the morning, the four small isles which lie to the northward of Bashee Island being in sight, we stood to the north-west. At noon, being in the latitude of 21° 25′ north, and the nearest isles bearing north 12° west, about thirty miles, we steered west. At two in the afternoon we lost sight of the four isles altogether. Towards night, as the weather continued unsettled and squally, I resolved to run only sixty miles to the westward from our observation at noon, and then to take a course to the west-north-west. This day, notwithstanding the unfavourable state of the weather, may be reckoned amongst the most fortunate of our voyage; since, exclusive of our entering into the Chinese seas, we completed our stowage, and brought the ship into a condition again to withstand any casual accident to which vessels are liable in these seas. From the Ladrone or Marianne Islands the current hitherto had tended to west-south-west, and carried the ship sixty-seven miles to the southward, and about five degrees to the westward.

The day following we cleaned the ship thoroughly, which we could not have done before, though she was uncommonly dirty every where. At noon we had an observation in 21° 42′ north, and in 240° 21′ west. At four in the afternoon we had passed about two miles from the place where a large rock is laid down in the East India Atlas, but we saw nothing of it. At midnight we came into soundings, as was expected, in fifty fathoms, fine white sand. Concluding from this, that we were not far from the island of Migrice, I kept off half a point: finding, however, at four in the morning the same depth, I steered as before to west-south-west. At day-light a Chinese boat was seen. It appeared about sixty feet long, with a high narrow stern, and a sail made of mats. At that time the weather was fine, and the ship was going west by north. In this course we kept till one in the afternoon, when, seeing the island of Pedro Branco about twelve miles to the northward, we shaped towards the Great Lema.

1805.
Nov.
29th.

30th.

The isle of Pedro Branco is situated, by our chronometers, in 244° of west longitude, and in latitude, by observation, 22° 24′ north. It is high, and, having a large rock to the westward, resembles at a distance a ship with all her sails set.

Though we had passed at least thirty Chinese coasters since the morning, I hailed none of them; as I had resolved not to take a pilot on board till we came near the Great Lema, expecting to obtain one there of superior skill. Being sufficiently near about four o'clock, I ordered a signal to be made; and, as the ship was surrounded by boats, I had no doubt that one or other of them would soon board us: I was,

1805.
Nov.

however, mistaken; for, though we fired many signals, they took not the slightest notice of us. As I could not procure a pilot, I determined to ply to windward till morning, and then to run close in shore.

During the night, we were driven by the currents to the southward of the Great Lema, and I was obliged still to ply to windward, to endeavour to enter the passage on the north side; but finding the swell too great for the ship to tack well, I changed my resolution, and made for the main channel. I had this day (the 1st of December) fourteen men on the sick list. As they all complained alike of extreme weakness, I attributed it to the same cause, the fatigue they had lately undergone; and had therefore little anxiety upon the subject, persuaded that rest was all that was necessary to their recovery.

Dec. 1st.

Towards noon we passed the rocks lying to the westward of the Lema group, and took our course to the Ladrones. Though I had been so near as within two miles of the Lema islands, no soundings could be found with a line of twenty-five fathoms: I have no doubt, therefore, that a ship may sail close to them with safety. At two in the afternoon, when we approached the north-west point of the small Ladrone, a pilot came on board, by whom we were informed that the Nadejda had arrived at Macao about a week ago, and now was in the Typa. We still worked to windward till ten in the evening; when, finding the ebb was making, we came to an anchor at the island of Shamshoo, in eight fathoms of water, oozy ground, where we were kept the whole of the following day by a calm.

On the 3d we had a northerly breeze, but it was so light that we did not arrive at Macao till the evening. After securing the ship, and giving orders to my first lieutenant to have all the guns loaded with grape-shot, and to be on his guard against the pirates that infest these seas, I went on shore to see captain Krusenstern, whom I found in good health, as were also all my other friends. I remained on shore the whole of the next day, in the enjoyment of their society, after a separation of nearly eighteen months.

The pirates I have mentioned are so daring, that they will sometimes attack a vessel under the very batteries. They are called here Ladrones, and are so numerous, that they are said to amount to two hundred thousand men. They plunder every thing in their power, as well on shore as at sea. It is probable that the boats we saw when we made signals for a pilot belonged to these robbers, who, finding our ship too strong, did not dare to molest us. Not long ago they contended with a Portuguese brig of war, and considerably damaged her.

The town of Macao is built upon a rising ground. It is tolerably clean, and has some handsome houses. It is defended by several batteries, and presents from the sea a very pleasant view. The environs appeared to be the very reverse of fruitful. Though I had resided but a day in the town, I could perceive plainly enough, that while the Portuguese were the professed masters, the Chinese in reality bore the sway; for nothing of any consequence could be done without their permission. Though the governor may attempt occasionally to defend his rights against the encroachments of the insolent mandarins,

1805.
Dec.

his garrison is too small for him to be able to enforce respect. I was told that there were as many monks and priests as soldiers, the number of which was about two hundred. It appears to me, that the Portuguese are themselves principally in fault in this subjection. Being badly provided with necessaries, they are continually dependent on the Chinese, who, on the smallest dissatisfaction, threaten to stop the supplies, and thus govern the town.

5th.

On the 5th I left this place, and proceeded for Whampoa. Captain Krusenstern, who, for reasons which I shall assign hereafter, could not accompany me with his ship, went with me as a passenger. This I deemed a happy circumstance; as, besides the pleasure of going with him to Canton, I should have an opportunity of learning from him the various events he had met with since we parted.*

6th.

In the night of the 6th we reached the Bocca Tigris, and there cast anchor. In the course of the day, we passed a large fleet

---

* Captain Krusenstern had had a very good passage from the Sandwich Islands to Camchatka, from whence, after refreshing his crew, he sailed for Nangasaky with the embassy. I was sorry to learn, that the object of the embassy, which was to establish a commercial intercourse with Japan, had entirely failed; which, I suspect, was to be attributed to the interference of the gentlemen of the Dutch factory, who were always jealous of strangers coming amongst them. The ambassador, on his return to Camchatka, left the Nadejda and proceeded to visit the Russian settlements in America. Captain Krusenstern had afterwards an opportunity of surveying the island of Sagaleen, whence he sailed for Camchatka, and then proceeded for China. During this multifarious voyage, his people had been in good health, though, except while in Japan, they had chiefly lived on salt provisions.

of war boats of the Chinese, who were preparing to go in search of pirates.

On the 7th two custom-house officers came on board in the morning. The wind was now so slight, that our sails were nearly useless. I therefore hired fifty boats to tow us. With this assistance we passed the first bar at ten o'clock in the evening, and the second about midnight; and at two in the morning were moored at Whampoa, with thirty fathoms of cable fore and aft.

The river Tigris is defended by two batteries, badly built, and badly furnished with artillery. Here ships must stop to wait for the custom-house officers and a pilot. The river is every where safe, except at its entrance, and at the two bars, the passage through which is a little difficult, especially for large ships, which should therefore, in case of a light breeze, always have recourse to the assistance of boats. The pay for such boats is two dollars each from Bocca Tigris, and one from the second bar to Whampoa.

Having placed the vessel in a snug birth, I gave orders for her to be unrigged, and in the mean time proceeded with captain Krusenstern to Canton, to find a purchaser for the cargo. On our arrival, we applied to Mr. Beal, an Englishman, an old acquaintance of captain Krusenstern's, who undertook the management of our business, and introduced us to Mr. Looqua, one of the hongs, or merchants privileged to trade with foreigners, who, as the custom of the country requires, became responsible for our good conduct, and the payment of the duties, and offered us the use of his warehouses. Without the

1805.
Dec.

intervention of a person of this kind, no goods are allowed to enter Canton. He is accountable to the government, for whatever is done by those whom he thus takes under his charge; and, in case of misbehaviour on their part, is sometimes heavily fined.

I might have landed with ease all my furs by the 16th of December, if the government had not interfered: but as we were the first Russians that had visited Canton for commerce, the viceroy of the province demanded a variety of explanations, before he would permit us to act. In consequence of this we were visited by all the inferior hongs, and at last by Mr. Panquequa, the chief, who put to us the following interrogatories:—Of what nation are you? Do you trade with China by land? What motives induce you to undertake so long a voyage from your own country? Are your ships, ships of war? To these questions he requested an answer in writing, which, he said, would be sent to Pekin, for the inspection of the emperor. Our reply was a tedious affair, as the hong was scrupulously attentive to every word of it. At first we were desired to write it in English; then it was to be changed to Russ: an indecision which occasioned many interviews, to the loss of much time.

As soon as this business was over, Mr. Beal waited upon us to say, that Mr. Looqua wished to have the refusal of our cargo, at the price which might be fixed by those who were to estimate its value.

The question of our ships being ships of war, originated in captain Krusenstern. On his arrival at Macao, as he had but few furs, he did not wish to proceed with them to Whampoa, but preferred waiting for me in the Typa. The Chinese, however, insisting on his going up the river, as all merchant vessels were obliged to do, he said that his was not a merchant vessel, which was immediately reported at Canton. For this reason, when he afterwards wished to take his ship to Whampoa in company with mine, the mandarin of the custom-house would not permit him. On our arrival at Canton, we endeavoured to set this matter right, by stating, that though the Nadejda belonged to the crown, she had been lent by the government to the American company, and by the laws of Russia was allowed to trade; that she had accordingly taken in a cargo, which consisted of furs. This circumstance had great weight with the Chinese. Being, however, suspicious by nature, they sent a custom-house officer to ascertain the truth of what we said, as to the vessel containing a cargo; and having received a report in the affirmative, a pilot was ordered to bring the ship to Whampoa, where she arrived on the 23d instant.

By this time the hold of the Neva was cleared of her goods, and we were preparing to examine the damage she had received when she grounded. She had previously been measured by the hopoo, or director of the customs of Canton, who came on board on the 18th, about ten o'clock in the morning, for the purpose, in a large handsome boat, decorated with different flags, and attended by three boats of the same size, and a great number of smaller ones. As was the custom on such occasions, I sent one of my officers and a Chinese interpreter to meet him. The measurement was soon effected; for it consisted merely in drawing a line from the fore- to the mizen-mast, and athwart-

1805.
Dec.

ship by the main-mast, which line was afterwards re-measured by a Chinese standard. After taking some refreshment in the cabin, consisting of wine and various sweetmeats, the hopoo expressed a wish to see the two Tartars he had been told we had on board. On their appearing, he addressed them in the language of the Chinese Tartars; but they did not understand a word of what he said. He was, however, very much gratified by seeing them; and, shortly after his departure, sent, as a present to the ship's company, two bags of flour, eight earthen pots of a spirituous liquor called shamshoo, and two small bullocks. As the measurement of vessels brings a great revenue to the government, it is always done by the director of the customs himself. Though our ship was only three hundred and fifty tons, she was obliged to pay three thousand nine hundred and seventy-seven Spanish dollars.

27th. On the 27th we laid the Neva down to repair her bottom. As she was broad on the beam, it required a very considerable force; and, there being no convenience for the purpose at Whampoa, I was obliged to make use of the Nadejda instead of a sheer-hulk, which occasioned much trouble. Her larboard side was soon repaired, but the starboard was a work of more time; because, to examine her properly, we had to heave the keel out of the water. Every thing, however, was finished in 29th. two days, and on the 29th we began to rig her out. Meanwhile I went once more to Canton, to finish my commercial affairs.

The greater part of the cargo of the two ships had been disposed of to Mr. Lucqua, and a new cargo purchased with the proceeds, consisting of tea, china-ware, and nankeens. By the 11th of January, nearly the whole of the first article was stowed in the hold, and we were proceeding with alacrity, hoping to enter on our destined course homewards before the end of the month. On the 22d, however, when the last packages of goods were about to be sent off from Canton, Mr. Lucqua informed us, that an embargo was laid on the vessels, and that they would not be permitted to depart till an answer to the report, which had been sent respecting us to Pekin, should arrive; and he added, that, to prevent our sailing clandestinely, a guard was ordered to be placed over each vessel.

This intelligence was equally unexpected and mortifying, and we were at a loss how to act in it; but, whatever might be the result, we resolved to act with spirit. As a first step, therefore, we determined that no Chinese soldiers should enter either of the ships: and we carried this point; for when they attempted to come on board the Nadejda, they were treated so roughly, that they quickly retired, and never ventured on a second intrusion, but contented themselves with keeping watch in their boats at a distance, to prevent any of the Chinese in our employ from coming to us.

The next step we took was the drawing up a remonstrance to the viceroy, against the injustice and arbitrariness of the proceeding: but this remonstrance we were not permitted to present, as, by the custom of the country, no European could have any direct communication with the great officers of state. In this dilemma, we applied to Mr. Drummond, president of the factory of the English East-India Company, who is held

1806.
Jan.

in high respect, and who kindly and readily undertook our cause. He sent for the hongs to his factory, and insisted on their presenting the remonstrance to the person, whoever he might be, by whose order the embargo had been laid on. This, however, they refused to do; alleging, that they did not dare to present a document of any kind, that arraigned the proceedings of government as unjust and arbitrary. We then threatened to deliver it ourselves, in person, to the viceroy; upon which they altered their tone, and expressed their willingness to comply with Mr. Drummond's request.

The next day we met these personages again at the factory, when they told us, that they had given our paper to the hopoo, who had informed them, that the vessels had been detained by express order of the viceroy, to whom he advised us to write in more polite terms, if we wished our application to be successful. We were at first unwilling to do this; but reflecting on the injury we might sustain by our voyage being protracted, and doubtful of obtaining justice in any other way, we complied; and the result was, the release of the vessels, the removal of the guard-boats, and permission to proceed with our stowage, and to sail when we pleased.

This unpleasant business had occupied an entire week; and would probably have extended to a much longer period, but for the interference of Mr. Drummond, to whose friendly conduct, in this and many other instances, we were largely indebted. From the European merchants in general, we also received much kindness. In this class of the inhabitants of Canton, there is a cordiality with one another that was extremely gratifying to me, and which I had never seen equalled. Though belonging to different nations, nations too that were at war with each other, one might have supposed them to be subjects of the same prince, and even members of one family.

CHAPTER XIV.

DESCRIPTION OF CANTON.

Houses. Population. Commerce. Despotic and mercenary Character of those in Authority. Productions. Wretchedness of the lower Class of Inhabitants. Sumptuous Fare of the Rich. Customs as to eating. Dress. Character. Religion. Temples. Military Force. Boats. Laws. Country-house of a Mandarin. Price of Provision. Weights and Measures.

1806.
Jan.

The town of Canton is situated on the river Tigris. It is large, with narrow streets, which, however, are kept clean. In the part which we were permitted to visit, every house had a shop; and the streets were as much crowded from morning till night with passengers, as some of the public streets of London. The river-side is embellished with a row of handsome buildings, of which the English and Dutch factories are the most splendid. The best Chinese houses in Canton will bear no comparison with those of the European inhabitants; and the houses of the poor are mere huts, in general without windows, and having for a door only a bamboo matting. A house of the first class, beside the main building, has several square courts paved with brick, against the walls of which bowers are erected, furnished with tables, chairs, sofas, and China pots containing flowers and fruit-trees. In the middle of some of the courts, a small pond is dug, or a large porcelain bason is placed, to contain gold-fish, of which the

Chinese are extremely fond. The houses are commonly two stories high. The apartments of the upper story are considered as private; since it is in these that the women of such as are not rich enough to have a separate seraglio commonly reside. Strangers are therefore not allowed to enter them. From what I could observe of the interior of the houses in general, I should suppose the inhabitants not remarkable for cleanliness. The Chinese temples, which are numerous, contribute but little to the embellishment of the town.

Several Europeans have endeavoured to ascertain the population of Canton; but it is a task not easily effected with exactness, from the great influx of non-residents for the purposes of commerce during the shipping season; and from the number of residents who in the summer betake themselves to a distance, to work in the fields; so that there is in this respect a continual fluctuation. The number of such as live constantly in the town, is not so great as has generally been supposed. Amongst the poor, are many who have no other property, and no other habitation, than a small boat, with a covering of mats. I have been told that the number of these distressed beings is immense in China; and as for the river Tigris, it is full of such boats. Some carry passengers; others row constantly about the ships, in the hope of finding some dead animal, or offal of any kind, that may have been thrown overboard, and which serves as food; while others are employed in raking up from the bottom of the water rags, pieces of rope-yarn, and other trifling articles, which however they sell, and thus obtain the means of being able to prolong a miserable existence.

1806.
Jan.

Canton may be divided into two parts; that in which the viceroy of the province and his officers of rank reside, and that which is inhabited by the people in general. Into the first no European is allowed to enter, though persons from the East Indies, and other Asiatics, are admitted freely. For the extent of its commercial concerns, there are few towns in any quarter of the world that surpass it. Besides European and American vessels, the East Indies and all the neighbouring countries largely trade with it; and such is the state of its population, that if the ships which frequent it should be doubled, there would be no want of hands. The business of loading and unloading is effected with great expedition; unless the government interferes, when the delay is sometimes intolerable. The officers of government, instead of protecting a commerce so advantageous to their country, think only of enriching themselves, and thus injure, by plundering it. The abject state in which the people are held by their rulers is such, that every species of injustice, however great, must be submitted to. The first merchant of Canton is, in reality, little better than a steward both of the viceroy and the hopoo, whom he is obliged to furnish gratis with whatever they may want: and should he refuse, his back may suffer for his refractoriness; as it is well known, that by the customs of this country, formerly so highly extolled for its just laws, no one is exempted from the liability to corporal punishment, from the heir to the throne down to the lowest subject; and that an individual of a higher rank can inflict, at his pleasure, chastisement on one of a lower, without evidence to convict, or any formality of trial. While these things exist, there will necessarily be a passive obedience in every description of the people to their rulers, whose thirst for wealth must be satisfied: and the heaviest contributions are thus laid on foreigners, on whose goods the hongs fix whatever value they please.

Spanish dollars are the best article that can be brought here for commercial dealings, as goods may be purchased with them at a cheaper rate than with any thing else; and they have the further advantage, that they cannot be undervalued by the hongs.

Furs vary so much in value, that it is difficult to form an estimate of the price that may be expected for them. Such immense quantities are imported by American ships, that the market is often glutted with them. During the present season they imported no less than twenty thousand sea-otter skins, which were sold at from seventeen to nineteen Spanish dollars a skin. We received for some of ours, the last price, in exchange for tea only; and for others the first, taking half in tea and half in money. Another reason of the little profit of furs to the importer, arises from the plundering system of the hopoo, who appropriates to himself a certain number of the best out of every ship, or makes a bargain with the merchant who buys the cargo, to receive a sum of money instead. Mr. Lucqua, who purchased ours, gave him seven thousand dollars, and thought himself well off. This abominable extortion, together with the heavy duty on measurement, and other unavoidable expenses, reduce the price of furs so much, that the gain reasonably to be expected by the commander of a vessel is greatly diminished.

1806.
Jan.

If this system does not soon change, the European merchants must suffer greatly. It would seem, indeed, as if the Chinese themselves were desirous to put a stop to European commerce; for a year scarcely passes in which they do not invent some grinding law to its prejudice; imagining, no doubt, that no quarter of the world can exist without the productions of their country.

In Canton no stranger can furnish himself with any thing he may want, either on board his ship or on shore, without employing a compador, who charges whatever he pleases for every thing he buys; and, when he has cheated as much as he can in this way, requires a handsome present for his trouble. In a word, fraud and deceit are the prevailing practice here; and the misfortune is, that, to whatever extent it may be carried, no justice can be obtained: for a European cannot see the viceroy of the province; nor, without extreme difficulty, get a letter conveyed to him. This regulation is productive of incalculable mischief; and if any European power should have influence with the court of Pekin, it could not be more beneficially exerted than in attempting to remove the evil.

This country abounds in every thing that can be wanted by man, whether flesh, fowls, fish, fruits, or vegetables; and every thing is excellent in its kind. The common food of a Chinese is rice, which grows in great plenty. This nourishing grain is equally necessary for the rich and poor. The rich consume great quantities of it, while the poor are satisfied with an allowance of two or three pounds a day.

The Chinese have a drink called shamshoo, which is extracted from rice. The best is palatable enough; but the inferior, disagreeable to the taste, and, when drank to excess, very pernicious. The common beverage, however, is tea, which is used in general without sugar or other mixture. It is made in cups with covers, answering the purpose of our tea-pots, and drunk at all hours of the day.

It has been said by many that China is extremely rich; yet, judging from what I saw, and from what was related to me, there is not a people on the globe among whom such misery is to be found, as amongst the lower class of inhabitants of this vast empire. Besides the poor families I have mentioned, who are obliged to pass their lives in small boats, and gain their livelihood as they can, the streets of Canton are always crowded with beggars. This poverty does not arise from the imposts of the government, as there is hardly a nation in Europe that pays fewer taxes; and is, in my opinion, ascribable to the oppressive nature of the laws, and the corresponding oppression of those who execute them. There is scarcely any production in nature, that the human stomach is capable of digesting, which this wretched class of the Chinese do not sometimes eat. Rats are even esteemed as a delicacy. On the contrary, the officers of government and rich merchants live in the extreme of luxury. They have large houses, fine gardens, and sumptuous tables. At their public dinners, not less than forty or fifty different dishes are served up, some of which are very costly. They are particularly fond of all sorts of stimulative dishes; as, for example, the fins of the shark, and the nests of a particular species of bird, both of which are extremely rare. An entertainment, on any extraordinary occasion, without these, would be thought mean; and they must be obtained, at whatever price. Their method, as to their meals, I did not like. They dine at separate small tables, in parties of from four to six. All their viands are served in small basons, one for each, out of which the party at the same table eat together. Each person has two bone sticks, called at Canton chop-sticks, which are about a foot long, and serve both for knife and fork. A Chinese is very expert in the use of them; and will empty a bason of rice with them in as short a time as he would with the best spoon in the world. He has, however, a china spoon, and by his side is a small cup, containing shamshoo, of which he drinks after every dish. The rice is generally served up in separate basons. Table-cloths are not used; and in place of napkins small pieces of paper are substituted, which often serve the purpose also of a pocket-handkerchief. Mr. Panquequa, the first merchant in Canton, always wiped his nose with such scraps of paper; which was to me the more disgusting, as he was much in the habit of taking snuff.

The Chinese might be called in general a sober people, if they were not so greatly addicted to sensual pleasures, to which they are perfect slaves. The rich spend vast sums in the purchase of women, of whom each has a seraglio, containing as many as he is able to support.

The Chinese are of an olive complexion, the northern inhabitants excepted, who are tolerably fair, but have none of the carnation in their cheeks that distinguishes Europeans. They have small black eyes, the form of which is rather long. Their hair also is black; but they shave it all off, except a small portion on the crown of the head, which is platted and hangs down behind: its length constitutes its beauty.

Their dress consists, first, of long trowsers and a loose garment, made of thin stuff, instead of a shirt: next, a sort of cassoc with long narrow sleeves, and over this another with short but broad sleeves. This dress belongs alike to persons both of the first and middling rank; but the poor and labouring class wear only trowsers and jackets. These jackets are increased according to the weather, some wearing even five at a time. In the winter many line the whole of the upper garments with furs, while others are satisfied with a fur collar and lappels. For this they use chiefly the furs of the sea- and river-otter and sea-bear: the skin of a sea-otter is preferred in China to every other, but is used only by the opulent; who, on common occasions, wear white lamb-skins. Foxes' paws, which, when sewed together, make a strong and warm fur, are greatly in vogue amongst the middling class of people.

The head-dress is very simple; it consists of a black satin cap, resembling those worn by the Jews, with a small silk ball on the top, which is black, red, or blue. They have a hat also, the upper part of which is covered with light blue silk, and the rims underneath lined with black velvet. From the crown hangs a tassel of red silk, over which is fixed a ball of gold, or of white, blue, or red glass. By these balls the ranks are distinguished. The red is considered as belonging to the first class; then follow in order the blue, the white, and the gold, or rather the gilt. The mandarins, besides this, wear on their breasts and back pieces of silk about six inches square, embroidered with different figures. These also show the class to which they belong, and may be distinguished at a great distance.

Their boots and shoes have a square shape; the sole is an inch thick. Boots are worn only by the higher class. They are made of black satin, lined with nankeen, and have worsted or bamboo under the soles. Shoes are chiefly worn by the lower class: they are often made of embroidered silk, and are worn over a stocking, the foot of which is of nankeen, and the upper part, or leg, of silk stuff. The Chinese are very fond of finery. Even servants are often seen dressed in silks from head to foot; and the middling class of the people seldom wear any thing else. Nankeen, of different colours, however, is the staple article throughout the empire. The generality of the people are clothed in it all the year round, and great quantities of it are therefore consumed in the country.

The Chinese women of the better class are guarded in so strict a manner, that I found it impracticable to get a sight of them. I cannot therefore say much about their dress. The poorer class wear loose trowsers, and an upper garment with broad sleeves, not unlike that worn by the men, and tie their long hair in knots behind. Their feet are curious. I saw some that were not more than six inches in length; and the Chinese say that the feet of their ladies of fashion do not exceed four inches. To this I could scarcely stretch my belief, though several shoes that had been worn, were brought to me of that measure, in confirmation of it. The real cause of this ridiculous custom is not known to us; unless it originates in jealousy. The women, however, are rendered such cripples by it, that they can scarcely walk. All their toes, except the great toes, are so bent under the sole of the foot, that the foot receives the form of a wedge; and to keep it in that form it is tied tight round, even beyond the ancle, from infancy. The Tartar women of China alone let their feet grow in their natural form.

In the arts of cunning and deceit, no nation can equal the Chinese; at the same time they have better qualities of the understanding. If they are ignorant as to matters that do not immediately concern them, it proceeds from their education: respecting what really concerns them, they are sure to have the requisite knowledge; and every one is master of whatever business he may follow. There is nothing they cannot imitate with astonishing accuracy. At Canton many copies of things may be found, executed with such delicacy and precision, that they cannot be distinguished from the originals. In their behaviour they are extremely polite; and their obedience is beyond example. Every thing is reduced to a rule, from which they cannot in the smallest degree deviate. All kind of novelties are forbidden, under the heaviest penalties; and as this originates in the policy of government, no one thinks of aiming at invention. Accordingly, their ships, guns, muskets, and various other things, are nearly in the same state, as when the use of them was first introduced.

Though the Chinese are educated from the cradle in notions of the most implicit obedience to the government, they have nevertheless a sovereign contempt for their present Tartar masters, and they never fail to show that contempt whenever they can do it with impunity. When the Tartars conquered China,

1806.
Jan.

they embraced the laws and customs of the conquered; yet are they obliged, for their own safety, to surround themselves with their own countrymen, who, in consequence, enjoy the highest offices, both civil and military, throughout the empire,—a preference which is regarded by the native Chinese with jealousy, and occasions great dissatisfaction.

The religion of China is idolatrous. It is divided into three sects; that of Confucius, that of Fo, and that of Taotsé. The court, however, and the Tartars, follow that of the grand Lama. It consists chiefly in different offerings to their gods, and in the casting of lots. This last is done by means of a set of small sticks, which are resorted to as oracles in every doubtful case. The Chinese burn candles before their idols, and sandal-wood in metal pans, which are placed at the entrance opposite the altar in every temple. Occasionally animals are presented as sacrifice; and there are also burnt-offerings, consisting of sandal-dust wrapped in paper, on the outside of which a piece of foil is stuck. A Chinese, on every instance of good fortune, thinks it his duty formally to thank his gods, either in his house or in the nearest temple. He likewise presents offerings of one kind or other, when he wishes to succeed in any undertaking. The commencement of the year is the grand day, when offerings are made through the whole empire. On that occasion every person is expected to offer something to their deity; and the rich, a sacrifice of value. At Canton, every house and every shop has a corner appropriated to its idols, before which candles are kept constantly burning, especially in the morning; an attention which seems to prove that its inhabitants are sincerely attached to their religion. This circumstance interested me the more, as it reminded me of the devout zeal of my own countrymen, by whom the same practice is observed towards their saints.

The largest temple which came under my observation, was one standing on the right side of the river Tigris, nearly opposite to the European factories. It had many divisions, or separate places of worship, the three principal of which were in the middle of a long court. It was laid out, in great measure, like a monastery. I passed several hours there, and was much pleased with the air of cleanliness and propriety that every where prevailed. The places of worship were full of idols. In some, there were three in the middle, and twelve on every side; in others, only one in the middle, and three or four on the sides. These idols were all gilded and lackered. Those in the middle were about ten feet long, and were represented in a sitting posture. Candles, of the dust of sandal-wood, burn always before them; and every person who comes to pray, makes some offering. My guides entered with their heads covered, and seemed to pay little respect to the sanctity of the places; though they endeavoured to persuade me, that, by making offerings to their gods, prosperity of every kind would attend me through life. One of them, pointing to a particular statue, told me, that if I would pray to him, I should not fail to have a pleasant voyage to Russia.

After examining the different temples, my guides led me to the apartments of the fraternity, who were in a large room at dinner. Each had a bason of rice before him. The members of this fraternity, I was informed, take an oath to renounce all com-

1806.
Jan.

merce with the female sex, and to abstain both from flesh and fish; and that a violation of this oath is punished with death. I was next introduced to a very different party, consisting of twenty large hogs, of which every possible care was taken. My guides informed me that these animals had been presented to the temple by different inhabitants, and were considered as sacred. They are well fed, and are kept till they die a natural death. One of them, which could hardly crawl, was represented as being about thirty years old. Near to the place in which these hogs were confined, is a large piece of ground, producing all sorts of vegetables. Towards the upper part of it is a burying-ground. In this burying-ground, the bodies of such of the fraternity as die, are burned, and the ashes and bones preserved in a place set apart for the purpose. I did not inspect this place: I saw, however, some bones where the burning is performed; but they were so disfigured by fire, that it was impossible to judge to what species of beings they had originally belonged. On coming out of the temple, I passed a place where stood a group of five statues dressed in red garments, and a candle burning before them. These were monuments erected to the memory of certain individuals of the fraternity, who had been distinguished for their exemplary lives.

The population of this extraordinary empire, is reckoned by the Chinese at three hundred million of souls; and its military force at nearly two millions of men. These accounts, however, are both very questionable. So immense an army would, in any other country, be very formidable; but in China, while it adds greatly to the expenses of the government, it is doubtful whether it would be able to defend its vast dominions, were they to be attacked with vigour by the neighbouring powers. From inspecting the cannon, muskets, and other implements of war which I saw at Canton, I may affirm, that, if aided only by these, the Chinese military force, however numerous it may be, would never alarm an European general, commanding an army of a few thousand disciplined troops. Compared with the artillery of Europe, their match-locks and cannon are contemptible. The naval force of the empire, for any effect it can produce, is also very insignificant. It consists of ill-built boats, some of which are armed with three or four small guns, while others carry long iron pipes or tubes, resembling those of muskets, fixed in a block of wood on the fore part of the vessel. The boats have commonly two masts, with sails made of mats, like all the vessels of this country. They resemble in form an arch or crescent. The rudder is fixed, like ours, or suspended, to act in the manner of a back-oar; but in both instances it is ill formed, and so badly fastened, that it is in danger of being struck off by the first heavy sea. The junks, which are of several tons burthen, are the largest of the Chinese vessels: but, like the others, have two masts only, with sails made of mats. The extent of their navigation is to Batavia, Japan, and Cochin China; and as these voyages are always performed in the best season of the year, they are in general tolerably successful. At other seasons, it would be dangerous to go out to sea in them; as, should a typhoon take place, which will try the stoutest European ship, the danger would be extreme. When a typhoon occurs on the river Tigris, it blows with great violence. About the time when we encountered the tremendous typhoon off the Marianne Islands, a similar one prevailed here, by which many vessels were driven ashore, and some of the streets of Canton

1806.
Jan.

deluged by the overflow of the river which it occasioned. The Chinese anchors are no better than their rudders. In form they resemble ours, but are made of wood. Instead of a proper stock, a strong pole of wood or bar of iron is driven through the shank, at a little distance from the arms, which are also of wood, and fastened to the shank by cords. The flooks, or points of the arms, are sheathed with iron. Though the river boats do not differ from the sea boats in their construction, they answer the purpose they are intended for extremely well. They draw but little water, carry great burthens, and sail pretty fast. In calm weather they are rowed by four or six oars, and steered by one or two long ones, suspended from the stern; which, from being worked from side to side, greatly increase their velocity. The oars are not managed with the same regularity as in European boats, every waterman rowing as he pleases, without regard to order or method. The Custom-house boats, however, are an exception, and are built also in the European manner. For the river boats, the matting sails are better than canvass ones, as they shake less during light airs.

The European missionaries, in their account of China, speak highly of its laws. I know not what policy there may be in this; but sure I am, that there is no country in the world where the people are so much oppressed as in this great empire. The insolence, or rather cruelty of office, is such, that many bear their wrongs with patience, rather than apply for justice to mercenary and despotic mandarins. It often happens, that a person of rank takes a liking to some article of value belonging to an inferior, and appropriates it to his own use without ceremony. I was assured by one of the first hongs, that his reason for not wearing a watch was, the fear of its being taken from him, for he had already suffered once in that way. The viceroy of the province of Canton happening to see in his hands a handsome repeater, desired to look at it, when, making an inclination of the head, he put it into his pocket, telling the proprietor, with great gravity, that he would keep it as a mark of good will towards him. Mean as this conduct might appear, Chinese politeness required that the hong should kneel, and thank the plunderer for his condescension in accepting it, though at the same time he must detest him in his heart.

I had no opportunity of witnessing any of their capital punishments; but to judge from the drawings publicly sold at Canton, they appear to be very cruel. The most common are those of strangling and beheading. The former is effected by a rope passed two or three times round the neck, two men pulling it by the ends, a foot of each resting on the victim. The latter is performed with a sabre, and is seldom accomplished in less than three strokes. For capital offences against the government, still more barbarous punishments are inflicted; such as cutting off the arms and legs, and quartering the body. From this it would appear, as if the Chinese, who boast of having been enlightened when Europe was plunged in barbarism, have made but slow advances since in improvement. Another proof of the defective nature of the Chinese laws, is the great number of poor unprovided for in this vast empire. Of these, many, having no means of livelihood, are obliged to turn pirates, and whole fleets of them swarm at present on the coast, and commit terrible depredations. Whilst we lay at Whampoa, a fleet of three hundred boats belonging to these plunderers, at-

1806.
Jan.

tacked a fortified place in the vicinity of Canton, and entirely destroyed it.

Having expressed a wish while at Canton to see the form and fashion of some country-house of a rich Chinese, with its appendages of courts and garden, my friends procured me an opportunity of breakfasting with Mr. Panquiqua, whom I have mentioned before. To arrive at his house we had to cross the river Tigris, and then row up a canal that led directly to the outer door. The door was locked, and could not be opened till the master was made acquainted with our arrival, and had given orders for us to be admitted. From this door we were led, through a narrow passage, into a large square, on the left side of which was a very handsome building, and thence into a spacious garden, by a grand circular opening in a brick wall. Before we had reached the first arbour, Mr. Panquiqua made his appearance in his ordinary dress, or dishabille, that is, without the upper garment usually worn; but he had a mandarin's hat on his head, with a blue ball on the top of it. When the first civilities, of which the Chinese are profuse, were over, he led us through the garden, ordering that breakfast should in the mean time be prepared. The novelty of the objects, and the taste displayed in the arrangement, so different from ours, engrossed my attention. The walks were paved with bricks to the very trees, between which, on stands, were a great number of china vases, containing flowers and fruit-trees. In vain did my eyes search every where for a lawn: nothing of the kind was to be seen in this extensive place; the best parts of which, instead of containing, as in Europe, grass-plots variegated with beds of flowers, were taken up by ponds of stagnated water, which occasioned no very agreeable smell. The artificial stone-work of the garden pleased me extremely. It represented, on a small scale, precipices, and different excavations of mountains, with astonishing accuracy. During our walk we entered many arbours or summer-houses, which were only one story high, and open on one side. They were all furnished alike, chairs and tables being placed on the sides, and a couch opposite the entrance covered with thin matting or silk. On the middle of the couch was a table with short feet. In every corner hung a lantern of horn or painted paper. The horn lanterns were very curious from their size. They were each more than a foot in diameter, and appeared to be made of a single piece of horn. The Chinese, I understand, have the art of expanding horn till it becomes as thin as writing paper.

Mr. Panquiqua, whose politeness induced him to show us every thing belonging to his establishment, led us to the arbour in which he sometimes sleeps. It differed from the rest, in being two stories high. In the upper story we saw a narrow bedstead, on which was a thin mattress covered with coarse blue woollen cloth, and over that a mat. At the foot of the bed were eight coverlets of different colours, placed there to be used, one or more at a time, according to the coldness of the weather. The Chinese, our host told us, never use either sheets or pillow-cases: in warm weather they sleep in their shirts on mats, and in cold weather on woollen cloth. He told us also, that the inhabitants of Nankin, when they go to bed, take off every article of clothing and lie perfectly naked: a custom that implies little sense either of delicacy or cleanliness.

1806.
Jan.

Having finished our walk through the garden, and partaken of a very sumptuous breakfast, Mr. Panquiqua introduced us into his seraglio. On passing a large gate ornamented with garlands, we entered a gallery terminated by a balcony, adjoining to which was a long spacious hall, the roof supported by a double row of columns, between which chairs were placed. The chairs were covered with English scarlet cloth, embroidered with silk, and the walls hung with china pictures. Near the walls were drums and other instruments for theatrical representations, of which, as well as of all sorts of spectacles and games, the Chinese are very fond. At the upper end of the hall was a sort of cupboard, with a candle burning before it. Mr. Panquiqua opened this cupboard, which contained five small boards fixed on pedestals, with Chinese characters on them. They were placed there, he observed, in commemoration of so many of his ancestors; and he added, that on certain days, established by religion, he made offerings to them. On turning round, from some noise I heard while engaged in this scene, I saw at a side door, which was open, three very handsomely dressed women looking at us. As soon, however, as my eye met theirs, they vanished. It was manifest, that the curiosity common to the fair sex was awake in them; for the same door was opened and shut several times; and when we came from the hall into the gallery, two of the females made their appearance with less reserve. One was of a certain age, the other young; but the faces of both were so daubed with paint, that they were more like pictures than the living countenances of human beings. After we had seen the seraglio, our host proceeded to show us his domestic economy; but as this differed but little from our own, I shall not trouble the readers with a description of it.

PRICES OF DIFFERENT ARTICLES OF PROVISIONS DURING OUR STAY AT CANTON.

	Tales.	Maces.	Candarins.
For a picul of rice	3	9	0
For a ditto of the best white flour	6	0	0
For a goose, per catty	0	1	4
For a capon, per ditto	0	1	5
For a duck or fowl, per ditto	0	1	4
For beef, per ditto	0	0	$7\frac{1}{2}$
For mutton, per ditto	0	3	6
For pork, per ditto	0	1	4
For sweet potatoes, per ditto	0	0	4
For European potatoes, per ditto	0	1	0
For a salad, per ditto	0	0	4
For greens, per ditto	0	0	4
For green peas, per ditto	0	0	8
For butter, per ditto	0	5	0
For a cabbage	0	1	5
For half a pint of milk	0	0	6
For twelve eggs	0	0	8

MONEY OF CHINA.

A tale contains ten maces; a mace, ten candarins; a candarin, ten cash; a Spanish dollar, seven maces and two candarins.

WEIGHTS AND MEASURES.

A catty is twenty-one ounces and a quarter; a pecul, a hundred catties, or a hundred and thirty-three pounds English.

CHAPTER XV.

PASSAGE FROM CANTON TO CRONSTADT.

Departure of the Nadejda and Neva from Canton. Islands and Straits in the Chinese Seas. Advice to Navigators respecting them. Island of Two Brothers. Make the Islands of Java and Sumatra. Erroneous Situation of several Places rectified. One of the Crew of the Neva dies. Strait of Sunda. The two Ships separate. Navigation round the Cape of Good Hope. Currents. Make the Western Islands. Pass immense Quantities of Sea-weeds. Arrival and Stay at Portsmouth. Arrive at Cronstadt. The Ship visited by the Emperor Alexander and the Empress-mother. Honours and Rewards conferred on the Officers and Crew.

1806.
Feb.
9th.
On the 9th of February, having received our passports from the Chinese government, both ships, the Neva and Nadejda, weighed anchor. As the wind was contrary, and Whampoa full of vessels, we were obliged to hire boats to tow us out.

10th. On the 10th, at midnight, we anchored at Bocca Tigris. Behind the second bar were a great many East-India-men, drawing upon an average twenty-five feet of water. As vessels of such burthen cannot take their whole cargo on board at Whampoa, they are obliged to come here to complete their lading. It was not our intention to have stopped at this place; on the contrary, we had resolved to take advantage of the evening tide, and pass it: but the knavery of the pilots, who clandestinely dismissed the boats that were towing us, prevented it; and as the wind, which was light, bore the ship towards the shore, we had no resource but to anchor, in four fathoms of water. The object of the pilots, in this underhand proceeding, was to extort from us more money; but instead of gaining their ends, I had the good fortune to procure for them a just and wholesome correction.

On the 11th, at sun-rise, with the wind at north-west, we were again under sail, and about eight o'clock passed an English ship of the line called the Blenheim, which was waiting to convoy a fleet homeward. As the wind freshened considerably, we were apprehensive of a bad night; however, we contrived to reach Macao in the evening.

During the night the wind shifted to the east, and at six in the morning we sailed. Having passed Macao at nine, we dismissed our pilot, and steered for Macklesfield Bank; which we were near, as we supposed, on the 15th; and at one in the afternoon of that day we made for the island of Poolo Sapata.

On the 19th, reckoning the island of Poolo Sapata to be north of us, we took a course for Poolo Aroe; and at six in the afternoon had soundings in thirty-five fathoms, with bottom of gray sand.

On the 23d the weather, which had been hazy at sun-rise, cleared about seven o'clock, and we saw the island of Poolo Teoman to the south-west. The south end of it appeared first, and next the north end, the part between being buried in clouds. At nine the island of Poolo Pambilang made its appearance, and shortly after that of Poolo Aroe. They seemed to be of dif-

1806.
Feb.

ferent elevations, but on our near approach were reduced to a level. At noon I had observations in latitude 3° 6' north, and longitude 255° 10' west; from which it appears, that the north point of the island of Teoman is in latitude 2° 59' 30", and in longitude, by the chronometers, 255° 22' 30"; but taking the mean between the chronometers and the lunar observations, which gave 255° 34', the real longitude will be 255° 28' 15" west. By our bearings, the island of Poolo Pambilang is south 22° east eleven miles from the north point of Teoman; and Poolo Aroe south 33° east nineteen miles and a half. The north end of the last therefore is 2° 44' north, and 255° 16' west, or fourteen miles more to the northward than Mr. Robertson has placed it. Hitherto the depth of water had been thirty-six fathoms, oozy ground.

24th. On the 24th we had a light breeze at north-east, and fine weather. By the lunar observations of this day, it was proved, that the mean longitude of the north point of the island of Teoman is 255° 34' west.

25th. The next day the weather was still fine. In the morning we crossed the line for the third time, in company with a strange sail, which was steering for the strait of Banca. At noon I had observations in 43' south, and 253° 37' west. Totty Island then bore south 64° west about fifteen miles. Being sure of this, and having nineteen fathoms of water, over a bottom of white sand and shells, we steered for the north point of Banca. We now found that the south-east current, which has been represented as being occasionally very strong in the Strait of Gaspar, was already acting upon our vessel; for she moved forward so fast, that at half after three the north point of Banca, or Point Pesant, appeared in sight. At the same instant Totty Island was seen like a small hillock, and bore west of us. The depth of water was then eighteen fathoms, white sand and shells. A little before, I had been surprised by the water all at once changing its colour; which proceeded, as we afterwards found, from a quantity of spawn swimming on the surface. Towards sun-set, the north point bore south twenty miles distant; but the wind being light, and the weather fine, I resolved to steer to the south-east, so as to keep during the night in a depth of eighteen fathoms.

On the 26th we had a fresh breeze from the north. At daylight the Nadejda was so far astern, that I was obliged to lie-to for her till seven o'clock; when, having brought the north point of Banca to bear north 70° west, and the second point south 20° west, we took our course to the south-east by south. At noon our latitude was 2° 3′ south, and longitude 253° 7′ 30″ west. The second point bore then south 77° west, the island of Gaspar, appearing like a small lump, south 55° east. From this place we steered south-south-east, and soon perceived the rock Navire right a-head. Before we saw the island of Gaspar, I had been sailing entirely by the lead, which gave constantly sixteen fathoms, sand and shells. I was under the necessity of doing this; for the shore to the westward was so unlike what is represented by Marchand, and so much farther off, that his chart was of no assistance to me. Point Brisé, instead of being the first after the north point, as Marchand states, proved to be the second; which excited strong doubts in my mind respecting it. At four in the afternoon we passed the island of Gaspar, and steered southeast by east, which led us near the Navire. About this time the

1806.
Feb.

depth of water continued from fourteen to fifteen fathoms, with bottom as before.

The Navire is a pretty large rock, and has trees growing on different parts of it. The east point of Banca is woody, and has a ridge of high mountains nearly contiguous to it.

As the depth of water increased from fifteen fathoms to nineteen, we kept our course to the southward, till we brought the east point of Banca to bear north 53° west, and the island of Gaspar north 19° east. We then came to an anchor in nineteen fathoms and a half, sandy bottom. At eight o'clock, having tried the current, I found its velocity to be a mile and half an hour, to the south-south-east.

27th.

During the night the wind blew from the north, and the current flowed still to the south-south-east, but at the diminished rate of a mile and a quarter an hour; and in the morning it changed to south-east, and was only three quarters of a mile an hour. About seven o'clock we weighed.

In passing between the Middle Island and the south-east point of Banca, I kept nearer the last, and at eleven was clear of all danger. At the Narrows we had from twenty-seven to thirty fathoms of water, over a bottom of gravel and shells; but having passed them, the depth decreased, and the ground was much finer. I was sorry I had not an opportunity this day of taking a meridian observation, as my survey of the Strait of Gaspar would then have been complete; however, we had reason to be perfectly satisfied with what we had done in other respects. In the afternoon we saw a small island, which we took for Shallow Island; but it proved to be five miles more to the westward than the situation given to that island by Marchand.

1806. Feb.

The Strait of Gaspar is, in my opinion, less perplexing to the navigator than has generally been supposed. From the island of Totty to the island of Gaspar, he should keep in eighteen fathoms of water, with bottom of sand, and sometimes of sand with shells. The northerly or southerly winds may incommode him when lying at anchor, by producing a heavy sea: but, with all its disadvantages, it is far preferable to the Strait of Banca.

By our chronometers, and by lunar observations taken on four successive days, from the 23d inst., we determined two principal points of the Gaspar Strait: namely, the island of Totty, which is in latitude 53′ 30″ south, and longitude 254° 7′ west; and Gaspar Island, the latitude of which is 2° 22′ 30″, and longitude 252° 50′ 30″.

The night of the 28th was both rainy and squally, but the weather improved in the morning. At nine o'clock the depth of water, which had never been less than from sixteen to thirteen fathoms, decreased of a sudden, and a low shore appeared to the west. In consequence of this we bore eastward, and lost some hours in regaining the proper depth; yet the wind favoured us so much, that we reached the islands of the Two Brothers about six in the evening, and at eight anchored beyond them in fifteen fathoms, oozy ground. In passing the Two Brothers, we had a heavy rain, accompanied with thunder

28th.

1806.
Feb.

and lightning; but by keeping the depth of eleven and ten fathoms we escaped every danger. The circumstance chiefly to be guarded against is the current, which sometimes changes its course from south-east to north-east. Both islands are high and woody. In fine weather they may be seen at a distance of more than twenty miles.

March 1st.

On the 1st of March, at seven o'clock in the morning, we steered south-west by south, having in sight the islands of Java and Sumatra, and Middle Island. At nine North Island was perceived under the shore, and at noon we came up with it. Finding that the wind was dying away, and the current acting against us, we anchored, at two in the afternoon, in eighteen fathoms, sandy ground. North Island was then north 16° west, and the coast of Sumatra west about three miles. The Nadejda also brought-to, in twenty-four fathoms, about a quarter of a mile from us.

3d.

On the 3d we attempted to sail; but the wind, by changing to the south, prevented us: however, the Nadejda was fortunate enough to double the Toca Point, leaving us to ourselves.

At midnight a breeze sprang up from the north-west, and we immediately got under way; but on approaching the Toca Point, we were becalmed, and were obliged once more to anchor close to the shore, in twenty-three fathoms, rocky ground.

4th.

In this situation we remained till two in the afternoon, when, with the wind at west-south-west, we preferred sailing rather than remain in so dangerous a place. Being assisted by a south-east current, we passed the Stroom Rock at three, and towards sun-set were about six miles from Middle Island; so that we were better off than could have been expected. Having a moon-light night, I resolved to keep under sail, and not to anchor, though the depth was thirty-five fathoms. Till eight o'clock in the evening the current was favourable, when it took a quite contrary direction.

Shortly after midnight, it again became favourable; and at four o'clock in the morning, the wind shifted to the north-west. At day-light we made sail, and steered for Prince's Island, between which and the island of Java we intended to pass. While working to windward last night, I kept near the shore of Java, and did not stretch farther to the north till Middle Island bore east-north-east, supposing that shore to be better placed on the chart of Dapré in the East-India Pilot, than the islands of Kracatoa, Samburicoo, or Point Toca, with which our bearings, when placed together on the chart, though taken with great accuracy, never agreed. This supposition was confirmed at last by our survey, and the following places were shifted accordingly:

North Island	- - to	N. 50° W. 7 miles.
Bottom ditto	- - to	N. 15 E. 4½ ditto.
Point Toca	- - to	N. 55 W. 6 ditto.
Cape St. Nicholas	- to	N. 15 W. 4 ditto.
The Island of Kracatoa	to	N. 23 W. 4½ ditto.

The islands of Samburicoo and Sabese, and the Bay of Batavia, have in like manner changed their position.

The Stroom Rock consists of three long rocks, against which

1806.
March.
we perceived a heavy sea was breaking. Between them and the island of Sumatra one may easily work to windward with a favourable current, as the channel is nearly five miles broad. At noon we were a-breast of the north point of Prince's Island; and at three o'clock approached the rocks called Carpenters. Considering the run of the ship, we expected to be soon in the ocean; but the wind died away suddenly, and we had afterwards only light westerly airs, which just enabled us to double, with difficulty, the first point of Java. At that time the Nadejda, which we had joined in the morning, was in a situation much worse than ours. At four o'clock, when five miles from the first point, we were perfectly becalmed, and were therefore obliged to tow the vessel a-head with all our boats, till the point bore north-east by north seven miles.

During our passage through the Strait of Sunda, one of our sailors, Stephen Konopleff, died. He was seized with a diarrhœa at Canton, which reduced him so much, that he was at last a mere skeleton. Nothing was neglected to effect a cure, but every remedy failed; and when we were a-breast of the west point of Java, we committed his body to the deep.

6th.
In the night of the 6th the ship was driving by the current towards the west point of Java, and, but for a seasonable breeze springing up from the north-east, might have been placed in a very disagreeable situation. At day-light the Nadejda was at a little distance to the west. During the time we were becalmed, she had had favourable winds, by means of which she had been able to reach us. At six in the morning we lost sight of the shore.

In the Strait of Sunda there are only two places to which navigators need pay particular attention, which are Middle Island and Prince's Island. In future, I should prefer passing between them and the island of Sumatra; though the passage I took between Prince's Island and Java is perfectly unexceptionable, if caution be observed on approaching the Carpenters Rocks; as, in case of calm weather, or a change of wind, the south-east current may force the vessel to the lee shore. In the middle of the Strait of Sunda a ship may work to windward in the darkest night, or come to an anchor during a calm, though not every where in a small depth of water. However, in coming from China, I would always wait for a steady breeze at North Island, where a vessel may lie quietly at anchor, and then sail through the passage. The shores of the Strait are woody and clear of rocks, except in a few places. We found the rate of the tide to be about two miles an hour; but the prevalence of strong winds may increase it. The anchorage about Prince's Island is very near to the shore. In passing it, at the distance of a mile and a quarter, we were only once able to get soundings in forty fathoms.

In her run from Canton to the Strait of Gaspar, the ship was much assisted by the currents, which acted throughout to the south-west, at the rate of sixteen miles a day. In the Strait itself it changed to south-east and south-south-east, as mentioned before.—The squally and rainy weather we experienced in the night of the 7th, plainly proved that we had not yet arrived in the tract of the trade-winds.

1806.
March.
8th.

On the 8th, at five in the afternoon, Christmas Island was seen south 39° east. We took bearings, and found that, from our observation at noon, its latitude was 10° 17′ 30″ south, and longitude 253° 57′ 50″ west. At sun-set the weather was still squally; and the night proved so dark, that we could hardly see one another on deck. At midnight it cleared up a little; but as the wind then died away, and the ship was driven towards the shore, I was obliged to bend two of my cables to the bower-anchors, which were already stowed in the hold.

9th.

At day-light, Christmas Island was north-east fifteen miles; and, as the weather was fair, we did not lose sight of it till night. During this day we saw none of the water-snakes which had amused us so often in the Chinese seas. These snakes greatly resembled those which I had formerly seen on the coast of Coromandel.

11th.

On the 11th we had a light breeze from the south-east quarter, and fine weather. At noon our latitude was 11° 33′ south, and our longitude 256° 54′ west. Supposing myself now to be in the trade-winds, I spent the whole of the day with captain Krusenstern, who informed me, that the Nadejda would certainly have been driven on shore at Cape Friar, if a northerly breeze had not fortunately sprung up, which extricated her from a very perilous situation. This confirms my idea, that a steady wind is necessary to a safe passage through the Strait of Sunda.

22d.

On the 22d we had a strong wind at south-east by south, and thick rainy weather. At noon we found ourselves in 19° 14′ south, and in 278° 36′ west. From the 11th to this day, the weather had been uniformly wet and disagreeable, which I conceive to be the reason of our not having seen, since we quitted the Strait of Sunda, either birds or fish.

On the 1st of April we had a light breeze; but the weather, which had been tolerably fine for the last five days, became again both squally and rainy. We this day left the south-east trade, and came into the tract of variable winds.

At day-light on the 12th, we were surrounded by different sorts of butterflies, which I suppose to have been blown off from the coast of Africa, though it was then 2° 40' from us. By the lunar observations of yesterday, finding that our chronometers were much to the eastward of the true longitude, I added to them 2' 27", intending to keep their former rate of going till we should see the shore.

On the 15th we had fresh breezes at south-east, and foggy weather. In the night we had lost sight of the Nadejda. Though I fired guns and burned blue lights, it was to no purpose: when day-light came, we found that we were left alone. I spent some time in endeavouring to find my companion; but a fog coming on towards noon, I relinquished the pursuit. The wind, besides, was fair; a circumstance that was not to be neglected, in a place where the loss of a few hours might occasion serious difficulties. Thus for the third time were we involuntarily separated from our friends.

Having formerly spent two years at the Cape of Good Hope, I was pretty well acquainted with its Bank, and concluded that

1806.
April.

to run alongside of it was preferable to passing it in the middle, or nearer the shore. I therefore shaped my course between the latitudes of 36° and 37°. Though this way was the farthest route, we gained by it, on account of the strong favourable currents that prevail there. As, during the last twenty-four hours, we had finished our circumnavigation from the meridian of Cronstadt, I added a day to our reckoning, which we had lost by our westerly course; and the 16th of April was accordingly called the 17th.

18th.

On the 18th we had light airs from the south-east quarter, and fine weather. At eight o'clock in the morning we had soundings in a hundred-and-ten fathoms, fine yellow sand and broken shells. At noon our latitude was 36° 18′ south, and longitude 338° 37′ west. In the course of the morning we saw a great many gulls, and the water had very perceptibly changed its colour. At five in the afternoon we had ninety fathoms, fine yellow sand; and at seven passed a rippling, which proceeded no doubt from the action of contrary currents on the surface of the water. This contrariety, giving quicker motion to the luminous animalcules, produced a fiery appearance in the sea, that, from the darkness of the evening, had a beautiful effect.

20th.

On the 20th we reached the latitude of 35° 31′ south, and the longitude 341° west. The wind blew fresh from the south-east, and we continued steering north-west with all sails set. During the day some shags were seen.

24th.

On the 24th, we had to congratulate ourselves, not only with having passed the southern promontory of Africa, but with having at length reached again the south-east trade-winds. On examining our stock of provisions and water, I found that we had still enough of both for three months; and as my people were all in good health and spirits, I resolved not to call at the island of St. Helena, as had been proposed, but to proceed straight to England. My only regret, as to this proceeding, was, that I should of necessity be separated from the Nadejda, who intended touching at the Cape, and should not see her again till our arrival in Russia.

1806.
April.

As, in the course of this run, few events occurred worthy of being recorded, I shall be brief in my account of it.

On the 1st of May we passed the meridian of Greenwich, and on the 11th, in the morning, found ourselves on the equator, with a light breeze from the south-east, and agreeable weather. At noon we observed, in latitude 37′ north, and longitude 16° 48′ west. I crossed the line in this longitude, in order that I might be enabled to get a stock of fresh-water for our washing and brewing; knowing that the rains are more prevalent there than farther to the westward. I also wished to keep near the Cape de Verd Islands. From the first of this month, the weather was beautiful, and the trade-wind blew fresh. We were daily surrounded by a great quantity of birds and fish, and every thing seemed to give fair hope of our speedy arrival in Europe.

May 1st.

On the 12th our longitude, by the lunar observations, was 18° 31′ west; which proved, that from the Strait of Sunda to the line, the vessel had been pushed by the current 1° 23′ to the north, and 12° 15′ to the west. On leaving the west point of Java,

12th.

1806.
May.

the current had acted for the first few days to the south-east. It then changed to the north-west, and occasionally to the south-west; so that in the latitude of 33°, and longitude of 329°, the ship was 4° 42′ to the west. From this place, the direction of the current was to the south-west as far as the Cape of Good Hope, pushing us 46′ to the south and 3° 6′ to the west. At last it turned to the north-west, and continued so as far as the equator, where we found ourselves again 2° 9′ to the north, and 4° 27′ to the west.*

16th.

On the 16th we were in 6° 48′ north, and 21° 5′ west. At day-light the wind was favourable; and the weather, which had not been fair since our entering the northern hemisphere, became very fine. This change was extremely acceptable, after the rains and squalls we had encountered, especially in the night of the 13th, when the gusts were so heavy, that, during the lightning, which broke continually over our heads with tremendous violence, the sea, as if on fire, resembled the boiling-over of a volcano. Notwithstanding this, we contrived to fill thirty casks with excellent water, and to get clear of a situation in which mariners are sometimes obliged to remain for weeks together.

---

* Captain Krusenstern, in the narrative of his voyage, says, that from the Strait of Sunda to the Cape of Good Hope, he found the currents chiefly to the east, the south-east, and the north-east; and that from thence to the island of St. Helena and the equator, it was constantly to the east with him. This differs greatly from my observations on the motion of the sea. Respecting the first point, that is, from the island of Java to the time of our separation, the difference must arise from the difference of our reckonings; and respecting the second point, from the Cape of Good Hope to the line, it may probably be owing to my having kept nearer the coast of Africa, though I passed the equator only five and a half degrees more to the east than the Nadejda.

The north-east trade continued with us till the 31st of May, when we reached the latitude of 28°. It commenced from the north, inclining by degrees to the east, and favoured us greatly. From the above-mentioned parallel we had light airs for four days, and then a north-west wind, by the assistance of which we made the Western Islands. On the 9th, at nine in the morning, the islands of Corvo and Fleury appeared to the south-east by south, thirty-five miles distant. I now took twelve lunar distances, by which the longitude of the south point of the first was calculated at 31° 6'. At noon our latitude, by observation, was 40° 13' north, and the south point of the island of Corvo bore south 27° east, thirty-five miles. During the day we were informed by an English privateer, of our country being at war with France. Although we had papers from the French government, ordering all its subjects not only to respect our ships, even in case of such an event, but to afford us every assistance that might be wanted; I thought proper to be prepared for all occasions, yet intended carefully to avoid falling in with any vessels of the enemy.

In crossing the equator we had a pretty strong westerly current; but it soon changed to the south-east, and so continued till we reached 9° north. It then took a direction to the south-west, and occasionally to the north-west, pushing us on as far as the tropic, at the rate of fifteen miles a day. From the tropic, till we had variable winds, it was constantly to the south-west, when it returned again to the south-east, and kept to that point till we made the Western Islands, where we found that, from the line we had been borne by currents, altogether, thirty miles to the south and 3° to the west.

1806.
June.

Between the parallels of 21° and 36½° north, we passed continually a quantity of sea-weeds, which appeared like large floating islands. These weeds were full of small fish and crabs, of which we caught a great number, chiefly from curiosity.

24th.

On the 24th, we found ourselves, by observation, in latitude 48° 23′ north, and longitude 9° 40′ west; and at night had soundings in ninety fathoms, fine gray sand with shells. Since our departure from the Western Islands, we had seen many armed vessels; but one only, a lugger, came up to us, the commander of which, Mr. Wilkinson, kindly sent me some newspapers and a quantity of potatoes; presents that were very acceptable.

25th.

We were chased, during the whole of the 25th, by a large ship; and at night, though it was extremely dark, and a strong gale blew from the south-west, we were obliged to carry all possible sail to escape, which was the more difficult, as we had to sound pretty often.

26th.

About noon, on the 26th, the weather cleared up sufficiently to allow us an observation in 49° 48′ north: the depth of water being forty-two fathoms, sand and shells. Concluding from this, that we had passed the Lizard Point, I steered for the Start. Towards evening the weather became hazy. This was extremely vexatious, as we had seen no land since our entrance into the Channel. However, a Jersey passage-boat came up to us and brought us a pilot, who took fifty guineas for carrying the ship into Portsmouth.

With an easterly wind we brought to anchor at Portsmouth on the 28th, about nine o'clock in the afternoon. We thus finished our long and troublesome voyage from Canton, without touching at any port; my people enjoying good health, and an abundance of every thing, during the whole passage.

1806.
June.
28th.

In the morning I paid my respects to sir John Prevost, governor of the town, who received me with great politeness, offering me, at the same time, every assistance in his power, of which I might stand in need. The fatigues of the voyage and the repairs necessary for the ship, required our remaining at Portsmouth for a week at least; which time, as my presence was not necessary, I chiefly spent in London.

29th.

On the 13th of July we weighed, with a fresh westerly breeze.

July 13th.

On the 14th, the wind blew so strong from the east, that we were obliged to anchor in the Downs, where we found lord Keith's squadron; and the next day we again set sail.

14th.

On the 20th, at day-light, we saw the Naze; and towards sunset the Robersnout appeared, which, however, we could not see distinctly, on account of the haziness of the weather.

20th.

On the 21st we reached the Skaw Light. This day one of our sailors, Jhon Gorboonoff, died. During the last Swedish war he had been wounded in the breast, and on the passage home had often complained of acute pains in that part of the body.

21st.

1806.
July.
23d.

On the 23d, at midnight, we anchored at Helsinher, and remained there till ten o'clock in the morning.

24th.

On the 24th we cleared the Sound. As the wind blew from the east we were obliged to work to windward under all sail.

26th.
August
3d.

On the 26th, having passed the island of Bornholm, we had foggy weather, which continued till the 3d of August, when we reached the island of Dago. The weather now became fine, and the wind so fair, that towards evening we came up with the island of Hogland.

4th.

On the 4th of August, at midnight, we had so strong a westerly breeze, that we went at the rate of eleven miles an hour, with hardly any sails set, and in the morning cast anchor at Cronstadt.

On our arrival, we were received by the commander-in-chief, admiral Hanicoff, and all the officers then in port, with the most ardent congratulations. As soon as the news of our return reached Petersburgh, persons of all ranks hastened to Cronstadt for the purpose of seeing us. I ordered the ship to be kept at all times ready, and that every possible attention should be paid to the visitors. But so constant was the succession of new comers, so abundant their compliments, and so insatiable their desire of learning the particulars of our voyage, that for several days I was nearly exhausted by fatigue, and could scarcely find time for the necessary meals, or for sleep.

When the vessel was secured within the mole, the emperor

honoured us by a visit in person, and expressed himself highly satisfied with the appearance both of the ship and of the crew; observing, as to the crew, that they even looked better than at their departure from Russia. This was indeed the fact; for there was not an individual on board either sick or diseased; and the feelings naturally arising from the prosperous termination of the voyage, gave to every one an animation, which added greatly to his general clean and healthy look. As to the Neva itself, I shall be excused, if, with the warmth of a sailor I declare, that there never sailed a more lovely vessel, or one more complete and perfect in all its parts. So little had it suffered from the length of the voyage, and even from the disaster of striking on the coral rocks at our new-discovered island, that in a few weeks it was again ready for sea, and was dispatched to the north-west coast of America.

Among the refreshments presented to his imperial majesty while on board, was some Russian salt beef, which had stood the test of the whole voyage, and was still more juicy and less salt than the Irish beef which I had lately purchased at Falmouth. His majesty quitted us with the most gratifying expressions of approbation, and flattered us with the promise of a visit from the empress-mother.

The visit of the emperor had been unexpected, and things were nearly in their usual state; but for the honour now intended us, we were better prepared. I had not permitted a single sixpence to be drawn by any one of the sailors, till our arrival at Canton, where six months pay was allowed to each, to purchase a complete suit of clothes, and to lay out the remainder in adventures. Our illustrious visitor was accordingly received by them in this their best attire, and their appearance greatly surprised her majesty, who, with the most gracious condescension, addressed a few words of kindness and congratulation to every individual on board. She was then conducted through the different parts of the ship, and was pleased to declare herself much gratified and entertained with all that was pointed out to her notice. On retiring, she presented me with a costly diamond ring, and afterwards sent to each of the officers a gold snuff-box or a watch, and to each of the crew ten ducats.

It now only remains to mention the permanent honours and rewards which were bestowed, by imperial munificence, upon the several individuals who had thus accomplished the voyage. As commander, I was promoted to the rank of post-captain in the navy. I had also the honour of being knighted with the order of St. Vladimer of the third class; and, besides different valuable presents from the imperial family, received an annual pension of three thousand rubles. In like manner, all my officers were promoted to the rank next to that which they before held in the service, with pensions from a thousand to five hundred rubles each: and lastly, the petty officers and sailors were allowed, if they pleased, to retire from the service, and enjoy their liberty for life, exclusive of pensions from seventy-five to fifty rubles. This may indeed be considered as the greatest of all rewards, on those on whom it was bestowed, and was truly our emperor's own gracious act. It will be hailed by every grateful heart, as one amongst the many instances of that paternal care, which leads him to regard the happiness and consult the comforts of the lowest of his subjects. His majesty was pleased to declare, that those who, by their ready obedience to orders, and steady perseverance in good conduct, had so materially contributed to add new honours to the Russian flag, deserved to be gratified in the point in which every man places his chief happiness, the enjoyment of ease in the bosom of his family. To every individual was also presented a silver medal, which he is entitled to wear on the breast: it is of an octagon form, impressed with the bust of the emperor Alexander I. on one side, and on the reverse with the ship under full sail, encircled with the inscription, " *For the Voyage round the World in* 1803, 4, 5, *and* 6." These tokens of honour will no doubt excite many to emulation, who would otherwise never have entertained a thought of the naval service; and, when the present wearers shall have completed their voyage of life, they will be valued by their posterity as interesting memorials of their fathers, who first carried the flag of Russia round the globe.

I cannot finish this narrative, without expressing my warmest acknowledgment to my ship's company for the present they have made me of a gold sword, with an inscription of thanks on the handle of it. This sword shall always remain in my family, as a testimony of the character of the people I had the honour of commanding in this memorable expedition.

APPENDIX.

APPENDIX, No. I.

A VOCABULARY

OF

THE LANGUAGE OF NOOCAHIVA.

A.

Afterwards	Mamoohé
Angry	Matatooma
Angry, do not be	Hakay, hakay, *or* Eboo-eboo
Away, go	A-dedahatahatoo
Axe, of iron	Toké tooé
Axe, of stone	Toké maooé

B.

Bad, that is	Ao midaggé
Be, it will	Ena ebo
Bird, a land-	Teté
Bottle	Hooiaki
Boy	Boiti
Brave	Toa
Bread-fruit	Mey
Brother	Toonané
Burying-ground	Meray
Buttons, *or* Playthings	Pipi
Buy, to	Ehogo

C.

Canoe, *or* Boat	Evaka
Catch and bring him here	Ate hooté my
Chief, a	Eiki
Cloth, made of bark	Ekagoo
Club, for war	Eoo
Cock	Moa vahana
Cocoa-nut,	Ehi
Come, do not, here	Ovita my-iné

D.

Day	Boha mahé
Day, to-	Kabo
Do, how do you?	Atika
Door, the	Pohoo
Dull	Vivio

E.

Ears	Pooann
Earth	Ebo
Eat, will you?	A-ky maooté ky
Enemy	Eheama
Enemy, do you eat your?	Gigoi nada?
European	Heytoo, *or* Eytoo
Eye	Gigo mata

F.

Farewell	Eba
Father, *or* Uncle	Matooa
Fingers	Eima
Fish	Eeka
Follow me	Amy tato
Foreign	Monahi
Friend	Ehoa

G.

Girl	Pahoé
Give me	Atoomy
Go and bring it here	Adaha kahé mya
Go to the devil	Tororoo
God	Heytoo, *or* Eytoo
Grandfather	Eta boona
Grandson	Moboona
Grass	Totouha
Gun	Pooi
Gun, do not touch that, it will kill you	Ovhé maoohé

H.

Hair	Ovoho
Hand	Eema
He	Oyana
Head	Ehobogoo
Heart	Hoboo
Hen	Moa vaheenee
Hog	Booaga
House	Ehy
Hungry, I am	Maté de oggé

I. J.

I	Ooaoo
Joyful	Enavé
Iron	Toké
Iron, a small piece of	Toké
Iron, I will give you some	Toogo ato toké ya-a-o-e
Island	Motoo

K.

Kill	Maté
Knife	Goggi, *or* Gooa

L.

Lips	Kinootoo
Liver	E-até
Lobsters or Crabs, three sorts:	
1	Kyitaké
2	Poto
3	Toe toe

M.

Man	Enata
Man, you are an honest	Ineta mitaggé
Mat	Moin
Month	Ete mahama
Moon	Maheena
Morrow, to-	Oy-oé
Mother, *or* Aunt	Ekooi

N.

Nail	Poohi-poohi
Neck	Katé ehi
Nose	Eishoo
Nostrils	Ebohama eishoo

O.

Oar	Hoi-hoi

P.

Plantation	Henoo
Priest	Edaoo
Prohibition	Taboo

R.

Rat	Kioré
Red	Kahoogooyar

S.

Saw, a	Heeka
Sea, *or* Salt water	Itaé
She	Tahova hené
Sister	Tooi heena
Sit down here	Ata nohoo
Sleep, will you, on-board?	Amoynoo devaha
Spear	Paggeo
Step, a	Tabooay
Stolen, have you not, something?	Hay kamo goé
Stone thrown from a sling	Kea *or* Kya
Sun	Eomaté

T.

Take this	Akaveeatoo
Tatooing	Teeka
Teeth	Neehoo

VOCABULARY OF NOOCAHIVA.

That is past	Oovayoo
That will be	Ena ebo
They	Ato
Thief, he is a	Ekamoo
Thigh	Pooha
Thou	Koé
Tongue, hold your	Tooi tooi
Tree	Toomoo

W.

War	Etou
Water	Vy
Water, is there no?	Hamtivy
We	Mato
Well, that is	Midaggé
What do you call it?	Ehadené
What is that?	Ea ha
Where do you go?	Anoigé
Where is he?	Ihé
Where is your king or chief?	Ha kyiriké
White *or* Yellow	Tava tava
Who is that?	Ooy
Why	Meyaha
Wife	Evehené
Woman	Vehené
Work	Hanamydehana
Wounded	Vootoo

Y.

Year	Etahetau
You	Taoe
I am	Ooaoo
Thou art	Koé enaveshoo
He is	Oyana
I was	Ooaoo houné
You were	Koé houné
He was	Oyana houné
She was	Tahova hené houné
I will do it	Ehaooney
You will do it	Atahagoé
He will do it	Tyé hanha aooné
I have	Eia
I had	Iua oo houné
I will have	Eyna ateetahé

Numerals.

1	Eytahé
2	Eynoo
3	Eyto
4	Eyha
5	Eyma
6	Eyono
7	Ehitoo
8	Evahoo
9	Eyva
10	Hanhoo.

N. B. By the inhabitants of Noocahiva the letter *h* is not always sounded. The vowels *a, e,* and *i,* are pronounced as the French pronounce them, except where the *e* is doubled.

APPENDIX, No. II

A VOCABULARY

OF

THE LANGUAGE OF THE SANDWICH ISLANDS.

A.

Afterwards	Mamooree
Angry	Hoohoo
Axe	Koeereepee

B.

Bad, that is	Eyo ino
Belly	Opoo
Black	Ereré
Boy	Taatee
Bread-fruit	Ooloo
Bring hither	Omy
Brother	Tay tyina
Button	Opeehee
Buy, to	Tooay

C.

Cabbage	Tabetee, *or* Kabekee
Cannon	Kooniahi
Canoe, single	Hevaha
Ditto, double	Mokorooa
Cat	Popokee
Cloth of the country	Tapa
Cloth which men tie round the waist	Maro
Ditto for women	Paoo
Cock	Moakanee
Cocoa-nut	Neoo
Come hither	Heré mayoé
Cry, to	Avé

D.

Dance, to	Ahoora
Dart, a small	Ihee
Day	Erapoo
Dead	Makeroa
Do, how do you?	Aloha
Dog	Rio
Door	Pooka
Dry, I am	Pimy vy

E.

Ears	Pepeiaoo
Earth	Ehonooa
Eat, will you?	E-ay-oé
Enemy	Aoree maka maka
European	Ehaouri
Evening	Aheeahee
Eye	Maka

F.

Farewell	Aloha
Father	Makooakanee
Finger, fore	Limameke poe
Ditto, middle	Limoaina
Ditto, third	Limapeelee
Ditto, little	Leemyitee
Fingers	Leema-leema
Fish	Heyo
Friend	Makamaka

G.

Girl	Ty tamaheenee
Goat	Riokao
Go away	Herapera
Go with me, or Follow me	Mamooreeaio
God	Kooa
Good	Myty
Grandfather	Toopoonakanee
Grandmother	Toopoonoaheenee
Grass	Mou
Green	Omomao
Gun	Poo

H.

Hair	Lavohoo
Hand	Leema
Handsome	Nanee
Hat	Papalé
He or she	Oera
Head	Pou
Hen	Moa vaheenee
High	Roeehee
Hog	Pooa
House	Haree
Hungry, I am	Pororeevou

I.

I	Vou
Island	Motoo, or Mokoo

K.

Kill, to	Papahee
Knee	Koolee
Knife	Okeeokee

L.

Lie	Punee punee
Lips	Elehelehé
Little	Poupou
Looking-glass	Aneeanee

M.

Mad	Hehena
Man	Kanaka
Man, he is a good	Ayakanaka myty
Mat (to sleep on)	Moena
Mat (used for clothing)	Ahoo
Melon	Ipoopaeena
Melon, a water-	Ipoohoeoree
Moon	Maheena
Morning, the	Tikaekaney
Morrow	Abobo
Mother	Makooaheenee

N.

Nails	Mayo
Night	Aoomoé
Noise, why do you make a?	Kooreekoore
Nose	Ehu
Nostrils	Pokyhu

O.

Oar	Ehoee

P.

Pay you, I will	Oreema reema
Plantains	Myo
Plantation	Ayna
Potatoes, sweet	Oovara
Priest	Kahoona

Q.

Quickly	Veetee

R.

Rat	Ioré
Red	Ooraoora

S.

Salt	Paky
Saw, a	Paheeoroo
Scissars	Oopa
Sea	Ty
Sheep, a	Rio hoolloo, or Rio veoveo
Shew what is that	Nana meereemeeree
Sister	Tay tooaheenee
Sit down	Noho
Sky	Heranee

Spear	Pororoo	Work, to	Hanahana
Stay a little	Noohoo mareea	Wounded	Tooitahee
Step, a	Vavy		
Stone	Poohakoo	**Y.**	
Sun	La	Yam, a root	Oohee
Swine, have you?	Aori pooaoé	Year	Makahity
Swine, I have no	Aoreepooa paha	Yellow	Orena
Swine, I have	Pooano paha	Yes	Ay
		You	Oé

T.

Take that	Erové
Teeth	Neeho
Temple	Heavoo
Thief	Ayhooé
Thigh	Ooha
Thumb	Limanui
Tired, I am	Manaka
Tongue	Alelu
Tongue, hold your	{ Hamaoo noohoo maria
Touch it not	Noohoo mareea
Tree	Laaoo

Numerals.

1	Akahee
2	Arooa
3	Akoroo
4	Aha
5	Areema
6	Aono
7	Aheetoo
8	Avaroo
9	Yva
10	Aoomi
20	Iva koorooa
30	Kana koroo
40	Kanaha
80	Arooa kanaha
120	Akoroo kanaha
160	Aha kanaha
200	Areema kanaha
240	Aono kanaha
280	Aheeto kanaha
320	Avaroo kanaha
360	Yva kanaha
400	Aoomi kanaha
1000	Manoo

W.

War	Taooa
Water	Vy
Water, is your, good?	Vymyty
Well, that is	Eio myty
What is that?	Ehara teyna
What, *or* Where	Eara
Where is he?	Ahvea
White	Keokeo
Who is it?	Vaynoa eia kanaka
Woman	Vahené

N. B. The inhabitants of the Sandwich Islands speak in a soft tone of voice: *m*, in speaking, is sometimes substituted for *k*, and *g* not sounded at all, or very slightly.

APPENDIX, No. III.

VOCABULARY OF THE LANGUAGES

OF

THE ISLANDS OF CADIACK AND OONALASHCA, THE BAY OF KENAY, AND SITCA SOUND.

English.	Island of Cadiack.	Island of Oonalashca.	Bay of Kenay.	Sitca Sound.
A.				
Apple-tree	. . . . . .	. . . . . .	. . . . . .	Kootst
Arrow	Hok	Ahathak	Iz-zeen	Choonet
Autumn	Ooksvoak	Sakoodee Kinham	Nak-lé	Takooneehaté
B.				
Bad	Aseelnok	Machheedolekan	Tsooheelta	Sliakooshké
Bargain	Youoho	Toomhidada	. . . . . .	Naoo
Basket	Haggek	Ahiahatsak	Hakki	Hinahkakaakee
Bason	Aludak	Kalukak	. . . . . .	Tseek
Bath	Maggeyveek	. . . . . .	Nallee	. . . . . .
Bathe yourself	Hohé	Keecheeheeda	. . . . . .	Etashooch
Bay, the	Kanhiak	Oodok	Botnoo	Key
Bear	Pagoona	Tanhak	Hank-ta	Hoots
Beat	Ahtoho	Toovvada	Neelchah	Chok
Believe	Ookheekeeu	Looceda	. . . . . .	Klehakek avaheen
Belly	Akcehka	Sanhoon	Schboot	Kayu
Berry	Keeoolhet	. . . . . .	Kakká	Knatagget
Birch-tree	Kadzouleek	. . . . . .	Tshoo*kía	Attaggé
Black	Toonhoohalee	Kahchehzeek	Taltashé	Toochaheté
Blackberry	Tshoovavak	Ooneehnok	Kaantsa	Kanettá
Bladder	Keelmak	Sanhook	*Kbis	Athooktee
Block of wood	Kobohak	Yahamkaka	Keyheytsakh	Shaak
Blood	Aook	Amak	Kootaalthin	. . . . . .
Board	Alcku	Aleiok	Opitgaalé	Ta
Boots	Peenadeek	Oleeheek	Sestlia	Hvon

2 U

English.	Island of Cadiack.	Island of Oonalashca.	Bay of Kenay.	Sitca Sound.
Bow		Saeheek	Tsalthan	Saks
Boy	Tanohak	Anektok	Ts*kanik-na	Hattakoo
Bracelets	Talik vahhat	Tameek		Chikatooh
Bragger, a	Sahkvatoolee	Adaluke	Htahootetnash	Hatektsaátee
Brave	Chak fiak	Ehatooleekan	Astsa*kan	Hikaaká
Brother		Aheetoken	Kallá	Ahhonoh
Brother, eldest	Angaha	Luthan		
Brother, youngest	Oouaga	Kee*n*heen		
Burn	Kvahkaho		Teenhkluté	Kahcekan
Bush	Iliahenot		Kankya	
Buy	Youoho	Akeeda		Hanasliahoon

C.

English.	Island of Cadiack.	Island of Oonalashca.	Bay of Kenay.	Sitca Sound.
Canoe	Palayak	Ek-yak	Ktsekooa	Yakoo
Cap	Shaliohnok	Chahoodak	Stcheekeetsá	Saahva
Catch		Sooda	Inlhkit	Alshit
Cheat	Eklunváho	Adalúceda		Kooltooehiheneska
Cheek	Taholskok	Oolloohak	Shinkoosha	Kavvosh
Child	Oodzveelhak		Shareehkahan	Tookonahee
Chin	Tamelok	In*l*akoon	Shtoonee	Kakatatsahí
Come here	Tykeena maoot	Athemeenahkada	Oontsa	Atkoon kehekoot
Copper	Kanooya	Kannooyak	Choochoona	Esk
Cough	Kooek		Khas	Iskohok
Coward	Mamoo keelnok	Ehatoolik	Chaitsk	Kootliahitchan
Cry	Keya	Kithada	Nchah	Kaah
Cure		Oohaeda	Shtatnooliah	Ootoohanakoo
Cut, a	Kiléhtok	Teenoonhaseeteé	Hootnaanltoo	
Cut down	Chaggidzu	Toohoda	Kitsalg	At-hoot

D.

English.	Island of Cadiack.	Island of Oonalashca.	Bay of Kenay.	Sitca Sound.
Dance	Seelga	Aiuhahada		Atleh
Darkness	Tamleek	Kahihakaiuleek	Heelhaklé	Kaoocheekeet
Day	Ahanok	Anneliak	Chaan	
Day, to-	Aganahvák	Vanaeeneliak	Chaan	Ittat
Devil	Yack	Ahlikay	Tskannash	Tseekiekaoo
Die	Togoo		Cheennah	Eenena
Dig	Hahoo	A*n*hooheda	Kookeelia	Ekahek
Dog	Piuhta	Aykok		Kekle
Door	Ommeek	Aheelrek	Tooka*k	Voldt-haak
Down, lay it	Leyhue	I*n*hanoon ahada	Neeneeltalh	Chavveke
Drink	Tanha	Idhootsiá	*Keet-noo	Itanná
Drown	Keeten		Tgataalnan	Ootahoo
Dry	Keenhtsiaho	Keechheeda	Nooletsooh	Kahook
Ducks	Saholheet	Sakeedak	Tinaaltga	Kaoohoo

E.

English.	Island of Cadiack.	Island of Oonalashca.	Bay of Kenay.	Sitca Sound.
Eagle	Koomaheak	Tehlok	Youkh	Chyak
Ear	Chiune	Tootoosak	Stseel-oo	Kakook
Ear-rings	Akhleetot	Neetokák	Stsakeel-a	Ahkookootlee
Ear-rings for the nose	Mydak	Suklook	Sneeh-a	

APPENDIX, NO. III.   331

English.	Island of Cadiack.	Island of Oonalashca.	Bay of Kenay.	Sitca Sound.
Ears	Chiudok	Tootoosakeen	Noolteehastseel-oo	
Earth	Nooná	Chekeke	Alshnan	Sleenkeetaanee
Eat	Peedoho	Kada	*Keeoolh	Hha
Ebb	Keendok	Agook		Hinnahlene
Eggs	Manneet	Samlokamnaholik		Kvoto
Ermine	Ameetadook		Kaholgena	Taa
Evening	Akfoak	Anneliak Ki*nh*an	Haalts	Hanna
Eye	Inhalak	Thak	Shnash-a	
Eyebrows	Kablute	Kamteenchnáneen	Sheentook	Kaatsá
Eyelids	Koomoogaenga	Thankah-senee	Snoutootsa	Kaokahekhoo
Eyes	Inhaliok		Shnashaika	Kavvák

F.

Fall, let	Ihtshu	It-heeda	Nootthilneeh	Nakeek
Farewell	Hvy-ey	Ang-an	Nootheetoosh	Tekooshkee
Father	Adaga	Athak	Tookta	Kyesh
Father, a grand-	Abaga	La-Tohen	Chata	Ahleelhkoo
Father-in-law	Chaggiga		Shpatssa	Ahgoo
Feather	Chooluke	Samaká		Taoo
Fever	Oknehvahtok			Kootsiti-iet
Find	Igoohoo	Ilhada	Nooinlheesh	Akakooshee
Fingers	Sváanga	At-hooneen	Slutska	Katlek
Finger, fore	Teekhá	Choohvahozik		Katlehonee
Finger, middle	Agoolpaga	Teeklok		Katlehtlen
Finger, third	Ahanovyaha			Katlaekakoo
Finger, little	Iggelekogá	Icheelokacheedon		Kavoonkachek
Fire	Knok	Keyhnak	Taaz-ee	Haan
Flood	Tooneehtok	Chehdootoóleek		Takeenatén
Flower	Pateehnet	Chehogniak		
Fool, a	Oosvilnok	Dahkaheholuke		Khleakooshké
Foot	Io-oga	Keetok		Kahooss
Footstep	Toomeet	Cheemek		Kahoosicté
Forehead	Tatka	Tannyak	Sheent-hooboonoo	Kakah
Fox	Kabiák	Ookcheen	*Kanoolsha	Nakatsé
Frost	Nunhlá	Keychók		Koossaát

G.

Gather	Aohkee	Tahseda	Inhtat	Kooteet
Get up	Nanhahtoon	Ankada	Htaneelcheet	Keetan
Girl, a young	Aggeahak	Aehadok	*Keisen kooya	Shaact
Give	Taho		Shla*kanhoot	Ahcheeté
Give me to drink	Tanhamook cheeggeedna	Teen taanak cheheda	Hashnooshect-ye	Atevat-hcen
Give me to eat	Nakmeek cheeggidna	Teen achhooda	Hashoolhinda	Ahehatneté
Go	Keada	Icha	Htsaneeltooh	Kooshté
Go away	Aooha	Inahanehooda	Tsaneeltoosh	Ahkootsoohoo
Go, let	Peedzu	Ihneeda		Cheennah
God	Ahyun	Ahoh	Na*kteltaané	Els

English.	Island of Cadiack.	Island of Oonalashca.	Bay of Kenay.	Sitca Sound.
Good	Aziglee	Mach-heeseleek	Pohallen	Tooaké
Gown, or Parka	Atkook	Sakeen	Shtak-a	Koototst
Gown, made of intestines	Kanahluk	Cheehdan	Keystah-a	At-hoshtee
Grass	Booit	Keyhak	*Katshan	Chookván
Green	Choonhahlee	Chidhaiok	*Kteelt-heen	Neeheenteeahenté
Gull, a sea-	Kadaiat	Slookak	Baach	Kekliatee
Guts	Kelut	Anhek	Shintsika	Kanassí

H.

English.	Island of Cadiack.	Island of Oonalashca.	Bay of Kenay.	Sitca Sound.
Hail	Kouhdat	Tahenem dahskeetoo	Choochoon kalt*ka	Katetst
Hair	Neoet	Imleen	Stseahoo	Koshahaoo
Hand	Taleha	Chianh	Shcoona	Kacheen
Head	Naskok	Kamhek	Shangg-e	Ashaggee
Healthy	Chacheedok	Anhahaseehelek	Pohallen	Klekahluneekoo
Heart	Oongooatagá	Kannuheen	See*ktee	Kateh
He, or she	Ooná	Ikoon	Hhoon	Youta
High	Kanahtoolee	Kaelik	Treélhnoz	Klyahie kooleeké
Hill, a small	Poonhok mihlenok		Koonalthishi	Koocha
Hold your tongue	Nuhneelu	Toonook Talhada	*Ktooteelcheet	
Hook, a fish-	Sagoliak	Imhazeen	Ekshak	Shalhootet
House, a	Naa, or Chekhliok	Oollon	Youiah	Heat
How much	Kouhcheen	Kannahen	Toonaalt-hé	Koonsa

I.

English.	Island of Cadiack.	Island of Oonalashca.	Bay of Kenay.	Sitca Sound.
Iron	Chyavik	Komlyahook	Tayeen	Kayez
Just	Eklunolnok	Adaloohooluke		Klekilhyitaek

K.

English.	Island of Cadiack.	Island of Oonalashca.	Bay of Kenay.	Sitca Sound.
Knee	Chiskoohka	Cheedheedak	Scheesh	Kakeeh
Knot of a tree	Avyak	Yahoomtalee	Kzeekna	
Know, do you not, me?	Nalsvahpoonha-ka	Teen ahkatah-kohteen-ee	Heet a shitneetoo	Hateesekooggé

L.

English.	Island of Cadiack.	Island of Oonalashca.	Bay of Kenay.	Sitca Sound.
Lake	Nanooak	Hanyak	Ban	Aaká
Leaf	Pelu	Yahamoleé	*Kat-oon	Kahanee
Lie, to	Eklu		Heentseet	Hataakeehoon
Light	Aggiek	Anhalyak	Keetsool	Ooteekaan
Lion, a sea-	Adahluk	Kavooak	Atahhlut	Taan
Lips	Hluhká	Athek	Ezak	Kahak-a
Liver	Aeenga	Ahhek	Sezzeet	Kakeykoo
Live, where do you?	Nanee-cheet	Kananhoon a-koot-hín	Ndah tokee-eetgan	Kooksehheté
Loose	Tamaho	Ihkeecha	Keeliahtoonah	Kotooveeh
Louse	Naaeta	Keetok	You	Betst
Low	Achahkeelnok	Kasloken	Tzeelhkats	
Lungs	Kamaganok	Hoomehek	Stsat-tska	Kakahakoo

APPENDIX, NO. III.   333

English.	Island of Cadiack.	Island of Oonalashca.	Bay of Kenay.	Sitca Sound.
M.				
Man	Shook	Tayaho	Teenná	Chakleyh
Mat	Pehat	Sootok		Toots
Moon	Yaalock	Tooheedak	Ne-é	Teess
Morning	Oonoak	Keelyam		Keskhé
Morrow, to-	Onnoago	Kelliohen	Neelkoonda	Sekanneen
Moss	O-ot		Naan	Tsikahá
Mother	Anaha	Annak	Anná	Aklee
Mother, grand-	Maga	Kookanh	Choota	Ahlilhkoo
Mother-in-law		Satemheen	Sh-o	Ahchaan
Mountain	Poonhok anhlee	Koothook	Teheylé	Shahata
Mouth	Kanok	Aheelrek	Shnaan	Kak-e
Murderer	Tohodgisnoolée	Alcet-hoozok	Cheekilhuhe	Chakooté
Muscles	Kabeeliot	Vyhak		Haak
N.				
Nails	Stoonga	Kaahelren	Skanna	Kahakoo
Neck	Ooyakoga	Oouk		Kasetá
Needle	Meenhon	Inukak	*Klean*kheen	Taakatel
Nephew	Ootsooga	Omnin	Shooja	Ahkeelk
Net, a fish-	Agaloo	Koozmahek	Tahveelh	
Night	Oonuke	Amak	*Kaa*k	Taat
Nose	Keenaga	Anhozin	Tsanalleetga	Kaclu
Nostrils	Padzifahka	Anhozin Hookik	Shneek	Kaslutoo
O.				
Oar	Chaheeyoun	Ahkadvoozeek	Khaneetsté	Ahhá
Old	Kaneehlak	Ollek	Keychee	Ooteeshen
Otter, a river-	Aakooya	Aakooya	Tact-hin	Kooshta
Otter, a sea-	Ahná	Cheenatok	To*k-es	Youhch
P.				
Palm of the hand	Toomága	Chankala	Slya*ka	Kachentak
Pay, to	Nalsyaho		Kiushilhnah	Agakenesnee
People	Shoot	Tayahoamnaholeeh	Koht-ana	Hsleenkeet
Pillow	Aggin	Kanheetak	Tset-aazdeen	Shehet
Pine-fir	Anknahaleet		Tspaalla	Aasé
Plant, to	Lseelahkee	It-heeda		Tankanakoo
Play, to	Vooamee	Meehkada	Cheenleool	Achkoolhiat
Poor	Nakhee nahalee	Itonasak	Pa*khool	Slshaan
Poplar-tree	Cheehoo		Esnee	Tokoo
Porpoise	Manhak	Alladok	Kooosheé	Chee-each
Pregnant	Aksaluke	Idmaheleek	Halkhoon	Hetehahoo
Q.				
Quick	Choogalee	Ayahohodooleek	Naheylhkeet	Chayoukoo
Quilt, a bed-	Oolik	Kallooheen		

English.	Island of Cadiack.	Island of Oonalashca.	Bay of Kenay.	Sitca Sound.
R.				
Rain	Kedok	Chehtak		Seevva
Raspberry	Alagnak	Halohnak	Koolhkaha	Kleakoo
Raven	Kalnhak	Kalkahyon	Cheenshla	Els
Red	Kaveeglee	Oolluthak	Tahalteley	Haniaheté
Rein-deer	Toondoo	It-Hayok	Patchih	Tavvé
Rejoice	Noonaneehsaha	Kaanooda	Nookooeelthoonh	Nashook
Rich	Kaskok	Toohkooleek	Kashkanlan	Antlinkintee
River	Kooyk	Chéhanok	*Katnoo	Hateen
Roe of fish	Chijoot, or Ah-majoot	Kamheesoo	Kin	Kaakoo
Roof	Padoo	Oolankamoon*h*een	Kan*ka	Hanatané
Root	Nooggihluke		Chan	Ahhaátee
Rope	Cavahtsee	Oomnak	*Keelh	Tikh
Rude	Kamanahlee	Koosootooleek	Tggeeknash	
S.				
Sack, a	Haggek		Oolks	Koelh
Sand	Kabea	Choohok	Soohoo	Klue
Sea	Eemák	Allaook	Noot-hé	Teyké
Seal, a	Izuik	Izok	Kootsaheyls-é	Tsa
Sell	Aggeechakue	Nooahada		Ihoon
Send	Tyskue	Ahkáneeda		Koonaká
Shoot	Peedeedzue	Toomheda	Teehkat	Atoont
Sick	Knal-ha	Takeehzeek	Cheennah	Haneekoo
Sing	Atoová	Oonuhada	Katalyash	Atkashee
Sister		Oon*h*een	Ootalla	Ahklyak
Sit down	Agomee		Neetsoot	Kannoó
Sky	Keliok	Innyak	Youyan	Haats
Sleep	Kahvá	Sahada		Nattá
Slow	Chookalnok	Aiahohlokan	Tsoonaheylkeet	Takeynah
Slumber	Kavahanee		Neeltseelh	Ahekho
Snow	Annué	Kanneeh	Ajjah	Kleyt
Snuff	Proshka	Ihdooteen	Ktoona	
Soft	Oonelnok	Ka*nh*a Heydoloken		Katlyaheté
Son-in-law	Neengouga	Naahoon		Ahcehoh
Spark	Kalski	Keyhnak Kalmeehzeek	Chatalahi	Heektlya
Spoon	Alugoon	Tahozek	Spata	Shelh
Spring	Oobnohkak	Kaneekee*nh*an	Klek	Takooité
Stars	Ageke	Stan	Sceen	Kootahanahá
Steal	Tecgleeha	Chhada	*Knazzeen	Ataoo
Step	Toomeenha	Keeton Keydhooneen		Kakoostak
Stick	Pekhodák	Ayaook	Tgats	Kaats
Stone	Yamak	Koovvanak	Kaleekneekee	Té
Straight	Nalekeeglee	At-hádeehaleek	Tsehalkhé	Klyakavoostiek
Strong	Tookneelee	Kayoutooleek	Talt-hey	Hleetseen
Summer	Kiek	Saakoodak	Shaan	Kootaan
Sun	Madzak	Ahhapak	Channoo	Kakkaan
Swim	Quima	Hoochihada	Niba	Echkootetecha

APPENDIX, NO. III.

English.	Island of Cadiack.	Island of Oonalashca.	Bay of Kenay.	Sitca Sound.
T.				
Tail		Samchehcheheteenee*nh*	Pka	Koohoó
Take	Tehoo	Suda	Ilhkeet	Shee
Take away by force	Aloodzhu	Ilyasuda	Ktooshecheet	Ashtseet-henesnee
Tear	Chaktaho	Oonháseda	Chaanhklut	Astcheetoot-hoot
Teeth	Hoodeit	Keahoozeen	Shreek-ha	Kaooh
That	Ooná		Keenee	Eta
That is mine	Hvy Pigá	Vaya-myou*nh*	Shish-iti	
That is yours	Hvy lspitpin	Inne-yemayou*nh*	Non-iti	
Thief	Toogluna galee	Chhaaheleek	*Kaneesh	Ataootsaté
Thin	Ameelnok	Annatoolookan	Trelteet	Klyahiekoossá
Thread, made of the intestines of the whale	Keepak	Ihachahsyak	Kattsah	Tehkatassé
Throw	Idzhoo	Anooséda	Yatsteeltuh	
Thumb	Kamlugá	Hooták	Slukts	Kaakoosh
Tongue	Oolue	Ahnak	Stseelue	Katnoot
Touch, do not	Chagnilu	Anehtaganan	Tgaa	
Touch me, do not	Chahin nilnha	Teen anehtahanok	Ltoosilhan	Henkatetsen
Tree	Kobohak tsbalakua	Yahak	Tsbalacooya	Shaak
U.				
Urchins, sea-	Ootoot	Ahohnok		Neets
V.				
Valley	Maak	Chanhanak		Shecheekeeka
Vein	Noogak	Ya-meekhap	Tsah	Tass
Venereal	Idoonak		Tsooeestat	Katluke
Volcano	Inhyak	Kiehozim Keegnáhee	Tokoge-hnoohalley	
W.				
Walk	Quinhdeen		*Kanoontoosh	Haacacoo
Wash	Ohtohó	Cheoohoda	Tnoonleah	Naootst
Water	Tanak	Tanak	Veelhnée	Ieen
Weak	Tookneelnok	Kauhaleeken	*Ktakhooleen	Klekhleetseen
Wet	Moodzok	Chahtakohalik		Ooteekek
Whale	Agvok	Allok		Yaaga
What	Chashtoon		Tsatoo	Vasaet
What are you afraid of?	Chay aleeksiu	Alkok Ehagteleet-heen	Tsatsaeentsk	
What is your name?	Namat-hoon		Ntecneegee	Coosisaggé
Where are you going?	Natmen-ayouit	Kananoomeen	Ndah teenue	Kootéseheenakooh
Where were you?	Nahin puden	Kanaliok Teleet-heen	Ndah toozitoo	Kooteseheekooteen
White	Katogalee	Oommeleek	Talkaé	Kletyaheté
Why	Chalooden	Alkomeen	Tsatskoo	Takotkaasa

English.	Island of Cadiack.	Island of Oonalashca.	Bay of Kenay.	Sitca Sound.
Wide	Ayanahtooleé	Slakseek	Trelt-han	Klyakié-koohoo
Wind	Kyaeek	Kycheek	Kakneeoon	Keelhcha
Winter	Ookseeok	Kanák	Hhee	Taakoo
Wipe	Alshue	Kidhooda	Knin*kash	
Wise	Oodzveetoolee	Akamkahek	Heet-aneezzan	Hakootseké
Wizard	Tonanok	Koohok	Chaanchoo	Eht
Woman	Aganák	Anhahenak	Mokelan	Shavvot
Work	Chená	Avvada	Heetnoo	Echenené
Wound	Keeye		Skoo*kha	Eeyeté
Y.				
Year	Cheeoolek	Elok	Shantto	
Yellow	Choonhahlee	Madelohnok	Taltsahé	Kandgeheenya-henté
Young	Soonhak	Soohonazak	Kooteehazalheen	Isvat
Numerals.				
1	Ataoodzek	Atoken	Tseelgtan	Klek
2	Azlha	Arlok	Nootna	Teh
3	Peengasvak	Kankoo	Too*k-e	Notsk
4	Stameek	Seecheen	Tan*k-e	Tackoon
5	Taleemeek	Chaan	Tskeel-oo	Keecheen
6	Ahoi-lune	Atoon	*Koojtonee	Ketooshoo
7	Malehonheen	Oolloon	Kants-e-hé	Tahatoushoo
8	Inglulun	Kancheen	Ltakool-e	Neetskatooshoo
9	Koolnhooen	Seecheen	Lkeetseet-hoo	Kooshak
10	Koolen	Atek	*Klujoon	Cheenkaat
11	Athahtok	Ateem atoken seehnohta		Cheenkaat avan-hak klek
12	Malhognook	Ateem arlok seehnohta		Cheenkaat avan-hak teh
13	Pinga-you-nook	Ateem kankoo seehnohta		Cheenkaat avan-hak notsk
14	Stamanook	Ateem seecheen seehnohta		Cheenkaat avan-hak tackoon
15	Talee manook	Ateem chaan seehnohta		Cheenkaat avan-hak keecheen
16	Ahoyeloogge-nook	Ateem atoon seehnohta		Cheenkaat avan-hak ketooshoo
17	Mals-honhee-nook	Ateem oolloon seehnohta		Cheenkaat avan-hak tahatoushoo
18	Inglu lugnook	Ateem kancheen seehnohta		Cheenkaat avan-hak neetskatooshoo
19	Kooln hooya-nook	Ateem seecheen seehnohta		Cheenkaat avan-hak kooshak
20	Koolnook, or Svinák	Alhatiah	Tsilhatna	Klek-ka
30	Sveenák koolnook azluke	Kankoodem atek	Toot klujoon	

APPENDIX, NO. III.

English.	Island of Cadiack.	Island of Oonalashca.	Bay of Kenay.	Sitca Sound.
40	Sveenák mallok	Seecheedem atek	Tange klujoon	
50	Sveenák mallok koolnook pin ha youlook	Chaanheedeematek	Tskil-oo klujoon	
60	Sveenet pinhaion	Atoonhidim atek	Koojts klujoon	
70	Sveenet pinhaion koolnook	Oolloonheedeem atek	Kankehoh klujoon	
80	Sveenet staman	Kancheenheedeen atek		
90	Sveenet staman koolnook	Seecheenheedeem atek		
100	Sveenet taleéma-loot	Seesak	Tgastlun	
200	Sveenet kooleen	Alhim seesak		

N. B. In the Vocabulary of Oonalashca, the letters *nh*, printed in Italics, and *k* and *n*, when final letters, should be half-sounded only. The inhabitants of this country have this singularity, that they pronounce the *th* with the same facility and precisely like the English.

The Sitcans observe three tones in every word of length, of which the middle one is the lowest.

The language of Kenay is very difficult to be expressed: k, with an asterisk preceding it, has a sort of double sound, not unlike the clucking of a hen.

APPENDIX, No. IV.

TABLES

OF

THE ROUTE OF THE NEVA,

DURING

THE YEARS 1803, 4, 5, & 6:

FROM

THE TIME OF ITS LEAVING EUROPE TO ITS RETURN.

N. B. In these Tables are set down the Situation of the Ship, the Temperature of the Atmosphere by Fahrenheit, and the Height of the Barometer, at Noon. The Latitude is given from Observation, and the Longitude from the Chronometers.

TABLE I.

PASSAGE FROM FALMOUTH TO TENERIFFE.

Time.	Lat. N.	Long. W.	Barometer.	Ther.	Variation of the Compass West.	Winds, Weather, and Remarks.
1803.	° ′	° ′	Inch. Line	°	° ′	
Oct. 6	49 5	6 30	30 1	58	....	Light breeze at N. E., and pleasant weather. At half past four P. M. set sail from Falmouth: at eleven, a-breast of the Lizard Point.
7	....	....	29 9	61	....	Strong breeze at S. E., and cloudy.
8	....	....	29 8	62½	....	Strong breeze: towards night more moderate, and hazy.
9	41 28	....	29 8	61½	....	Strong breeze from the eastward, and cloudy.
10	38 44	13 55	29 7	66	18 12 azim.	Strong breeze from the E. S. E., and cloudy: towards night, more moderate.
11	35 55	14 48	29 6	69	....	Fresh easterly gales, and squally.
12	34 47	15 1	29 6	70	19 16	Variable and squally, with occasional lightning and rain.
13	34 8	13 50	29 6¼	71	19 2	Moderate breeze at S. W., and fine weather: during the night, squally and rain.
14	....	....	29 6½	71	....	Light airs and serene weather.
15	33 23	13 47	29 7¼	71	....	Light airs and squally, with occasional rain.
16	32 43	13 47	29 8	72	16 22	Light westerly airs.

TABLE I.—Continued.

PASSAGE FROM FALMOUTH TO TENERIFFE.

Time.	Lat. N.	Long. W.	Barometer.	Ther.	Variation of the Compass West.	Winds, Weather, and Remarks.
1803.	° ′	° ′	Inch. Line.	°	° ′	
Oct. 17	31 23	14 48	30	72	....	Fresh breeze from the N. E. to N. W., and fine weather.
18	30 8	15 14	30	72	....	Light breeze from the N. W., and fine weather.
19	28 58	15 50	29 9½	75	....	Light breezes from the eastward, and clear. At three P. M. saw the Salvages. At noon, the north end of the island of Teneriffe bore S. W. twenty miles.
20	....	....	29 9	74	15 22 azim.	About noon anchored in the harbour of Santa Cruz.

APPENDIX, NO. IV.   343

TABLE II.

PASSAGE FROM TENERIFFE TO THE ISLAND OF ST. CATHARINE.

Time.	Lat. N.	Long. W.	Barometer.	Ther.	Variation of the Compass West.	Winds, Weather, and Remarks.
	° ′	° ′	Inch. Line.	°	° ′	
1803. Oct. 28	27 48	....	29 5	75	....	Light airs and fine weather. At one P. M. sailed from Teneriffe: at six, the Peak of Teneriffe bore N. 86° west.
29	26 13	....	29 5	75	16 11 azim.	A light breeze from the N.W. At half after six the Peak of Teneriffe bore N. by E. three quarters E.
30	24 53	18 9	29 9	75½	15 21	Fresh breeze from the N. W., and fine.
31	23 52	....	29 9	75	....	Fine breeze from the N. E., and cloudy.
Nov. 1	23 9	19 32	29 9	84	....	Light airs from the N. E.
2	22 37	20 2	29 9	79	15 14	Light airs from the eastward, and close weather.
3	21 49	20 46	29 9	80	15 4 amp. az.	Light northerly breeze, and pleasant weather.
4	20 12	22 26	29 8½	79	14 22 (azim.)	Pleasant breeze, and cloudy weather, which cleared up in the night.
5	18 48	24 9	29 9	80	13 40 amp.	Fine breeze from the N. E., and cloudy.
6	17 58	25 23	29 9	81	....	Fresh breeze from the N. N. W., and cloudy. At five A. M. the island of St. Antony bore S. half E. twenty miles.

TABLE II.—Continued.

PASSAGE FROM TENERIFFE TO THE ISLAND OF ST. CATHARINE.

Time.	Lat. N.		Long. W.		Barometer.		Ther.	Variation of the Compass West.		Winds, Weather, and Remarks.
	°	′	°	′	Inch.	Line.	°	°	′	
1803. Nov. 7	17	7	....		29	9	82	10 azim.		Light airs from the N.E., and cloudy. At noon, S. point of St. Antony E. S. E. ½ E. 56 miles.
8	15	34	26	36	29	9	81	7	58	Light breeze at E. S. E., and cloudy.
9	14	54	27	7	29	8½	83	6	38	Light breeze at S. E., and clear: rain in the morning.
10	13	53	27	13	29	9	82	....		Light easterly breezes, and cloudy.
11	12	47	26	23	29	9	83	5	55	Winds and weather the same. At midnight rain.
12	11	13	25	10	29	9	84	11	7	Fresh breeze at E. N. E., and fine.
13	9	45	23	27	29	8½	83	13	38	Strong breeze at N. E. by E., and cloudy.
14	8	5	21	57	29	8½	84	....		Strong breeze at E. N. E., and cloudy. At night thunder and lightning.
15	7	3	21	31	29	8½	84	10	35	Light breeze from the eastward, and squally; with thunder and lightning.
16	6		21	8	29	8¼	85	11	4	Light easterly breeze and squally, with occasional rain.
17	5	35	21	18	29	8	80	....		Light variable airs, and calm. In the morning squalls and rain.

TABLE II.—Continued.

PASSAGE FROM TENERIFFE TO THE ISLAND OF ST. CATHARINE.

Time.	Lat. N.	Long. W.	Barometer.	Ther.	Variation of the Compass West.	Winds, Weather, and Remarks.
1803.	° ′	° ′	Inch. Line.	°	° ′	
Nov. 18	5 46	21 18	29 8	83	11 43 azim.	Calm and cloudy. Rain in the afternoon.
19	5 36	....	29 8	80	....	Light airs and clear. At nine A. M. squally.
20	....	....	29 8	80	....	Light airs from the S. E. quarter, with rain towards midnight.
21	....	....	29 7¼	79	....	The same.
22	4 42	21 28	29 7¼	81½	....	Calm and rainy.
23	4 13	22 7	29 8	83	10 50	Light airs at S. S. E. with rain.
24	....	....	29 8½	75	10 43	Variable winds, with rain.
25	1 34	22 57	29 8	81	9 40	Strong breeze from the S. E. and rainy.
26	Lat. S. 10	24 9	29 8	81	8 18	Fine breezes at S. E. by S. and cloudy.
27	1 45	25 12	29 8½	82	7 22	Strong breeze from the S. E. and fine weather.
28	3 21	26 10	29 8½	81	7 21	The same.
29	4 57	27 15	29 8	81	7 32	Strong breeze and squally.
30	6 30	28 16	29 8½	81	6 44	Pleasant breezes at S. E. and clear.

TABLE II.—Continued.

PASSAGE FROM TENERIFFE TO THE ISLAND OF ST. CATHARINE.

Time.	Lat. S.	Long. W.	Barometer.	Ther.	Variation of the Compass West.	Winds, Weather, and Remarks.
1803.	° ′	° ′	Inch. Line.	°	° ′	
Dec. 1	8 27	29 11	29 8	83	5 40 azim.	Moderate gales at S. E. and cloudy.
2	10 30	29 45	29 8½	82	5 46	Moderate gales at S. E. by E. and clear.
3	12 18	30 24	29 8¼	80	4 55	Strong breeze at E. by S. and clear.
4	14 45	30 53	29 9	80	4 27	Moderate gales at E. S. E. and fine weather.
5	16 30	31 18	29 8¾	82	2 46	Pleasant breeze from the E. N. E. and fine.
6	....	....	29 9	78	2 23	Variable breeze, and fine.
7	19 48	31 53	29 9¼	79½	....	Fine breeze from the N. E. and cloudy.
8	20 51	....	29 9½	81	....	Fine breeze from the N. E. by E. and cloudy.
9	20 43	35 50	29 9	82	....	Moderate breeze from the northward, and cloudy.
10	21 45	38 12	29 7	79	....	Strong breeze at N. by E. towards morning N. by W.
11	22 43	39 30	29 6	79	Var. E. 4 21	Fresh gales at N. N. W. and rainy: towards night light airs.

TABLE II.—Continued.

PASSAGE FROM TENERIFFE TO THE ISLAND OF ST. CATHARINE.

Time.	Lat. S.	Long. W.	Barometer.	Ther.	Variation of the Compass East.	Winds, Weather, and Remarks.
1803.	° ′	° ′	Inch. Line.	°	° ′	
De 12	....	....	29 6	78	4 azim.	Light airs and pleasant weather. At eight P.M. sounded in fifty-five fathoms: at five A.M., saw Cape Frio, in S. 85° W. At noon the depth of water was forty fathoms, green oozy ground and shells.
13	....	....	29 8	74	5 40	Pleasant southerly breeze and fine weather. During the night the wind freshened: at eight A. M. Cape Frio bore N. 57° W. distant thirty or forty miles.
14	24 14	42 17	29 9½	77	4 57	Fine breeze from S. E. and clear. At six P. M. Cape Frio bore N. half W., twenty-two miles.
15	....	....	29 8½	79	....	Fine breeze at E. N. E. and cloudy.
16	26 19	47	29 8½	77	8 55	The same.
17	....	....	29 8½	78	9 45	Fine breeze and clear. At four A. M. saw the land to the S. S. W. At ten A. M. hazy: depth of water from twenty to twenty-five fathoms.
18	26 59	48 5	29 8	75	10	Light airs, and rain. Depth of water from twenty-two to thirty-five fathoms.

TABLE II.—*Continued.*

PASSAGE FROM TENERIFFE TO THE ISLAND OF ST. CATHARINE.

Time.	Lat. S.	Long. W.	Barometer.	Ther.	Variation of the Compass East.	Winds, Weather, and Remarks.
1803. Dec. 19	° ′ 26 52	° ′	Inch. Line. 30	° 77	° ′	Fine breeze at N. E. and clear. At five P. M. strong southerly gales, and heavy sea.
20	26 59	....	29 9½	74	....	Moderate gales from the southward. At seven A. M. depth of water thirty-five fathoms, and the island of Alvaredo S. by W. fifteen miles.
21	27 5	....	....	......	....	Calm and pleasant weather. At noon the island of Alvaredo bore S. half E. about six miles.
22	....	....	....	......	....	Light airs, and fine. At six P. M. came to an anchor in six fathoms, oozy ground; fort of Santa Cruz, bearing N. 15° W. and the fort of Ponta Grossa, N. 71° E.

APPENDIX, NO. IV.

TABLE III.

PASSAGE FROM THE ISLAND OF ST. CATHARINE TO EASTER ISLAND.

Time.	Lat. S.		Long. W.		Barometer.		Ther.	Variation of the Compass East.		Winds, Weather, and Remarks.
1804.	°	′	°	′	Inch.	Line.	°	°	′	
Feb. 5	....		....		29	8	77	....		Light airs and cloudy. At two P. M. weighed and made sail: at five doubled the north point of the island of St. Catharine. Towards night fresh gales, and thirty-five fathoms of water.
6	28	5	....		29	8	78	....		Fresh gales and rainy: in the evening, moderate and clear.
7	30	16	46	50	29	9	79¼	....		Moderate gales, and fine.
8	32	50	47		29	9	77	S 40 azim.		Fine breeze at E. N. E. and pleasant weather.
9	34	39	47	27	30		77	....		Fine breeze from the N. E. and clear.
10	36	44	49	14	29	5	75½	....		Strong breeze at N. E. and cloudy, with rain during the night: in the morning stronger breeze and hazy.
11	38	19	50	47	29	6	71½	14	30	Fresh gales and heavy sea, with hazy weather.
12	....		....		29	8½	64½	....		Moderate gales at S. W. and squally, with heavy swell.
13	40	6	50	48	29	9½	70	14		Light breeze and thick weather.
14	40	37	50	43	30		64	14	17	Light breeze and pleasant weather.

TABLE III.—Continued.

PASSAGE FROM THE ISLAND OF ST. CATHARINE TO EASTER ISLAND.

Time.	Lat. S.	Long. W.	Barometer.	Ther.	Variation of the Compass East.	Winds, Weather, and Remarks.
1804.	° ′	° ′	Inch. Line.	°	° ′	
Feb. 15	40 58	53	30	70	....	Fine breeze, and cloudy.
16	42 26	54 21	30	69½	16 44 amp. az.	Fine breeze from the E. S. E. and cloudy.
17	43 56	56 12	30	68½	18 8 amp.	Light airs, and cloudy.
18	45 29	58 32	29 8½	63	18 10 azim.	Fine breeze from the N. E. and clear: in the morning more fresh, from the N. N. E.
19	....	....	29 6½	58	....	Fresh gales from the northward: at ten A. M. squalls and fog, with rain.
20	48 27	63 1	29 7	58	19 38	Variable breezes. At four P. M. the fog cleared up: sounded in seventy fathoms, sandy bottom.
21	....	....	29 4	57	....	Fresh gales from the S. E. and cloudy. At noon sounded in sixty fathoms, the wind at S. W.
22	50 33	65 33	29 5	59½	21 16	Fine breeze from the S. W. quarter.
23	51 44	65 37	29 3½	58½	....	Fine breeze at W. by N. and cloudy weather. At seven P. M. sounded in seventy fathoms, sandy bottom.

TABLE III.—*Continued.*

PASSAGE FROM THE ISLAND OF ST. CATHARINE TO EASTER ISLAND.

Time.	Lat. S.	Long. W.	Barometer.	Ther.	Variation of the Compass East.	Winds, Weather, and Remarks.
	° ′	° ′	Inch. Line.	°	° ′	
1804. Feb. 24	53 24	64 45	29 1	58	21 16 azim.	Pleasant breeze at W. N. W. and fine weather. At six P. M. sounded in seventy fathoms, pebble stones.
25	54 11	63 38	29	56	23 47	Variable winds and cloudy. At seven P.M. sounded in sixty-eight fathoms: at four A.M. saw Staten Land to the S. S. E.: at nine the depth of water seventy-five fathoms, small pebble stones.
26	56 12	62 37	28 5	47	21 37	Pleasant breeze and clear weather: in the morning fresh gales from the S. W.
27	57 16	63 38	28 7½	45½	....	Fresh gales from the westward.
28	58 22	64 2	28 7½	37	....	Fresh westerly gales, and squally weather, with hail: at night strong gales.
29	....	....	29 3	34	....	Fresh westerly gales, and squally weather, with snow and hail: at night strong gales and heavy sea.
Mar. 1	....	....	29 3½	36	25 9	Fresh gales from the N. W. to S. W. and hazy weather.
2	59 2	63 45	29 6½	38½	....	Fine breeze at S. W. and cloudy: in the morning light airs from the eastward.

TABLE III.—*Continued.*

PASSAGE FROM THE ISLAND OF ST. CATHARINE TO EASTER ISLAND.

Time.	Lat. S.		Long. W.		Barometer.		Ther.	Variation of the Compass East.		Winds, Weather, and Remarks.
	°	′	°	′	Inch.	Line.	°	°	′	
1804. Mar. 3	....		....		29	1¼	44	26	30 azim.	In the evening pleasant breeze at N. N. E. In the night the wind shifted to the N. W. and blew fresh.
4	....		....		28	8½	41	....		Pleasant breeze from the westward, hazy.
5	....		....		28	9	41	....		Light variable airs, with heavy sea and foggy weather.
6	....		....		29	1½	41	....		Light airs, with a heavy westerly swell, and hazy weather.
7	59	20	71	22	29		41	....		Fine breeze from the westward. In the night moderate gales.
8	59	10	71	5	28	9	44	....		Light airs from the S. W. quarter, and rainy weather, with a swell from the westward.
9	59	32	72	35	28	7½	41	....		Fine westerly breeze, and cloudy.
10	59	30	73	5	28	8	40	25	47	Light airs from the S. W. quarter.
11	58	40	75	32	29	1	40	....		Light airs. At night a fine breeze from the S. S. W. and squally.
12	57	48	78	43	28	9¼	46	....		Light breeze from the E. S. E. and cloudy. In the morning a fresh easterly breeze.

APPENDIX, NO. IV.

TABLE III.—*Continued.*

PASSAGE FROM THE ISLAND OF ST. CATHARINE TO EASTER ISLAND.

Time.	Lat. S.		Long. W.		Barometer		Ther.	Variation of the Compass East.		Winds, Weather, and Remarks.
	°	′	°	′	Inch.	Line.	°	°	′	
1804. Mar. 13	57		80	53	29	2¼	44	24 azim	45	Pleasant breeze from the S. E. and clear weather. Towards night light variable airs.
14	56	12	83	14	29	½	46	....		Pleasant breeze from the northward, and cloudy weather. In the morning moderate gales.
15	55	34	86	6	28	8	46	....		Fresh gales from the northward. In the morning moderate gales.
16	55	9	87	3	28	8	47	22 az. & amp	40	Light breeze from the N. W. and hazy weather. Towards midnight fresh gales.
17	....		....		28	6	44	....		Fresh gales from the N. W. and cloudy. In the morning more moderate.
18	55	44	89	27	28	9	57	....		Calm and clear weather.
19	55	46	90	6	29	½	46	23 azim.	38	The same.
20	54	13	91	28	29	7	44½	....		Light airs and clear weather. At night a fine easterly breeze.
21	51	33	93	29	30	2	45	....		Fresh variable winds and cloudy, with occasional squalls.
22	49	25	95		30	3½	47	....		Fine breeze from the S. W. and squally.
23	48	10	95	52	30	3	48	14 az. & amp.	33	Variable breeze and fine weather.

TABLE III.—Continued.

PASSAGE FROM THE ISLAND OF ST. CATHARINE TO EASTER ISLAND.

Time.	Lat. S.	Long. W.	Barometer.	Ther.	Variation of the Compass East.	Winds, Weather, and Remarks.
	° ′	° ′	Inch. Line.	°	° ′	
1804. Mar. 24	....	....	29 7	52	....	Fine breeze from the E.N.E. At night fresh gales and squally, with fog and rain.
25	47 15	98 6	29 6	54	....	Fresh gales from the N. W. and foggy weather. Lost sight of the Nadejda.
26	45 43	97 15	29 7	58	15 22 azim.	Fresh breeze from the westward, and hazy.
27	....	....	29 3	54	....	Light breezes from the N.W. and clear.
28	43 11	97 18	29 3	54	....	Fresh gales from the N. E. At night strong gales from the S. W.
29	43 18	....	29 1½	54	11 4	Fresh gales from the N. W. and clear weather, with a westerly swell.
30	41 49	97 37	29 6½	54	11 55	Fresh gales and clear weather.
31	39 20	98 42	30	58	10 49	Moderate gales from the W. S.W. and hazy, with heavy sea.
April 1	38 1	....	30	62	11 5	Light breezes from the S. W. and cloudy weather.
2	37 44	100 24	29 7	65	9	Light airs. At night a fine breeze from the northward, with occasional rain.

TABLE III.—Continued.

PASSAGE FROM THE ISLAND OF ST. CATHARINE TO EASTER ISLAND.

Time.	Lat. S.	Long. W.	Barometer.	Ther	Variation of the Compass East.	Winds, Weather, and Remarks.
	° ′	° ′	Inch. Line	°	° ′	
1804. April 3	37 2	101 5	29 6	65	....	Light variable breezes, and cloudy.
4	35 50	101 15	29 6¼	64	8 22 az. & amp.	Light breeze from the N. W. quarter, and cloudy.
5	....	....	29 7	63	8 17 amp.	Light breeze, and clear.
6	33 12	100 55	29 9	74	....	Moderate gales from the W. S. W. Towards night still more moderate.
7	33 4	102 45	29 4½	70	....	Moderate gales from the N. N. W. and cloudy.
8	33 7	103 38	29 6¼	68½	7 57 azim.	Fresh gales at N. W. and squally. At night more moderate, and fine weather.
9	....	....	29 6¼	68	....	Light airs from the N. W. quarter, and cloudy.
10	31 53	103 23	29 7	71	....	Light airs and cloudy, with a swell from the N. W.
11	31 48	104 5	29 7	73	8 46 az. & amp	Light breeze, and cloudy.
12	....	....	29 6	66	....	Light breeze from the N. W. Towards noon stronger breeze.
13	29 45	104 49	29 7½	67	8 30 azim.	Fresh gales from the N. W. and rainy.
14	28 33	106 13	29 9	71	....	Fine breeze from the S. W.

TABLE III.—Continued.

PASSAGE FROM THE ISLAND OF ST. CATHARINE TO EASTER ISLAND.

Time.	Lat. S.	Long. W.	Barometer.	Ther.	Variation of the Compass East.	Winds, Weather, and Remarks.
1804.	° ′	° ′	Inch. Line.	°	° ′	
April 15	27 47	107 32	29 9½	75	7 9 azim.	Variable airs.
16	27 13	....	29 8¾	71	....	Fine breeze from the N. E. and cloudy. At eleven A. M. saw Easter Island to the W. N. W. half W. forty miles distant.

TABLE IV.

PASSAGE FROM EASTER ISLAND TO THE WASHINGTON ISLANDS.

Time.	Lat. S.		Long. W.		Barometer.		Ther.	Variation of the Compass East.		Wind, Weather, and Remarks.
	°	′	°	′	Inch.	Line	°	°	′	
1804. April 22	25	17	111	8	29	9½	73	5	56 azim.	Pleasant breeze at S. W. At six P. M. steered for the Marquesa Islands.
23	24	7	113	51	30		77	5	37	Pleasant breeze at S. E., and clear weather.
24	23		116	22	29	9½	79½	3	58	Pleasant breeze at E. S. E., and cloudy.
25	21	43	118	21	29	9½	77	3	15	Pleasant breeze, and fine weather.
26	20	47	119	56	29	8½	76½	....		Light variable breezes, and cloudy.
27	20		121	26	29	9	78½	5	8	The same. In the morning a calm.
28	19	21	122	45	29	7¾	84	4	28	Light breeze, and fine.
29	19	6	123	33	29	8	84	4	12	Light airs, and clear.
30	18	30	124	31	29	8	80	5	35	The same. In the morning fine breeze at N. E.
May 1	17	21	126	25	29	9	81	5	31	Fine breeze at N. E., and pleasant weather.
2	15	50	128	50	29	8½	81	5	20	Pleasant breeze from the N. E., and clear weather.
3	14	30	131	21	29	7½	82	5	46	Strong breeze at N. E., and fine.

TABLE IV.—Continued.

PASSAGE FROM EASTER ISLAND TO THE WASHINGTON ISLANDS.

Time.	Lat. S.	Long. W.	Barometer.	Ther.	Variation of the Compass East.	Wind, Weather, and Remarks.
	° ′	° ′	Inch. Line.	°	° ′	
1804. May 4	13 25	133 41	29 7	84	....	Fine breeze at N. E., and clear. In the morning squalls and rain.
5	12 30	135 35	29 7½	84	5 33	Fine breeze, and squally weather.
6	11 18	137 28	29 7¼	84½	6 32	Fine breeze, and clear.
7	10	138 16	29 7	84¼	5 52	The same. At six A. M. saw the island of Fatoohiva, or Stª. Magdalena to the westward. At noon the south end of Motané, or St. Pedro, bore W. fourteen miles.
8	8 54	....	29 7	84¼	4 34	Fine easterly breeze, and pleasant weather. At eight P. M. the island of Fatoohoo, or Hood's Isle, was S. W. seven miles. At noon the island of Ooahoona, or Riou's Isle, was E. by S. about six miles.
9	8 52	....	29 7½	85	....	Light airs, and cloudy. The north point of Noocahiva was N. W. about six miles. Night squally.
10	....	....	29 7	86	....	Light airs and rainy weather. In the morning fine northerly breeze. At noon entered the bay of Tayohaia, where we found the Nadejda.

TABLE V.

PASSAGE FROM THE WASHINGTON ISLANDS TO THE SANDWICH ISLANDS.

Time.	Lat. S.		Long. W.		Barometer.		Ther.	Variation of the Compass East.		Winds, Weather, and Remarks.
	°	′	°	′	Inch.	Line.	°	°	′	
1804. May 18	9	1	....		29	7	85	....		Light breeze and squally, with rain. At 10 P. M. got out of the bay of Tayohaia. In the morning moderate gales, and squally.
19	9	30	141	30	29	7½	86	....		Moderate gales from the eastward, and fine weather.
20	7	19	143	5	29	7½	85	6	9 az. & amp.	Moderate gales, and cloudy weather.
21	5	39	144	7	29	7	85	4	25 azim.	Pleasant breeze from the eastward, and cloudy.
22	3	28	144	46	29	6	84½	6	2	The same.
23	1	46	145	22	29	6	79	4	46	Pleasant breeze from the N. E., and fine. In the night squally, with rain.
24		59	145	59	29	6½	79½	3	46	Light airs and rainy weather. In the night the weather cleared up.
25		5	146	12	29	7	80½	4	40	Light airs, and pleasant weather.
26	Lat. N.	56	146	12	29	7	80	4	34	The same.
27	1	59	146	30	29	7½	84	5	7	Light breeze from the N. E. quarter, and clear weather.
28	3	1	147	18	29	7½	85	4	32	Fine breeze at N. E. and pleasant weather.

TABLE V.—Continued.

PASSAGE FROM THE WASHINGTON ISLANDS TO THE SANDWICH ISLANDS.

Time.	Lat. N.		Long. W.		Barometer.		Ther.	Variation of the Compass East.		Winds, Weather, and Remarks.
	°	′	°	′	Inch.	Line.	°	°	′	
1804. May 29	....		....		29	7½	78¼	4	35 azim.	Fine breeze and cloudy. Rain at noon.
30	4	55	148	25	29	7	80	5	26	Light airs. In the night rain.
31	6	3	148	33	29	7	80	5	12	Light airs, with occasional rain.
June 1	....		....		29	7½	75½	....		Light airs and rainy.
2	8	17	149	8	29	7½	80	6	52	Variable breeze, and rain. In the night clear weather: the wind at E. N. E.
3	9	59	149	50	29	7½	79	5	49	Moderate gales at N.E., and beautiful weather.
4	11	44	150	29	29	8	77	5	58	Pleasant breeze from the N. E. quarter. At night moderate gales and clear weather.
5	13	23	151	25	29	7½	79	5	58	Fine breeze at N. E. by E., and clear.
6	15	10	151	57	29	8	75	6	36	The same.
7	17	16	152	41	29	9	75	6	10	The same.
8	19	10	153	51	29	9	75	7	13	The same. At nine A. M. saw the east end of the island of Owyhee to the N. W. At noon it was N. 3° W. twenty miles.

APPENDIX, NO. IV.

TABLE V.—*Continued.*

PASSAGE FROM THE WASHINGTON ISLANDS TO THE SANDWICH ISLANDS.

Time.	Lat. N.	Long. W.	Barometer.	Ther.	Variation of the Compass East.	Winds, Weather, and Remarks.
	° ′ ″	° ′	Inch. Line.	°	° ′	
1804. June 9	18 54 30	....	....	......	7 35 azim.	Pleasant breeze at E. N. E. At noon the south end of the island of Owyhee S. 73° E.
10	18 57 36	....	29 9	79	8 19	Moderate gales from the N. E. In the morning light breezes. At noon the south end of Owyhee N. 79° E. about twenty-five miles.
11	19 17 8	....	....	86	....	Light breeze, and cloudy. At eight P. M. the Nadejda parted company for Camchatca. At noon the bay of Caracacoa bore N. 15° E. ten miles.
12	....	....	....	......	....	Light airs, and clear. At five o'clock P. M. brought to an anchor in the bay of Caracacoa.

3 A

TABLE VI.

PASSAGE FROM THE SANDWICH ISLANDS TO THE ISLAND OF CADIACK.

Time.	Lat. N.	Long. W.	Barometer.	Ther.	Variation of the Compass East.	Winds, Weather, and Remarks.
	° ′ ″	° ′	Inch. Line	°	° ′	
1804. June 17	19 34 49	....	....	.....	....	Light airs from N. W. At nine P. M. weighed. At noon the bay of Caracacoa bore E. S. E.
18	20 20	157 42	29 9	78	....	Light airs. In the night strong breeze from the N. E., and cloudy.
19	....	....	29 9	79	9 45 azim.	Pleasant breeze from the E. N. E., and cloudy. At noon the Isle of Onihoo S. 84° W., and the south-west point of the island of Otooway S. 80° E.
20	23 6	160 11	30	74½	9 50	Calm weather. At night fine breeze from the N. E. In the morning no land in sight.
21	25 22	161 48	30 ½	71	10 24	Strong breeze from the N. E., and cloudy.
22	27 40	163 23	30 ½	73½	10 30	Strong breeze, and fine.
23	29 12	164 22	29 9½	76½	11 26	Pleasant breeze at S. E., and cloudy.
24	....	....	29 8¼	74½	....	Light breeze from the southward, and rainy.
25	32 55	163 57	29 7¾	67	....	Fine breeze from the southward, and rainy.
26	33 14½	164 2	29 9½	70	14 25	Light airs, and cloudy.

TABLE VI.—Continued.

PASSAGE FROM THE SANDWICH ISLANDS TO THE ISLAND OF CADIACK.

Time.	Lat. N.	Long. W.	Barometer.	Ther.	Variation of the Compass East.	Winds, Weather, and Remarks.
1804. June 27	36° 24′	164° 3′	Inch. Line. 30 ½	70°	15° 50′ azim.	Pleasant breeze at W. S. W., and hazy. In the morning clear.
28	....	....	30	65	....	Strong breeze at S. W., and foggy.
29	....	....	29 4¼	58	....	The same.
30	42 18	163 12	29 9½	50	....	Fresh gales from the westward, and hazy.
July 1	....	....	29 7	52	....	Light variable breezes and hazy, with occasional rain.
2	....	....	29 7	47	....	Pleasant breeze at S. by E., and thick weather.
3	48 20	160 41	29 8	47	....	Light airs from the westward, and foggy weather.
4	....	159 46	29 8	44	....	Strong westerly breeze, and cloudy weather.
5	....	....	29 6¼	46	21 54	Light variable breeze and hazy, with occasional rain.
6	53 7	156 23	29 7¼	47	....	Light breezes.
7	54 27	157 8	29 8½	49	24 37	Light breeze from the N. E. and cloudy, with fog at times.
8	55 16	156 7	29 9½	49½	....	Light variable airs. At noon sounded in eighty fathoms, gray sandy bottom.

TABLE VI.—Continued.

PASSAGE FROM THE SANDWICH ISLANDS TO THE ISLAND OF CADIACK.

Time.	Lat. N.	Long. W.	Barometer.	Ther.	Variation of the Compass East.	Winds, Weather, and Remarks.
	° ′	° ′	Inch. Line.	°	° ′	
1804. July 9	55 52	....	29 8	53	....	At two o'clock P. M. saw the isle of Cheericoff, bearing N. E. by N. Light airs.
10	55 58	....	29 6	57	25 45 azim.	Fine breeze at N. W. At two o'clock A. M. saw the island of Cadiack. At four, a-breast of the harbour of Three-Saints.
11	....	....	29 6¾	55	....	Light airs and calms, with fog. At noon forty fathoms, small stones.
12	....	....	29 8	49	....	The same. Depth of water, from thirty to forty fathoms.
13	....	....	29 7½	55	....	Fine breeze. Towards night foggy weather. At midnight brought the ship to with a cadge in the bay of Chiniatskoy. At eight A. M. weighed.
14	....	....	29 8	65	....	Pleasant breeze and fine weather. At two P. M. anchored in St. Paul's Harbour.

TABLE VII.

PASSAGE FROM THE ISLAND OF CADIACK TO SITCA OR NORFOLK SOUND.

Time.	Lat. N.	Long. W.	Barometer.	Ther.	Variation of the Compass East.	Winds, Weather, and Remarks.
1804.	° ′	° ′	Inch. Line.	°	° ′	
Aug. 16	57 14	148 34	29 4	54	26 7 azim.	Light breeze from W. S. W. At three o'clock P. M. set sail from the harbour of St. Paul. In the night fresh westerly gales.
17	56 54	143 20	29 3½	59	25 27	Fresh gales from the W. S. W., and clear weather.
18	56 38	138 58	29 6	59	27 23	Moderate gales from the S. W. by W., with occasional rain.
19	57 8	136 46	29 6	59	27 32	Fine breeze from W. S. W. About six o'clock A.M. saw land to the north half east.
20	57 4	....	29 6½	65	26 45	Light westerly airs and fine weather. About noon anchored in Sitca Sound, in fifty-five fathoms, oozy ground.

TABLE VIII.

PASSAGE FROM SITCA OR NORFOLK SOUND TO THE ISLAND OF CADIACK.

Time.	Lat. N.	Long. W.	Barometer.	Ther.	Variation of the Compass East.	Winds, Weather, and Remarks.
	° ′	° ′	Inch. Line.	°	° ′	
1804. Nov. 11	....	....	29 3	48½	....	Light airs. At eight o'clock P. M. Cape Edgecumbe bore N. 5° W. about five miles. Towards morning strong breeze from the eastward.
12	58 7	145 12	29 2	45	....	Fresh easterly gales and cloudy weather, with heavy sea. Rain at times.
13	....	....	29 ½	45	....	Fresh gales from S. E., and squally weather. At ten A. M. saw land from N. W. to S. W.
14	57 44	....	29 1	43½	26 44 azim.	Fine breeze: the depth of water from thirty-five to fifty fathoms. At eleven A. M. the Broad Point bore S. W. by S. about twenty miles.
15	....	....	29 ½	47	....	Fresh gales from the S. E. and squally weather, with heavy rain. In the morning saw the isle of Oohack. Towards noon reached the harbour of St. Paul.

TABLE IX.

PASSAGE FROM THE ISLAND OF CADIACK TO SITCA OR NORFOLK SOUND.

Time.	Lat. N.	Long. W.	Barometer.	Ther.	Variation of the Compass East.	Winds, Weather, and Remarks.
	° ′	° ′	Inch. Line.	°	° ′	
1805. June 15	57 45	147 51	29 4½	56	27 28 azim.	Light airs. At five P. M. we were clear of the harbour of St. Paul. In the evening fine southerly breeze. Cape Chiniatskoy S. 6° W. twelve miles.
16	....	....	29 4½	52	....	Pleasant breeze from the S. E., and hazy weather.
17	57 50	141 42	29 5¼	54	....	Light airs, and hazy.
18	....	140 34	29 3½	50	....	Light airs, and cloudy.
19	57 13	....	29 2½	......	....	Fine breeze at N. E., and rainy. In the night fresh gales.
20	57 32	137 19	29 6¼	54	....	Pleasant breeze from the S. E. quarter. At noon saw land to the N. N. E.
21	57	....	29 8	54	....	Light airs. In the evening Cape Edgecumbe bore S. 86° E. about forty miles. At noon it was N. 69° E. five miles.
22	....	....	....	......	....	Fine breeze from the N. W. and pleasant weather. At noon brought to an anchor in the harbour of New Archangel.

TABLE X.

PASSAGE FROM SITCA OR NORFOLK SOUND TO CANTON.

Time.	Lat. N.	Long. W.	Barometer.	Ther.	Variation of the Compass East.	Winds, Weather, and Remarks.
	° ′	° ′	Inch. Line.	°	° ′	
1805. Sept. 3	....	....	29 2½	......	....	Light airs and calms, with rain. At midnight fresh gales. Cleared the Sound.
4	53 50	138 41	29 7	......	....	Fresh gales from the westward, and clear weather.
5	52 33	139	29 7	......	....	Moderate gales from the W. and S. W., and cloudy.
6	50 48	139 50	30	......	....	The same. In the morning fine breeze, and clear.
7	49 20	139 58	30 2	......	....	Light airs, and cloudy.
8	48 17	139 29	30 4	......	....	Pleasant breeze from the S. W., with hazy wet weather.
9	48 22	139 29	30 3¾	......	20 7 azim.	Light airs, and hazy wet weather. At noon strong westerly breeze.
10	....	....	30 2	......	....	The same. At noon fine breeze from the S. S. W.
11	47 21	143 8	30 2	......	....	Fine breeze at W. N. W., and cloudy.
12	....	....	30 ½	......	17 32	Fine breeze from the S. W., and drizzling weather.
13	....	....	30 1¾	......	....	Pleasant breezes from the W. and N. W., and foggy.

TABLE X.—*Continued.*

PASSAGE FROM SITCA OR NORFOLK SOUND TO CANTON.

Time.	Lat. N. ° ′	Long. W. ° ′	Barometer. Inch. Line.	Ther. °	Variation of the Compass East. ° ′	Winds, Weather, and Remarks.
1805. Sept. 14	44 24	147 32	30 2½	......	....	Pleasant breeze at N. E., and cloudy.
15	44 21	149 59	30 3½	......	17 13 azim.	Pleasant breeze at N.E., and cloudy. At noon, fine weather.
16	44 12	151 4	30 3¼	......	....	Light breezes from the northward, and pretty clear weather.
17	43 40	....	30 2¼	......	17 33	Light variable airs, and cloudy.
18	....	....	30 1¼	......	....	Light variable airs, and wet weather.
19	....	....	29 8½	......	15 40	Fine westerly breeze, and cloudy. At night squally.
20	....	....	29 4	......	....	Pleasant breeze from the S. W. At night moderate gales and wet weather.
21	45 9	....	29 8	......	....	Strong gales, and cloudy.
22	43 41	158	29 9½	......	....	Fresh breeze from the N. W., and cloudy. At night squally.
23	....	....	29 8½	......	....	Fresh breeze from the N.W. and W. At night squally.
24	....	....	29 5	......	....	Moderate gales from the S. W., and squally wet weather.
25	....	....	29 4	......	....	Moderate westerly gales, and wet squally weather.

TABLE X.—Continued.

PASSAGE FROM SITCA OR NORFOLK SOUND TO CANTON.

Time.	Lat. N.	Long. W.	Barometer.	Ther.	Variation of the Compass East.	Winds, Weather, and Remarks.
1805.	° ′	° ′	Inch. Line.	°	° ′	
Sept. 26	42 4	163 48	29 6½	……	………	Moderate gales from the W. and N. W. with squalls and rain.
27	………	………	29 3½	……	16 44 azim.	Fine breeze, and squally wet weather.
28	………	………	29 3½	……	………	Fresh gales, and squally, with rain, and heavy swell.
29	41 46	163 35	29 5	……	………	Fine breeze at S. W., and pleasant weather.
30	39 55	163 25	29 7½	……	15 7	Fine breeze from the W. and N. W., and fine.
Oct. 1	38 24	164 30	29 9½	……	14 58	Pleasant breeze at N. W., and fine clear weather.
2	36 53	165 30	29 9¼	……	15 15	Pleasant breeze at N. N. E., and fine clear weather.
3	36 19	166 44	30 ½	……	13 28	Light airs from the N. W. quarter, and fine.
4	36 25	167 45	29 8	……	14	Fine variable breezes, and clear.
5	33 53	167 53	29 6½	……	………	Fresh gales from the W.S.W., and cloudy weather.
6	32 3	169 46	29 8	……	………	Fresh gales from the W. and N. W., and clear.

TABLE X.—Continued.

PASSAGE FROM SITCA OR NORFOLK SOUND TO CANTON.

Time.	Lat. N.		Long. W.		Barometer.		Ther.	Variation of the Compass East.		Winds, Weather, and Remarks.
	°	'	°	'	Inch.	Line.	°	°	'	
1803. Oct. 7	31	4	....		29	8	......	....		Fine breeze at N. W., and clear.
8	30	30	170	21	29	9¾	......	12	35 azim.	Light airs and calms, with cloudy weather.
9	30	20	170	57	29	9	......	12	36	Light airs, and clear.
10	29	14	170	24	29	8½	......	12	23	The same.
11	28	57	170	19	29	9	......	11	42	Light airs in the S. W. quarter, and pleasant weather.
12	28	52	171	20	29	8½	......	12	26	Light airs, and fine.
13	28	37	172	30	29	7½	......	11	52	Fine breeze from the S. W. quarter, and cloudy.
14	27	47	....		29	7	......	....		Light airs, and fine: at night, rain.
15	26	43	173	24	29	6¾	......	12	13	Light airs, and fine.
16	....		....		29	6¾	......	11	36	Fine breeze at W. S. W. At ten P. M. the ship grounded. At day-light saw a small low island to the westward, about two miles distant.
17	26 2 35		....		29	7½	......	....		Light airs, and fine. Warped the ship to the northward. At noon the island bore S. 75° W. one mile and a half distant.

TABLE X.—Continued.

PASSAGE FROM SITCA OR NORFOLK SOUND TO CANTON.

Time.	Lat. N.	Long. W.	Barometer.	Ther	Variation of the Compass East.	Winds, Weather, and Remarks.
1805. Oct. 18	° ′ ″ 26 3 35	° ′	Inch. Line. 29 8	°	° ′	Light airs and fine. Warped the ship to N. by E.
19	° ′ 26 10	....	29 8	......	....	Light breeze from N.W., and fine weather. About ten A.M. set sail. At noon the island of Lisiansky was in sight from the mast-head.
20	25 23	172 58	29 7	......	....	Moderate gales from the N. E., and clear. At night squally.
21	24 5	174 24	29 7	......	11 35 azim.	Moderate gales from the N. E., and clear.
22	23 39	175 9	29 6½	......	12 10	Light airs, and clear.
23	22 15	175 32	29 6½	......	11 42	Fine breeze, and pleasant weather. In the morning, rain.
24	21 56	175 21	29 6½	......	....	Light airs, and cloudy. At one P.M. saw a great surf ahead. Soon after, squally and rainy weather.
25	21 25	175 47	29 6½	......	12 37	Light airs, and clear.
26	21 10	176 4	29 6½	......	11 33 amp. & az.	Calm, and fine weather.
27	21 5	176 42	29 7¼	......	12 4 azim.	Light airs, and pleasant weather.
28	20 25	177 25	29 7½	......	12 31	The same.

TABLE X.—Continued.

PASSAGE FROM SITCA OR NORFOLK SOUND TO CANTON.

Time.	Lat. N.		Long. W.		Barometer.		Ther.	Variation of the Compass East.		Winds, Weather, and Remarks.
1805.	°	′	°	′	Inch.	Line	°	°	′	
Oct. 29	19	37	178	26	29	7	......	....		Light breeze from the N. E., and clear.
30	19	27	178	56	29	6¼	......	11	54 azim.	Light airs, and pleasant weather.
31	18	34	178	56	29	6½	......	....		Light airs and calms: the weather fine.
Nov. 1	17	51	179	19	29	6½	......	10	40	The same.
2	16	31	180	32	29	6¼	......	12	28	Pleasant easterly breeze, and clear.
3	14	57	182	11	29	6	......	12	27	Strong breeze from the E. N. E., and clear.
4	13	39	184	5	29	5½	......	12	43	Fine breeze from the N. E., and clear.
5	13	26	186	36	29	5¼	......	11		Strong breeze from the E. by N., and pleasant weather.
6	13	27	189	32	29	5¼	......	11	38	Strong breeze from the N. E., and clear. In the night, rain.
7	13	28	191	44	29	5¼	......	12	47	Pleasant breeze from the E. N. E., and fine.
8	13	12	194	17	29	5½	......	11	40	Strong breeze from the N. E. The night rainy.
9	13	35	196	32	29	5½	......	11	40	Fine breeze from the N. N. E., and clear.

TABLE X.—Continued.

PASSAGE FROM SITCA OR NORFOLK SOUND TO CANTON.

Time.	Lat. N.	Long. W.	Barometer.	Ther.	Variation of the Compass East.	Winds, Weather, and Remarks.
1805. Nov. 10	° ′ 13 42	° ′ 198 25	Inch. Line 29 6	°	° ′	Fine easterly breeze, and cloudy.
11	13 57	200 29	29 5¼	......	9 45 azim.	Fine breeze, and pleasant weather.
12	14 4	203 4	29 5¼	......	9 9	Strong breezes from the E. N. E., and clear. At night, strong breeze from the N. N. E.
13	14 7	206 13	29 5	......	7 58	Moderate gales from the N. N. E., and pleasant weather.
14	14 29	209 14	29 5	......	7 43	Strong breeze from the N.E., and fine.
15	14 48	213 4	29 5	......	6 2	Moderate gales from the N. E., and fine.
16	° ′ ″ 15 1 52	....	29 5	......	5 51	The same. At five P. M. the island of Tinian was west twelve miles. The night squally.
17	° ′ 15 44	217 8	29 5½	......	4 30	Moderate gales at N. N. E., and pleasant weather. At two P.M. the Ladrone Islands were out of sight.
18	16 34	220 21	29 5½	......	2 33	Strong breeze from the N.E., and fine.
19	17 12	224 2	29 5½	......	....	Fresh gales from the N.N.E., and clear.

TABLE X.—Continued.

PASSAGE FROM SITCA OR NORFOLK SOUND TO CANTON.

Time.	Lat. N.	Long. W.	Barometer.	Ther.	Variation of the Compass East.	Winds, Weather, and Remarks.
1805. Nov. 20	° ′	° ′	Inch. Line. 29 3	°	° ′	Fresh gales. Towards noon, strong gales and cloudy.
21	....	....	29 2	......	....	The same, with occasional squalls and rain.
22	....	....	28 28 1 28 3	......	....	A heavy gale of wind. In the morning a typhoon, and dark weather.
23	16 10	....	29 5½	......	....	Typhoon from the W.N.W.: moderated by degrees, and towards morning blew a fresh gale.
24	....	....	29 5	......	....	Moderate gales from the W. and N.W. Cloudy weather, and a very heavy swell.
25	17 58	....	29 6	......	....	Moderate gales from the N.N.E., and cloudy, with rain.
26	18 48	231 39	29 6	......	....	Fresh gales from the N.E., and cloudy.
27	19 59	234 30	29 7	......	....	The same.
28	21 25	237 28	29 8	......	....	The same, with rain. At seven A.M. saw the Bashee Islands to the westward.
29	21 42	240 21	29 9½	......	....	The same. The Bashee Islands out of sight.

TABLE X.—Continued.

PASSAGE FROM SITCA OR NORFOLK SOUND TO CANTON.

Time.	Lat. N.	Long. W.	Barometer.	Ther.	Variation of the Compass East.	Winds, Weather, and Remarks.
1805. Nov. 30	° ′	° ′	Inch. Line.	°	° ′	Fresh gales, and clear weather. At noon saw land to the northward.
Dec. 1	....	....	....	......	....	Moderate gales from the N. E., and pleasant weather. At one o'clock P. M. the island of Pedro Branco bore N. about twelve miles. At noon, the south point of the Great Ladrone N. 56° W.

TABLE XI.

PASSAGE FROM CANTON TO PORTSMOUTH.

Time.	Lat. N.		Long. W.		Barometer.		Ther.	Variation of the Compass East.		Winds, Weather, and Remarks.
1806. Feb. 12	°	′	°	′	Inch.	Line.	°	°	′	Strong easterly breeze, and cloudy. At six A.M. weighed and set sail. At noon, a-breast of the Ladrones.
13	19	43	246	1	29	4½	74			Pleasant easterly breeze, and cloudy.
14	18	41	246	12	29	4¼	76	1	13 azim.	Pleasant breezes: towards morning, calm and cloudy.
15	16	45	245	16	29	4½	76			Pleasant breeze from the E. N. E., and cloudy.
16	15	7	246	25	29	5	76			Pleasant breeze at N. E. by E., and fine.
17	13	19	248	9	29	5	78			Strong breeze at E. N. E., and clear.
18	11	20	249	51	29	5	80			Strong breeze at N. E., and clear. At night rain.
19	9	9	251	21	29	4	77	2	8	Strong breeze at E. N. E., and clear.
20	7	2	253	34	29	3¼	78	3	6	The same. At noon sounded in twenty-seven fathoms, sandy bottom.
21	5	18	254	37	29	4	80	2	55	Pleasant easterly breeze, and fine. At noon the depth of water was thirty-six fathoms, sandy bottom.

TABLE XI.—Continued.

PASSAGE FROM CANTON TO PORTSMOUTH.

Time.	Lat. N.	Long. W.	Barometer.	Ther.	Variation of the Compass East.	Winds, Weather, and Remarks.
	° ′	° ′	Inch. Line.	°	° ′	
1806. Feb. 22	4 8	255 8	29 4	81½	3 24 azim.	Light airs, and clear. At noon forty-one fathoms, oozy ground.
23	3 6	255 10	29 4	81	………	The same. At noon the island of Poolo Teoman bore S. 63° W., eighteen miles.
24	1 27	254 35	29 4¾	80	2 8	Light breeze at N. E., and fine.
25	Lat. S. 43	253 37	29 4¼	82	3 5	Light airs in the N. E. quarter. At eleven A. M., saw the island of Tody to S. W.
From 26 to March 7	………	………	………	……	………	N. B. We were passing the Sound of Gaspar, and the Strait of Sunda. All this time we had light variable winds, and sometimes calm weather. The variation of the compass, out of the Straits of Gaspar, was 2° 36′, and off the Java Point, 2° 18′ west.
7	8 28	254 13	29 4	83	Var. W. 55	Light airs, and clear. In the morning, squalls and rain.
8	9 46	254 7	29 4	82	………	Fine westerly breeze, and squally wet weather.
9	………	………	29 3½	80	2 5	Light breeze, and rain. At four P. M. saw Christmas Island S. E. by S., about twenty-three miles.

TABLE XI.—Continued.

PASSAGE FROM CANTON TO PORTSMOUTH.

Time.	Lat. S.	Long. W.	Barometer.	Ther.	Variation of the Compass West.	Winds, Weather, and Remarks.
	° ′	° ′	Inch. Line.	°	° ′	
1806. Mar. 10	11 32	....	29 4	81	....	Light airs, and rainy.
11	11 33	256 54	....	......	....	Light airs, and cloudy. At noon, fine breeze at S. E.
12	11 41	257 12	29 4½	84	1 16 azim.	Light breeze in the S. E. quarter.
13	11 42	257 27	29 3¾	84	....	Light airs, and pleasant. At noon, calm weather.
14	11 52	257 50	29 3½	85	12 azim.	Light airs, and clear.
15	12 29	258 22	29 3½	84½	52	Calm and cloudy weather. At night, fine breeze from the S. E.
16	13 50	260 25	29 3½	83	22	Fine breeze, and clear. At night, rain. In the morning, moderate gales from the S. E.
17	....	....	29 3½	77½	....	Fresh gales at E. S. E., and rainy.
18	....	....	29 4	79	1 59	Strong breeze at S. E., and cloudy, with rain.
19	16 26	269 6	29 4	79	2 6	Fine breeze at S. by E., and cloudy, with rain.
20	17 35	272 33	29 4	79	1 43	Moderate gales at S. E. by S., and fine, with heavy sea.

TABLE XI.—Continued.

PASSAGE FROM CANTON TO PORTSMOUTH.

Time.	Lat. S.		Long. W.		Barometer.		Ther.	Variation of the Compass West.		Winds, Weather, and Remarks.
	°	′	°	′	Inch.	Line.	°	°	′	
1806. Mar. 21	18	41	275	22	29	3¼	79	....		Moderate gales at S. E., and cloudy.
22	19	14	278	36	29	4	79	....		Moderate gales from the S. S. E., and cloudy.
23	19	57	281	46	29	3	79	....		Fresh gales at S. E. by S., and thick rainy weather.
24	20	52	....		29	3	79	....		Fresh gales from the S. S. E., and cloudy.
25	....		....		29	4	76	....		Fresh gales, and squally, with rain.
26	22	27	292	19	29	3	79	....		Fresh gales at S. S. E., and squally, with rain.
27	23	23	295	40	29	3½	79	....		Fresh gales from the S. E. by S., and fine.
28	24	2	298	42	29	4½	78	10	21 azim.	Moderate gales from the southward, and clear.
29	24	49	301	26	29	4½	78	13	15	The same.
30	25	51	304	1	29	5	76½	14	47	Fine breeze from the S. S. E., and fine.
31	26	30	305	46	29	5	79	15	2	Fine easterly breeze, and pleasant weather.
April 1	....		....		29	4½	74	18	2	Light variable breezes. Towards noon, squalls and rain.

TABLE XI.—Continued.

PASSAGE FROM CANTON TO PORTSMOUTH.

Time.	Lat. S.		Long. W.		Barometer.		Ther.	Variation of the Compass West.		Winds, Weather, and Remarks.
	°	′	°	′	Inch.	Line.	°	°	′	
1806. April 2	26	24	307	9	29	4¼	74	19	10 azim.	Light airs, and cloudy, with rain.
3	26	40	308	15	29	5¼	74	....		Fine breeze, and cloudy. At night, squalls and rain.
4	27	52	310	44	29	7	75	20		Fine breeze from the S. E. quarter, and beautiful weather.
5	29	14	313	5	29	7	76	23	27	Fine easterly breeze, and clear.
6	29	42	314	35	29	7	74	24	43	The same.
7	30	25	316	49	29	8	73½	24	46	Pleasant easterly breeze, and fine weather.
8	30	41	318	27	29	8	71½	26	13 az. & amp.	The same.
9	31	17	321	16	29	7	74	26	25 azim.	The same.
10	31	45	....		29	6¼	75	27	44	Pleasant breeze from the N. E. quarter, and clear. In the morning, some thunder.
11	32	8	325		29	6	80	27	32	Light airs, and fine. Towards noon, strong breeze at N. N. E.
12	....		....		29	3¾	78	28	49	Fresh gales at N. by E., and fine.
13	33	8	328	52	29	3½	......	....		Light airs, and foggy, with rain.

TABLE XI.—Continued.

PASSAGE FROM CANTON TO PORTSMOUTH.

Time.	Lat. S.		Long. W.		Barometer.		Ther.	Variation of the Compass West.		Winds, Weather, and Remarks.
	°	′	°	′	Inch.	Line	°	°	′	
1806. April 14	....		....		29	7¼	64½	....		Fine westerly breeze. In the night, fresh gales at S. W.
15	....		....		29	6	68	....		Fresh breeze at S. E. Towards evening, fresh gales, with rain.
17	35	49	335	32	29	5¾	68	....		Fresh gales at S. E. by S., and hazy weather. At night, variable winds and unsettled weather.
18	36	18	338	37	29	6	69	25	55 azim.	Light airs from the S. E. quarter, and fine weather. At eight A. M. sounded in one hundred and ten fathoms, fine sand.
19	36	16	340	33	29	4	69	24	44	Light breeze from the N. E. quarter. At five in the afternoon, the depth of water was ninety fathoms, sandy bottom: at noon, found no soundings.
20	35	31	341		29	5	67	26	20	Pleasant variable airs. At noon, fresh breeze.
21	34	44	342	40	29	3½	66	....		Pleasant breeze at S. E. In the evening, the Cape of Good Hope bore S. 47° E. about forty miles.
22	34	15	343	33	29	3	......	....		Moderate breeze in the N. W. quarter, and fine.

TABLE XI.—Continued.

PASSAGE FROM CANTON TO PORTSMOUTH.

Time.	Lat. S.	Long. W.	Barometer.	Ther	Variation of the Compass West.	Winds, Weather, and Remarks.
1806.	° ′	° ′	Inch. Line	°	° ′	
April 23	32 11	345 5	29 6	60	21 6 azim.	Fresh breeze from the westward, and squally, with rain. In the night more moderate.
24	29 59	347 37	29 6	61	....	Moderate variable gales, with occasional squalls and rain.
25	27 54	350 35	29 5½	64	....	Fresh gale at S. S. E., and cloudy.
26	26 36	351 50	29 5	65	22 35	Pleasant variable breezes, and cloudy.
27	....	353 15	29 5¼	68	21 27	Pleasant westerly breezes, and clear.
28	22 31	354 58	29 6¼	68	20 9	Fine variable breezes, and clear.
29	....	....	29 6¼	71	21 32	Pleasant breeze at S. S. E., and fine.
30	18 56	....	29 6	71	....	Strong breeze at S. E., and cloudy. At night moderate gales.
May 1	17 31	1 15	29 6¼	74	20 36	Fine breeze at S. by E., and cloudy.
2	16 20	2 58	29 6	72	....	Pleasant breeze at S. E. by S., and cloudy.
3	14 48	4 36	29 6	72	20 26	Strong breeze at S. S. E., and pleasant weather.

TABLE XI.—Continued.

PASSAGE FROM CANTON TO PORTSMOUTH.

Time.	Lat. S.	Long. W.	Barometer.	Ther.	Variation of the Compass West.	Winds, Weather, and Remarks.
	° ′	° ′	Inch. Line.	°	° ′	
1806. May 4	13 1	6 27	29 5	74	19 23 azim.	Fine breeze at S. S. E., and clear.
5	....	....	29 5½	80	18 53	Strong breeze at S. S. E., and cloudy.
6	9 11	9 54	29 5	78	....	Strong breeze at S. E. by S., and cloudy.
7	7 17	11 34	29 5	79	16 54	Pleasant breeze at S. S. E., and clear.
8	5 21	13 9	29 4¾	80	16 12	The same.
9	....	....	29 5	80	....	The same. At noon, rain.
10	1 25	16 9	29 5	80½	15 18	Fine breeze at S. E., and pleasant weather.
11	Lat. N. 37	16 48	29 4¾	84	....	Light breeze at S. E., and fine.
12	2 15	18 26	29 5	82	15 2	The same.
13	....	....	29 5	77	14 40	The same. Towards evening, rain.
14	....	....	29 5	75	....	Light airs, and rainy.
15	6 11	20 35	29 5	82	....	Fine breeze from the eastward, with squalls and rain. In the night changeable weather.
16	6 48	21 5	29 5	85	15 46	Light airs from the N. E. quarter, and clear.

TABLE XI.—Continued.

PASSAGE FROM CANTON TO PORTSMOUTH.

Time.	Lat. N.		Long. W.		Barometer.		Ther.	Variation of the Compass West.		Winds, Weather, and Remarks.
	°	′	°	′	Inch.	Line	°	°	′	
1806. May 17	7	11	22	1	29	4½	83	12	32 azim.	Light airs from the N. E. quarter, and clear.
18	7	48	23	2	29	5	83	13	16	Pleasant breeze at N. E., and clear.
19	8	36	24	27	29	5	81	....		Fine breeze from the N. E. by N., and pleasant weather.
20	9	14½	25	43	29	5	79	....		Fine breeze at N. N. E., and cloudy.
21	9	41	26	12	29	5	78½	11	50	The same.
22	10	12	27	18	29	5	77	12	15	Variable breezes, and cloudy. In the night, clear weather.
23	11	15	28	26	29	5¼	78	11	56	Pleasant breeze at N.E., and clear.
24	12	50	29	45	29	6	77	9	26	The same.
25	....		....		29	6	76	9	44	Pleasant breeze at N. E. by E., and fine.
26	16	7	32	25	29	6½	75½	8	30	Strong breeze at N. E. by E., and fine.
27	18	26	34	10	29	6½	76	8	52	Moderate gales at N. E. by E., and cloudy. In the morning, fine weather.
28	21	5	35	34	29	7	75½	....		Moderate gales at E. N. E., and cloudy.

TABLE XI.—Continued.

PASSAGE FROM CANTON TO PORTSMOUTH.

Time.	Lat. N.		Long. W.		Barometer.		Ther.	Variation of the Compass West.		Winds, Weather, and Remarks.
	°	′	°	′	Inch.	Line.	°	°	′	
1805. May 29	23	26	36	9	29	7½	76	………		Strong breeze at E. by N., and cloudy.
30	26	10	36	33	29	8¼	75	10	39 azim.	Strong breeze from the eastward, and fine.
31	28	11	36	34	29	8½	75	11	7	The same.
June 1	29	53	37	11	29	8¾	75	12	41	Light easterly breeze, and fine.
2	31	34	37	49	29	5	75	13	44	Pleasant breeze from E. by S., and clear.
3	32	24	38	4	30		80½	14	22	Light airs and calms. Fine weather.
4	32	51	38	7	29	9	72½	14	52	The same.
5	34	21	37	7	29	8	76	16	44	Light breeze at N. W., and cloudy.
6	36	36	35	55	29	5	72	17		Light breeze from the W. N. W., and clear.
7	38	10	34	55	29	5	60	………		Pleasant breeze and cloudy, with rain at times.
8	39	41	34	16	29	6	64	………		Pleasant breeze, and rainy.
9	40	13	31	34	29	6½	……	19	53	Pleasant breeze from the N. W., and cloudy. At nine A. M. saw the island of Corvo, S. E. by S., thirty-five miles.

TABLE XI.—Continued.

PASSAGE FROM CANTON TO PORTSMOUTH.

Time.	Lat. N.	Long. W.	Barometer.	Ther.	Variation of the Compass West.	Winds, Weather, and Remarks.
	° ′	° ′	Inch. Line.	°	° ′	
1806. June 10	....	....	29 5	62	21 52 azim.	Light breeze at N. W. In the night strong gales from the southward, and squally weather.
11	43 58	24 45	29 5½	65	....	Strong gales at S. S. W. In the evening more moderate weather, and clear.
12	45 22	21 46	29 8	61	....	Fresh gales at S. by W., and cloudy.
13	45 53	19 26	29 7	61½	26 14	Fine southerly breeze, and pleasant weather.
14	45 36	17 8	29 9	60	27 13	Fresh breeze at N. E., and clear.
15	45 37	16 9	29 9	64	....	Light breeze at N. E., and cloudy weather.
16	42 26	14 17	29 9	60	....	Fine breeze at N. E., and cloudy.
17	45 30	13 28	29 8	60	....	Light breeze at N. E., and cloudy.
18	45 50	12 52	29 7	61½	....	Light breeze, with squalls and rain.
19	....	....	29 8	62½	....	Fresh gales from the eastward, and clear.
20	48 11	14 24	29 9	62	25 20	Strong easterly gales, and delightful weather.

TABLE XI.—Continued.

PASSAGE FROM CANTON TO PORTSMOUTH.

Time.	Lat. N.	Long. W.	Barometer	Ther.	Variation of the Compass West.	Winds, Weather, and Remarks.
	° ′	° ′	Inch. Line.	°	° ′	
1806. June 21	48 35	14	29 8½	59	25 12 azim	Pleasant breeze, and delightful weather.
22	48 20	13 16	29 8¼	59½	27 47	Pleasant breeze, and cloudy.
23	47 48	10 48	29 7¾	59½	………	The same.
24	48 23	9 40	29 7¼	57¾	25 56	Pleasant breeze from the N. E. In the morning, light airs and cloudy.
25	………	………	29 5½	60½	………	Fine breeze from the S. E., and cloudy. At eight o'clock P. M. the depth of water was ninety fathoms.
26	49 48	………	29 3½	63	………	Fine southerly breeze, and thick hazy weather. At night, strong gales from the S.W. At noon, forty-two fathoms, fine sandy bottom.
27	………	………	29 4	63	………	Light southerly breeze, and hazy. At ten A. M. the Isle of Wight bore to the northward.
28	50 31	………	29 5	……	………	Fine breeze from the N. E. quarter, and clear.
29	………	………	………	……	………	Light easterly airs. At nine o'clock P. M. anchored at Spithead.

Printed by S. Hamilton, Weybridge, Surrey.

RECORD OF TREATMENT, EXTRACTION ETC.

Shelfmark: 982.i.4.
S&P Ref No. RDW 1428/21270
Microfilm No.

Date	Particulars	
	pH Before or Existing	pH After
Feb 08	5.06	7.34

Deacidification: Mag-Bi-Carb / Methyl-Mag-Carb

Adhesives: Animal Glue, Wheat Starch Paste

Lined / Laminated: Jap Tissue

Chemicals / Solvents: Pure Gelatine Size

Cover Treatment: Leather.

Other Remarks:

BCG – 1

SHELFMARK 982:1:5

THIS BOOK HAS BEEN
MICROFILMED (1995

MICROFILM NO. PBM
1691